THE SIKHS AND THEIR LITERATURE

The Sikhs and their Literature

(A Guide to Tracts, Books and Periodicals, 1849-1919)

N. GERALD BARRIER

Foreword by

KHUSHWANT SINGH

MANOHAR
2026

First published 1970
POD reprint 2021, 2022, 2023, 2025
Reprinted 2026

ISBN 978-93-88540-72-8

Published by
Ajay Kumar Jain *for*
Manohar Publishers & Distributors
4753/23 Ansari Road, Daryaganj
New Delhi 110 002

Printed at
Replika Press Pvt. Ltd.

PREFACE

Among the religious communities of India the Sikhs of the Punjab probably possess the strongest sense of history and the most vital contact with past events. Sikh literature abounds with accounts of the Gurus, martial bravery, the glories of Ranjit Singh, and in the British period, the heroism and sacrifice surrounding the gurdwara reform movement, 1921-1924. Despite this historical consciousness, however, the Sikhs and students of Sikh history have paid little attention to two significant turning points in the life of the community—the eighteenth century when Sikh ideas on religion, society and politics crystallized and moulded the subsequent development of Sikhism and the period following annexation of the Punjab in 1849 when the Sikhs moved from defeat toward a new self-awareness and militancy culminating in the formation of the Akali Dal and the Shiromani Gurdwara Parbandhak Committee.

These historiographical gaps often are explained with claims that source materials do not warrant fresh research and interpretation. Admittedly, documents on the post-Guru period are scattered and difficult to evaluate, but this is not true of the Sikh resurgence in the late nineteenth century. Despite the prevalent view that the Panjabi language and Sikh literature in general went into eclipse following 1849[1], a survey of publications suggests that the Sikhs produced a wide range of books, tracts, and newspapers on almost every conceivable subject. By 1910, for example, there were over twenty Sikh newspapers and journals, supplemented by the literary products of publicists and scholars such as Bhai Vir Singh, Babu Teja Singh, Bhai Kahan Singh of Nabha, and Bhai Mohan Singh Vaid. At the same time Sikh educationalists and reformers founded organizations such as the Khalsa Tract Society and the

1. For example, discussion in Kulwant Singh Virk's "Panjabi : A Foresaken Language." *The Sunday Statesman Magazine Section*, Feb. 9, 1969. Also see I. Serebryakov, *Punjabi Literature*. (Moscow, 1967), pp. 62-67.

Panjabi Prachar Sabha which institutionalized the spread and popularity of Sikh literature in the Gurmukhi script. Not only were many Sikh publications circulating, they were being preserved and are available to scholars. Bibliographical information alone is lacking. With the exception of Dr. Ganda Singh's survey of five hundred years of Punjab and Sikh literature (*A Bibliography of the Punjab*. Patiala, 1966), no bibliography discusses the Sikh experience under the British *raj*.

This guide introduces the vernacular and English-language literature on and by the Sikhs written between 1849 and 1919. It has been designed to facilitate research on a neglected phase of Sikh history and to help scholars locate items relating to their special interests. An introductory statement on the individuals, organizations, and themes involved in the Sikh resurgence is followed by three sections surveying non-serial publications. Each entry contains bibliographical information, background on the items, and location if available. A concluding section treats Sikh periodicals. Appended are notes on collections of Sikh printed documents and proscribed works, a select bibliography of biographies, autobiographies, and histories relating to the period, and two indexes (subject-title and general).

The quarterly catalogue of Punjab publications prepared by the Punjab government after the enactment of the Registration of Books Bill in 1867 serves as the primary source for the non-serial entries. The Act required publishers to supply the British with three copies of every work printed in India. On receiving the books the Punjab and other local governments compiled lists or catalogues of publications with information on title, translation of title if vernacular, language, author, subject, number of pages, publisher and printer[1]. I prepared initial entry cards from the catalogues, 1868-1920, in the India Office Library and the National Archives of India and checked the cards against items in depositories of Sikh material (Bhai Takht Singh Library, Khalsa College Library, Punjabi University Library, December 1968-February 1969; India Office Library, British Museum, summers of 1968 and 1969). This procedure resulted in occasional modifications and additions to the original set of cards. Serious alteration of British entries was infrequent except for dates of first editions, and therefore if the entry cards could not be checked against the original work, they have been accepted as accurate.

British reports are also the major sources for the concluding section on periodical publications. I drew information from annual confidential reports

1. Background on the catalogues and the evolution of book registration system discussed in N.G. Barrier, "South Asia in Vernacular Books and Tracts," *Journal of Asian Studies*, August 1969. Also, see Appendix A.

on the Punjab press prepared by the Special Branch, Punjab Police Department, and cross-checked the cards, where possible, against back files of the periodicals.[1]

Three criteria determined the selections in the bibliography. First, all works pertain primarily to the Sikhs and were written in the period 1849-1919. For additional sources on Sikhism, the reader is referred to Dr. Ganda Singh's bibliography which surveys general works containing chapters or stray information on Sikhism. Decisions on the inclusion of several categories of publications also limit the selections. New editions of older works previously mentioned, reprints of Sikh scripture (except those with appended commentaries), Sikh prayers, eulogies of the Gurus, and miscellaneous items such as treatises on health and sanitation have not been included because they would have doubled the number of entries without contributing materially to the value of the bibliography. In this connection, the existence of hundreds of small four-sixteen page pamphlets on martyrs, often on the sons of Guru Gobind Singh, presents a special problem. I have included only the most important items or those which could be union-listed. Finally, with a few exceptions that are noted, the guide lists only items in British catalogues or ones personally examined by the compiler. Although biographies and newspaper articles provide stray reference to other titles, I left out those items unless I could verify the information and prepare a satisfactory entry.

Decisions on the scope of the study and the methodology employed in preparation limit its comprehensiveness. For example, internal evidence in organizational reports suggest that similar items exist which could not be traced for inclusion in the guide[2]. Moreover, the British press reports leave out information and give a prejudiced viewpoint. I think, however, that despite the limitations, the bibliography remains the most thorough survey of Sikh printed material in the late nineteenth and early twentieth century which can be prepared at this time. Gaps and inaccuracies inevitably exist, but hopefully they can be adjusted in a revised bibliography if such an edition seems warranted. I am aware of the deficiencies in the guide and welcome criticism and additional information.

Although specific comments on format and arrangement introduce each

1. For additional information on this source and its use, see the introduction to N. G. Barrier and Paul Wallace (eds.), *The Punjab Press, 1880-1905 : A Data Paper*. (East Lansing, MSU South Asia Occasional Papers Series, forthcoming, winter of 1969-70).
2. The Bhasaur Singh Sabha, for example, published five annual reports between 1893 and 1898, but only one year, 1898, could be traced. *Salana Report Sri Guru Singh Sabha Bhasaur*, 1898 (Lahore, 1898), p.l. Another striking gap is in the reports of the Ferozepur Singh Sabha which publi hed reports annually between 1902 and 1918.

section, several general points require highlighting at the outset. First, the reader should familiarize himself with the table of abbreviations utilized in the bibliographical sections before attempting to use the guide. Punjab personal and place names also present difficulties. Spelling of personal names in British catalogues has been followed unless altered in the light of spelling in original items. The spelling of place names follow usage prevalent in West Pakistan, Punjab State, and Haryana. I apologize to relatives or associates of authors whose honorific titles or spelling of names have been modified, but I trust that readers will appreciate the problem inherent in standardizing vernacular words and Punjab nomenclature. A final technicality concerns translation and romanization of vernacular material. The entries in British catalogues have been followed except for obvious misprints. Titles which I have transliterated follow romanization now in practice, with *ch* and *chh*, and with the omission of diacritical marks. Two factors influenced the decision to omit diacriticals. First, the British catalogues frequently left them out or placed the marks incorrectly (or so it seems—given the state of Panjabi spelling, one can never be sure). Unless the title of every work could be checked and romanized, adding or dropping marks would perpetuate inaccuracies because original titles might have been spelled in an unconventional fashion. Secondly, conversations with Punjabi and western scholars convinced me that incorrect diacritical marks create unnecessary problems for individuals familiar with the language. These arguments also weighed against the temptation to standardize romanization or to attempt to put British entries back into the vernacular character.

Many institutions and individuals contributed to the compilation of this bibliography. Grants from the National Endowment for the Humanities, the American Institute of Indian Studies, and the Research Council of the University of Missouri supported research and writing. In addition, the American Institute provided special funds for assistance and travel so that I could consult with historians and librarians on various bibliographical problems. My research assistants, Ashok Mahindroo and Sukhwant Singh (Devinder), helped at each stage of the project. S.P. Nirash assisted in preparing descriptions of vernacular items and laboured long teaching me Panjabi. I also wish to thank the authorities at the following institutions for extending facilities and permission to work in their collections : India Office Library; British Museum; Punjab Public Library, Lahore; National Archives of India, New Delhi; Khalsa College, Amritsar; Punjabi University, Patiala; Sikh Kanya Mahavidyala, Ferozepur. Professor Parkash Singh, Director of the Sikh History Research Department, Khalsa College, Amritsar, gave great assistance, as did Sardar Satnam Singh, Officer-in-Charge of the Bhai Mohan Singh Vaid Collection,

Punjabi University. Sardar Hakam Singh, librarian of Punjabi University, read a draft copy of the bibliography and provided helpful criticism. Sardar Gurbaksh Singh, manager of the Sikh Kanya Mahavidyala, took me into his home and threw open the treasury of Sikh newspapers and tracts collected by his father, Bhai Takht Singh. I also benefitted from discussions with Professors Ainslie Embree (Duke University), Fauja Singh (Punjabi University), and Kenneth Jones (Kansas State University), and Dr. Ganda Singh of Patiala. Sardar Nahar Singh and Dr. W.H. McLeod made special contributions to the study. Both read the draft manuscript and worked closely with me at all times. Nahar Singh was a travelling companion on several book-hunting trips through the Punjab, while Hew , McLeod's encouragement carried me past many low points. Khushwant Singh first introduced me to the study of the Sikhs during my initial research in India in 1964. I have appreciated his comments and help over the past years and am honoured that he has agreed to write a foreword to this work. Finally, I am indebted to two Sikh pioneers, Bhai Takht Singh of Ferozepur, and Bhai Mohan Singh Vaid of Tarn Taran, who had the foresight to collect and preserve the literature which some day will serve as a key to a fresh understanding of Sikh history. I dedicate the bibliography to their memory.

This bibliography is the product of a year of discussion and research with scholars and friends, but as compiler, I assume full responsibility for mistakes, omissions, and interpretations of material.

N. Gerald Barrier
University of Missouri

Columbia, August 1969

FOREWORD

The most important problem that has faced the Sikhs since their inception is that of identity and survival as a distinct community separate from the Hindus. Most Sikhs were converts from Hinduism, governed by Hindu law, inter-married with the Hindus, observed Hindu fasts and festivals, and when they abandoned the external symbols of the Khalsa tradition (the unshaven hair and beards) did in fact become Hindus believing in Sikhism.

Arjun, the fifth Guru, proclaimed : "We are neither Hindus nor Mussalmans". Gobind Singh, the last Guru, gave them a distinct look, a community name and started traditions which would make his following into a distinct people with an ethos of their own. The gurus had perhaps not reckoned with Hinduism's remarkable capacity to accept all variations of the religious theme. Hindus acclaimed Sikhism as a militant aspect of their own faith. Within a few years of the death of Guru Gobind, leadership of the Sikhs was in the hands of a Hindu bairagi, Banda Singh Bahadur. And by the time the Sikhs came to dominate the Punjab, Sikh ruling class had been thoroughly brain-washed by their mentors; they wore sacred threads, were married to the chanting of Vedic mantras, went on pilgrimage to Hardwar and Banaras, forced their widows to perform sati. Such was the state of affairs during the reign of the superstitious Brahmin-ridden Maharaja Ranjit Singh (1780-1839).

With the collapse of the Sikh Kingdom in 1849, it seemed to many that Sikhism had run its course and would soon become an episodic chapter in the history of Hinduism. Lord Dalhousie, The Governor-General, who annexed the Punjab was of the opinion that within a few years the Sikhs would cease to be. However, it was he more than anyone else who took measures to prevent a whole-sale sliding back of Sikhs into Hinduism. He made the observance of Khalsa traditions (long hair and beard) compulsory for Sikh soldiery. Every unit had a *granthi* (scripture reader) attached to it and attendance at gurdwara was made obligatry

The Sikh intelligentsia responded to the government gestures. Literature extolling the teachings of the Gurus and the heroism of the Khalsa began to be published in Gurumukhi, a script which came to be almost entirely used by the Sikhs. Separate ritual for birth, baptism, marriage and death was established. "*Ham Hindu nahin hain*—We are not Hindus" became the slogan. The Sikh separatist movement was helped by the resurgence of Hinduism under the Arya Samaj. In order to reclaim Sikhs as Hindus, Samajists had to emphasise the superiority of Hinduism over the teachings of the Gurus. Sikhs retaliated by denigrating the Arya Samaj. In the battle for survival two more fronts were opened—one against Christian missions who had begun to gain converts from the lower castes of Sikhs and the other against the Muslims who began to question the Sikhs over representation in services and grants of land. Out of this maelstorm were generated the Singh Sabha and its more aggressive successor the Akali Movement. And these two movements moulded the Sikhs' separate identity.

Of all periods the most neglected by scholars are the years between the fall of the Sikh Kingdom (1849) and introduction of democratic reforms (1909). N. Gerald Barrier fills this gap. His work is pioneering, painstaking and thorough. He has compiled a most valuable catalogue of source material for those who wish to fill the blank pages of Sikh history.

Khushwant Singh
Editor
The Illustrated Weekly of India

Bombay, January 15, 1970

ABBREVIATIONS

BM	...	British Museum
BTSL	...	Bhai Takht Singh Library, Ferozepur
CKD	...	Chief Khalsa Diwan, Amritsar
E	...	English
EC	...	Educational Committee, CKD
H	...	Hindi
HG	...	Hindi in Gurmukhi Script
IOL	...	India Office Library, London
KC	...	Khalsa College, Amritsar
KTS	...	Khalsa Tract Society
NAI	...	National Archives of India, New Delhi.
P	...	Panjabi
PBC	...	Punjab Book Catalogue
PE	...	Persian
PN	...	Panjabi in Nastaliq Script
PPU	...	Punjabi University, Patiala
U	...	Urdu
UG	...	Urdu in Gurmukhi Script

Note :- *Bilingual works are indicated by two symbols separated by a comma (e.g., H,E for a work in Hindi and English). Specialized abbreviations pertaining only to section four are found in the introduction to that section.*

CONTENTS

INTRODUCTION

THE SIKH RESURGENCE: THE PERIOD AND ITS LITERATURE

INTRODUCTION

THE SIKH RESURGENCE : THE PERIOD AND ITS LITERATURE

Sikh history can be divided into three phases. The first, beginning with the birth of Guru Nanak in 1469 and ending with the death of Guru Gobind Singh in 1708, witnessed the emergence of most of the distinctive features of Sikhism. Guru Nanak expounded a system of belief rooted in the Sant tradition of North India, a synthesis of Sufism, Vaishnava *bhakti,* and the ideas and discipline associated with the Nath yogis.[1] According to Nanak, God reveals himself through His creation. Man's duty is to meditate on this revelation, referred to as the *Nam* or the Name of God, so that he will grow more like his Creator. This meditation can be carried out in the daily routine of life and does not require rejection of the world. If a person persists in devotion and meditation, he will attain a mystical union with God and break from the cycle of transmigration. Man is able to understand this revelation through the voice of God in the human heart, the Guru, a term also appended to Nanak's name by his followers because he had perceived ultimate meaning and was qualified to instruct others.

Nanak's teachings were transmitted and elaborated by nine successors, each of whom bore the same title of Guru. By the death of the third Guru, Amar Das (1479-1574), the disciples of Nanak had become a distinct community with their own organizations, customs, and pilgrim places. The fifth Guru Arjan (1563-1606) compiled a sacred scripture, the *Adi Granth* or the *Granth Sahib,* a collection of hymns by the Gurus and other religious poets. Written in a new script, Gurmukhi ("Gur"-"Mukh"—from the mouth of the Guru), the *Adi Granth* gradually became central in Sikh life and in all religious observances. In 1699 the last Guru, Gobind Singh (1666-1708), transformed the Sikhs into a disciplined body or order, the *Khalsa (Panth).* The creation of the *Khalsa* at Anandpur, strengthened by developments in the eighteenth century, provided

1. A scholarly treatment of Guru Nanak's teachings is found in W.H. McLeod, *Guru Nanak and the Sikh Religion* (Oxford, 1968).

Sikhs who followed Guru Gobind with a new name, Singh ("lion"), and symbols, the wearing of the five "k's"—*kesh* (uncut hair), *kangha* (comb), *kara* (steel bangle), *kirpan* (sword or dagger), and *kach* (breeches). The succession of personal Gurus also ended with Guru Gobind Singh. Henceforth the function and authority of the Guru was vested in the *Adi Granth* and the corporate decisions of the community, the *Khalsa*.

The next period, 1708-1849, included the further evolution of Sikh institutions and complex socio-political developments—the appearance of the Sikh *misals* (warrior bands loyal to one chief but also united in a loose confederation), the ascendancy of Ranjit Singh's rule over the Punjab (1799-1839), and two wars with the British leading to annexation in 1849. A decline of the Sikh faith accompanied these tides of fortune. As a knowledgeable observer noted:

> The Sikh religion which has long since reached its zenith is now visibly on the decline. The Sikhs themselves say that the freethinking Sikhs who follow their own whims and fancies instead of the precepts of the Guroos are daily on the increase. Many disguise their long hair. Many wear the prohibited colours. A few trim their hair and smoke.[1]

The last century might be characterized as a period of Sikh resurgence. Today the Sikhs virtually control their own state, the Punjab. There, and in many parts of the world to which Sikhs have migrated, the term "Sikh" has become synonymous with progressive thinking and economic advance. Although still embroiled in debate over theology and custom, Sikhism has reasserted its identity and claim as a great world religion.

This essay introduces one phase of the Sikh revival, 1849-1919, during which time the Sikhs moved from political defeat and religious confusion toward the militancy and self-awareness preluding the gurdwara reforms after 1920. Its primary purpose is to present the personalities, organizations, and issues reflected in and producing the works discussed in the bibliography. Such a contextual statement should be helpful for placing the literature within historical perspective. Hopefully the survey also will stimulate discussion of research problems and interest in a neglected area of Sikh history.

Intellectual Crisis and Revitalization

Historians have tended to picture the Sikhs during the first decades of

1. Quotations from *"Notes on the Religion of the Sikhs and Other Sects Inhabiting the Panjab,"* by Major R. Leech, First Assistant Agent, Governor General of India, North-West Frontier, in For. Secret, Dec. 20, 1845, 144 (NAI).

British rule as a disspirited people bordering on economic and religious decline. The decline has not been examined systematically and probably is exaggerated, especially the alleged repercussions of the Sikh wars.[1] Available research nevertheless supports the general view that the Sikhs were enmeshed in forces which threatened their existence as a religious body. Embittered by abrupt loss of power, many Sikhs had difficulty in adapting to the circumstances accompanying British rule and fell behind in education and official employment.[2] The Sikh population also began to dwindle. A few high and low caste Sikhs converted to Islam and Christianity, but the Sikh tendency to abandon old customs and symbols and to move toward orthodox Hindu practices probably accounts for most of the loss in numbers. Beginning in the Ranjit Singh period, this erosion of Sikh ideals and institutions had accelerated to the point that in the 1860's observers felt that Sikhism might disappear. A survey at the time showed that even Sikh religious leaders were uncertain about interpretations of their scripture, their past, and the central question of "what does it mean be a Sikh ?"[3] As in the case of other Punjabis, the Sikhs faced a crisis of identity.

Sikh intellectual activity in the nineteenth century focussed on aspects of unsorting and understanding what constituted tradition and orthodoxy. Although Sikhism possessed an immutable scripture, the *Adi Granth* could be and was interpreted in different ways. One early English translation particularly offended Sikh theologians, Dr. Ernest Trumpp's *The Adi Granth or Holy Scriptures of the Sikhs*.[4] The following excerpt from correspondence with the Government of India, which subsidized the translation, summarizes the core of Trumpp's ideas :

> The greatest part of the Grunth contains a sort of devotional hymn, rather poor in conception, clumsy in style, and wearisome to read.........The writings of the old Hindu Bhagats (or devotees) are on the whole far superior to those of the Sikh Gurus themselves as regards contents and style, especially those of Kabir from whom Nanak and his successors have borrowed all they know and preach. In fact so much is clearly

1. For example, the British were more lenient toward the conquered Sikhs than is commonly realized. The government gave pensions to aristocratic families to use them as a device for controlling the Sikhs. Details on this policy and its results are in GI For. proceedings. NAI.
2. Discussed in Sikh memorial, GI Home Public, June 1883, 134-65A. It is difficult to generalize on employment and education because the British tended to lump Sikhs and Hindus together in statistical tables. Even if the Sikh situation also has been exaggerated, what is important is that the Sikhs felt they were lagging behind.
3. Correspondence in GI For. General, Sept. 1873, 6-10A; Jan. 1874, 1-5A.
4. *The Adi Granth Or Holy Scriptures of the Sikhs* (London, 1877, item 701).

> seen from the Grunth itself that the Sikh Gurus taught nothing new whatever, and if a separate religion and a partially new nationality was in the course of time sprung from it, this was not owing in any way to the doctrine taught by them, but to their financial and political organizations which they gave their disciples."[1]

Leaving aside Trumpp's gratuitous remarks on the value of the *Adi Granth,* his opinion that Sikhism was a Hindu sect whose separation from Hinduism occurred in the post-Guru period evoked a violent reaction from Punjabi Sikhs. Whether Sikhism was a separate religion and when this separation occurred remained vital questions for later theologians and historians. Some Sikhs, especially those following Hindu ritual and lax in maintaining symbols, argued that Sikhs were Hindu, albeit a special variety. Other Sikhs replied with a booming "Ham Hindu Nahin" ("We are not Hindus"). Quoting from historial accounts and the *Adi Granth* the two camps fought over the issue in debates, newspaper columns, and interchanges of tracts.[2] The defenders of separate Sikh identity found support in another European scholar, Max Arthur Macauliffe, who after fifteen years of research published a six-volume study of the Sikh Gurus and religion.[3] Macauliffe wrote his opus in consultation with leaders of the "neo-Sikh" or separatist group (Bhai Kahan Singh, Bhai Ditt Singh, Bhai Vir Singh), and the result can be taken as a statement of their viewpoint. Macauliffe criticized Trumpp, stating that Sikhism had been distinct from Hinduism since the time of Guru Nanak. He also preened the Sikhs for their loyalty to the British and rejection of "backward" Hindu practices :

> To sum up some of the moral and political merits of the Sikh religion : It prohibits idolatry, hypocrisy, caste exclusiveness, the concremation of widows, the immurement of women, the use of wine and other intoxicants, tobacco-smoking, infanticide, slander, pilgrimages to the sacred rivers and tanks of the Hindus; and it inculcates loyalty, gratitude for all favours received, philanthropy, justice, impartiality, truth, honesty, and all the moral and domestic virtues known to the holiest citizens of any country.[4]

1. Trumpp to the Sec. of State for India, Jan. 13, 1874, GI For. General, July 1873, 34-37A. Similar comments were included in the introduction to the published volume.
2. See, for example, items 37, 41, 52, 53, 135, 196, 215, 298, 318, 323, 333, 335, 396, 465, 484.
3. Macauliffe, *The Sikh Religion* (Oxford 1909, item 395).
4. *The Sikh Religion*, I, xxiii.

Theological discussion generated a secondary literature of commentaries and glossaries pertaining to the *Adi Granth*. The publication of each new study in turn generally led to more controversy over the nature of Sikhism.[1] Another offshoot was an assertion that Sikhism should be counted a universal religion. Sikh writers proclaimed that the Gurus' teachings contained the essence of religious understanding and the most valid analysis of human existence.[2] The Sikhs attempted to put this idea into practice by forming world-wide missionary teams.[3] They also actively began to purify (through *shuddhi* or ceremonies of ritual cleansing), and convert Christians, Hindus, and Muslims.[4]

It is not surprising that at the same time Sikhs were exhibiting fresh interest in their past and historical literature in general. Much of the theological discourse rested upon evaluation of history and documents. Scholars such as Professor Gurmukh Singh (1849-1898) and Bhai Kahan Singh of Nabha (1867-1938) toured the Punjab locating and publishing old texts. They discovered hither-to-unknown traditional biographies of Guru Nanak, *janam-sakhis*, and these fostered greater concern with the nature and reliability of sources.[5] By the end of the century at least two societies sponsored historical research, the Gurmat Granth Pracharak Sabha of Amritsar which prepared reports on documents and the Gurmat Granth Sudharak Committee of Lahore which examined sources and attempted to prevent the printing of unauthentic *janam-sakhis* and inferior editions of the *Adi Granth*.[6] Studies by individuals supplemented the work of organizations. For example, Giani Gyan Singh wrote several histories, while Bhai Kahan Singh produced a commentary on Sikhism, glossaries, and a substantial encyclopedia of Sikh religion and literature.[7] None could match Bhai Ditt Singh for sheer volume. Between 1880 and 1900 he wrote forty books on martyrs, history and theology.[8] These studies are not only sources on Sikh history and scripture,

1. The Faridkot commentary and the edition of the *Adi Granth* by the Bhasaur Singh Sabha were particularly controversial works (see items 56, 884, 919).
2. Reflected in speeches delivered at the annual Sikh Educational Conference.
3. See, for example, the proposal for the creation of a missionary unit: *Khalsa Baradari Unatti Ashram Dian Kunjian* (Rangoon, 1908, item 843).
4. The monthly issues of the *Shuddhi Pattar* (item 1230) contain reports on the conversions, 1896-98. Also, see items 239, 612, 936, 1229.
5. Background in McLeod, *Guru Nanak*, pp. 1-33. Also, essays in Harbans Singh and Jagjit Singh, "Singh Sabha Lahir," in Ganda Singh (ed.), *Panjab 1849-1960* (Ludhiana, 1962), pp. 123-40.
6. Munsha Singh Dukhi, *Jivan Bhai Sahib Bhai Mohan Singh Vaid* (Amritsar, n/d.), pp. 16-18; Harbans Singh and Jagjit Singh, "Singh Sabha Lahir", pp. 127-28, 139.
7. Giani Gyan Singh, *Panth Prakash* (Lahore, 1880, item 240); *Tawarikh-i-Guru Khalsa* (3 vols. Sialkot, 1892, item 243). Bhai Kahan Singh, *Gurmat Prabhakar* (Lahore, 1898, item 332); *Gurushabd Ratnakar Mahan Kosh* (1/ed. 1930; 2/ed., 4 vols., Patiala, 1960).
8. Shamsher Singh Ashok, *Bhai Kahan Singh Nabha* (Gurar, 1966), pp. 48-55; Giani Amar Singh, *Singh Sabha Lahir De Ughe Sanchalak Giani Ditt Singhji* (Amritsar, 1962), pp. 93-96.

they mirror the interests and interpretations of a generation trying to formulate a viable statement of Sikh doctrine.

Concern with orthodoxy and "what is a Sikh ?" led to a re-examination of current social and religious conduct. The first characteristic of the consequent reform effort was a highlighting of Sikh distinctiveness. Reformers believed that Sikhism's survival and prosperity depended on emphasis of "Sikh" custom and elimination of "non-Sikh" elements which had slipped into common usage. Sikh boundaries were to be demarcated and maintained. For example, celebration of memorable events in Sikh history should be substituted for participation in Hindu festivals.[1] The expression of Sikh identity in daily life was related to another object, the cultivation of a renewed sense of Sikh community and the strengtheing of that community against internal and external threats. Service for the *Panth*, progress of the community, defence of Sikhism, building the Sikh nation—these slogans filled the literature of the period. Reformers were not content to revive old forms and models, they also wanted to modernize their religion, adding or changing elements thought necessary for the late nineteenth century. Caste, for example, had to be eliminated for two reasons. Social restrictions were opposed to the doctrine of Sikh brotherhood, and they placed a check on the creativity of individuals, creativity necessary for the progress of the *Panth*[2] The move to revitalize Sikhism reflected this duality of purpose, a combination of utility and a desire to return to guidelines set by the Gurus.

Although calculated to strengthen the community, criticism of existing patterns split the Sikhs into warring factions. Intellectuals might become excited over theological points, but the application of "Ham Hindu Nahin" to everyday affairs affected the entire *Panth.* The labelling of norms and accepted activities (e.g., Brahmans officiating in rituals, Hindu idols in the premises of the Golden Temple, worship of Muslim saints, and pilgrimages to the Ganges) as "non-Sikh" understandably created turmoil.[3]

The streams of Sikh reform illustrate these patterns. Ceremonial procedure was a key issue for nineteenth-century Sikhs. Reformers urged that the Brahman-dominated and Hinduized rites of passage (birth, puberty, marriage, and death) be replaced with simple ceremonies emphasizing the *Adi Granth* and the corporate life of Sikhism. Such observances would have the added value of shielding Sikhs from exorbitant debts. The ensuing discussion produced compilations of rules for the conduct of Sikh rites, and in 1909 the

1. On festivals and holidays, see items 177, 668, 766, 806.
2. For example, discussion in Bhai Gurdial Singh, *Pisne Ka Pisna Rangraw Ka Rangraw* (Rajajang, 1914, item 216); *Sachcha Rahbar* (Gujranwala, 1910, item 910).
3. For example, items listed in the subject-title index under "Controversies among Sikhs."

legitimization of Sikh ceremony through the passage of the Anand Marriage Bill. As frequently happened, the victory of the neo-Sikh or separatist forces alienated others and stirred up the Punjab press.[1] Attempts to assert the equality of men and women were equally controversial. Educated Sikhs generally advocated instruction for Sikh girls and relaxation of severe restrictions on movements. These reforms were buttressed with appeals to tradition, particularly opposition to *purdah* or the Muslim seclusion of females, and with the pragmatic argument that a liberal attitude toward women would improve homelife and foster "progressive" thinking among children. A small but vocal group of radicals demanded that women be given equality in all ceremonies and wear the five "k's."[2]

The spread of Sikh education and Gurmukhi reflect similar concerns. Often Sikh leaders felt that the public schools "de-nationalized" students, who then strayed from religion and old allegiances. On the other hand, western education was requisite for the advancement of Sikh interests. Educationalists tried to deal with the problem by establishing separate institutions which synthesized theological and moral training with European subjects.[3] Appeals for Sikh schools were combined with a campaign to popularize Panjabi as a literary language and to have Panjabi in the Gurmukhi script made equal to Urdu in the British educational curriculum. Since the *Adi Granth* had been written in Gurmukhi, some argued, Sikhs must consider Gurmukhi their own script and use it in all transactions. At the same time Panjabi advocates realized that if Gurmukhi received further patronage, the Sikhs would be the chief benefactors. A third argument usually was found for Panjabi, namely that its universal adoption by Sikhs further unified the community and reinforced a spirit of Sikh nationalism.[4]

Emergence of New Sikh Institutions

Criticism of Sikh social and religious practice had begun prior to the introduction of British rule. The Nirankari sect, descended from Baba Dyal Singh (1783-1854), opposed idol worship and preached marriage reform, a tradition continued and elaborated by the Namdharis or Kukas. The founder of the Kukas, Bhai Balak Singh (1799-1862), set stringent requirements for his followers. They were expected to sing praises continually to the Guru, to

1. Background in K.S. Talwar, "The Anand Marriage Act" *Panjab Past and Present II*, Pt. 2 (Oct. 1968), 400-10.
2. For information on one such militant group, the Bhasaur Singh Sabha, see *Aduti Jivan Britant Panth Ratan Babu Teja Singh Overseer* (Amritsar, n.d.).
3. Reflected in the speeches on education at the annual Sikh Educational Conference. See the subject-title index under "Education-speeches."
4. Munsha Singh, *Mohan Singh Vaid*, pp. 186-89, 222; also, Mohan Singh Vaid, *Benati* (Lahore, 1903, item 425).

avoid marriage expenses and dowries, to contribute at least a rupee each month, to refuse meat, wine and tobacco, and to lead "a moral life." Under a *chela* of Bhai Balak Singh, Ram Singh (1816-1884), the Namdharis moved toward more militant reform. Although Ram Singh was deported in 1872 and the Kuka organizations disassembled following an abortive uprising, the spirit and some of the personnel connected with the Kukas and the Nirankaris played a role in the early years of the Singh Sabha movement.[1]

The founding of the Amritsar Singh Sabha in 1873 and a sister organization in Lahore (1879) marked a new chapter in the evolution of Sikhism. Earlier efforts at altering prevalent Sikh conditions had been limited to sects and groups considered heterodox or barely on the fringe of the Sikh faith. The Singh Sabhas occasionally met insults and charges of *manmati* (false or self-construed religion), but the fact remained that their membership included respectable and accepted leaders of the Sikh community. These men stood within the fold of Sikhism and avoided radical demands which might have led to their ostracism.

Sikh conversions to Christianity and the anti-Sikh speeches of Hindu propagandists precipitated the founding of the Amritsar Singh Sabha. Following a series of open meetings, Sikhs from Amritsar and surrounding districts adopted these principles as the basis for the association:

1. The purpose of the Singh Sabha is to arouse love of religion among Sikhs.
2. The Sabha will propagate the true Sikh religion everywhere.
3. The Sabha will print books on the greatness and truth of the Sikh religion.
4. The Sabha will propagate the words of the Gurus.
5. The Sabha will publish periodicals to further the Panjabi language and Sikh education.
6. Individuals who oppose Sikhism, who have been excluded from Sikh holy spots, or who have associated with other religions and broken Sikh laws cannot join the Sabha. If they repent and pay a fine, they can become members.
7. English officers interested in Sikh education and the well-being of Sikhism can associate with the Sabha, also those who support the Panjabi language.
8. The Sabha will not speak against other religions.
9. The Sabha will not discuss matters relating to the government.

1. For information see Ganda Singh, "Nirankari Sanpardai" and "Kuka Lahir," in *Panjab 1849-1960*, pp. 80-122.

10. The Sabha will respect well-wishers of the community, those who love Sikhism, and those who support truth and education in Panjabi.[1]

The Lahore Singh Sabha adopted a similar programme, followed by the one hundred and twenty other sabhas operative in 1899. Depending on local circumstance, the new organizations held religious meetings *(diwans)*, established schools and orphanages, and sent out preaching *(prachar)* teams. Financial support came from individual subscriptions, donations at conferences, and sporadic grants from rajas or wealthy "gentry." The sabhas were distributed throughout the Punjab and neighbouring provinces, with branches in both rura and urban areas. Membership included the classes and castes prominent in Sikhism: the aristocracy and landlords, zamindars, merchants, professional men, and menials, drawn from the Jat, Arora, Khatri and even "depressed" castes.[2] Sikh soldiers proved to be an additional source of strength for sabhas. The British deliberately maintained religious orthodoxy among Sikh troops to perpetuate their martial spirit, with the result that the soliders provided constant moral support and funds for the reformers.[3] Sabhas usually had a constitution which formalized internal arrangements and programme, illustrated by the rules and regulations of the Karachi Singh Sabha. Membership of the Sabha consisted of baptized Sikhs or *Sajhdharis* (clean-shaven Sikhs) "who are ready to declare that they adhere to the tenets of the Gurus, do not belong to any other religious sect, and pay a subscription of at least annas four per mensem."[4] Members could be ousted for nonpayment of dues or by a majority vote. A fifteen-man executive committee dealt with employees and prepared rules, budgets and annual reports. Of the fifteen, six positions were reserved for members who were not "Singh" (orthodox or *Keshdhari* Sikhs).

Each Sikh unit had its own personality and peculiar interest despite similarity in composition and programme. Often this colouring came from the man or the group of men instrumental in the sabha. A brief mention of a few such leaders would not be out of place because they moulded the issues and gave direction to the Singh Sabha movement.

The Amritsar Singh Sabha derived much of its ideology and spirit from the Maharaja of Faridkot (Bikram Singh) and Baba Khem Singh Bedi (1832-1905), a direct descendant of Guru Nanak. Both donated large sums to

1. Jagjit Singh and Harbans Singh, "Singh Sabha Lahir," pp. 124-25, 131-33.
2. Based on research in annual reports and the two Khalsa directories (items 846-47).
3. Harbans Singh, "Singh Sabha Lahir," pp. 133-34; Nahar Singh (ed.), "Developments in Sikh Politics, 1900-1911," *Gurduara Gazette* (P), April 1969, English section, p. 15.
4. *Rules and Regulations of the Siri Guru Singh Sabha, Karachi* (Karachi, n/d., c. 1909), p. 1. For other reports, consult section 3.

education and related projects. They tended to be conservative, however, looking down on the Lahore Singh Sabha and particularly its low caste leader Bhai Ditt Singh. Their demand for special reverence finally precipitated an open break between the two sabhas in 1883.[1]

Professor Gurmukh Singh and Bhai Ditt Singh led the Lahore association. Gurmukh Singh had been trained under the auspices of Kanwar Bikrama Singh of Kapurthala, a founder of the Amritsar Singh Sabha. Gurmukh Singh taught mathematics and Panjabi at the Oriental College, Lahore, publicized Panjabi literature, and helped found at least five newspapers. One of his greatest contributions to Sikh reform was the conversion of Bhai Ditt Singh (1853-1901) to the Singh Sabha cause. Ditt Singh quickly became the chief propagandist for the Lahore Singh Sabha.[2] Although he "exposed" and challenged non-Sikh writers, especially Arya Samajists, Ditt Singh's preoccupation was righting what he considered to be unpardonable defects within the Sikh community. Caste and "Guru-dom" received special blows. Ditt Singh personally had experienced the double social standard operating among Sikhs, and he incessantly denounced high caste Sikhs looking down at converts or "unclean" co-religionists. Caste controversy led to collisions with *pujaris* and members of the Amritsar Singh Sabha. Ditt Singh slashed at their pretensions of being "gurus" (holding a special place in the Sikh community) in a tract entitled *Sudhan Natak* ("A Dream Drama"). His ridicule of *pujaris* and other opponents such as Baba Khem Singh landed Ditt Singh in court, the first of many prosecutions arising from his publications.

Bhai Takht Singh (1860-1937) directed the programme of the Ferozepur Singh Sabha. Also a protègè of Professor Gurmukh Singh, Takht Singh devoted his life to female education and almost single-handedly built up the Sikh Kanya Mahavidyala (a high school and hostel for girls) in the 1890's when the idea of educating women was unthinkable in many Sikh circles. Given the title of "the living martyr" by those who stood in awe of his energy and devotion, Bhai Takht Singh was always ready to travel hundreds of miles to sing at a meeting or to collect funds.[3]

Babu Teja Singh Overseer (1867-1933) converted the sabha of a small village near Sangrur, Bhasaur, into a centre of Sikh militancy. If Bhai Takht Singh was labelled a "living martyr," Babu Teja Singh could well be termed the "human hurricane," a ceaseless source of ideas and sharply-worded pamph-

1. Harbans Singh and Jagjit Singh, "Singh Sabha Lahir," pp. 126-27, 137-38.
2. This sketch primarily drawn from Amar Singh's biography of Bhai Ditt Singh.
3. On Takht Singh, see Attar Singh, *Jinda Shahid Nun Moran Lai Vichar Te Tajwiz* (Lahore, 1916).

lets. Clad in rough *swadeshi* clothes and clutching an omnipresent sword, Teja Singh led his Bhasaur associates into ideological combat with Hindus, other Sikhs, and even rulers of princely states. He was obsessed with the revitalization of the Sikh religion, an ideal nowhere better illustrated than by an incident in which Teja Singh left an injured son to carry out a preaching schedule. When bystanders shouted that his son was moaning in pain, Teja Singh supposedly replied that while the boy was only one person, "many people are crying for baptism."[1] On another occasion Teja Singh founded his own school for girls because Takht Singh refused permission to proselytize among students at Ferozepur. Each girl in Teja Singh's school and ashram was encouraged to receive baptism, to learn parts of the *Granth* by heart, and to wear headbands resembling turbans.[2]

Bhai Mohan Singh Vaid (1881-1936) of the Tarn Taran Singh Sabha matched Teja Singh Overseer in spirit and rate of publication, but his leadership and journalism reflected a more gentle and conciliatory attitude toward current issues. Maturing in an age of controversy and pamphleteering, Mohan Singh early evolved a routine of work, worship and writing which continued through his life. He moved back and forth across the Punjab providing medical service, lecturing and distributing literature. In spare time he wrote literally hundreds of books and tracts on subjects ranging from religion and social reform to medicine and vice. Panjabi was a special passion, and to encourage its use, he formed Gurmukhi publishing organizations. A second concern was reform of Sikh gurdwaras, an activity precluding Akali efforts by over two decades.[3]

These Sikhs, and others like them, provided the motivation and continuity for the sabhas. They also served as links in an informal communication chain binding the dispersed organizations. Takht Singh, Mohan Singh Vaid, and Ditt Singh wrote to each other and discussed mutual problems while gathered at religious conferences. In addition, Teja Singh formed corresponding committees to relay information and opinion on pressing matters.[4]

The growth of Sikh journalism offered another means of communication. Quick to appreciate the potential of this channel for disseminating ideas and news, Singh sabha leaders rushed to set up presses and papers, often without experience or proper financing. This accounts for the experi-

1. *Aduti Jivan*, p. 76. Note that Babu Teja Singh and Principal Teja Singh are two different individuals.
2. *Ibid.* pp. 116-19.
3. Sketch drawn from Munsha Singh Dukhi's biography of Mohan Singh Vaid.
4. *Aduti Jivan*, pp. 55, 175-77; Munsha Singh Dukhi, *Mohan Singh Vaid*, pp. 62-63, 247-48, 252.

mentation and the rapid rise and fall of papers characterizing Sikh journalistic efforts prior to 1900.

Sikh newspapers tended to be started for a particular purpose, and unless subsidized by a raja or businessman, the enterprises ran on a slim budget. Accordingly, when interest in the cause waned, or when subscriptions dropped off, the papers suspended operation, to reappear again if circumstance permitted. Newspapers generally were in Urdu or Panjabi and had small circulations (150-400). They were weekly, bi-monthly or monthly with occasional bulletins or supplements. The papers shared a similar format—a page of scripture, editorials, perhaps a special article, local news, and a letter column in which correspondents challenged the editor and other writers on a variety of subjects.[1]

The background of several periodicals illustrate these patterns. Professor Gurmukh Singh and his Lahore friends established two early journals, the *Vidya Pracharak* and the *Gurmukhi Akhbar,* to foster Sikh education and Panjabi as a literary language.[2] Although the former collapsed, the *Gurmukhi Akhbar* ran from 1880 until 1895. In 1883 Gurmukh Singh joined with Bhai Jhanda Singh and Bhai Ditt Singh to found the Khalsa Press and the *Khalsa Akhbar.* With Ditt Singh and Bhai Maya Singh as editors, the *Khalsa Akhbar* became a chief spokesman for the Lahore Singh Sabha until Ditt Singh's death in 1901. The longevity of the papers can be attributed chiefly to the efforts of Gurmukh Singh and Ditt Singh, and sustained financial backing from Hira Singh, the Maharaja of Nabha.[3] Other Sikh papers were short-lived, as for example, the *Nanak Parkash* (Urdu, 1887-89 ?) of Kapurthala, Bhagat Lakshman Singh's English-language *Khalsa* (1899-1901), and the Panjabi *Shuddhi Pattar,* an organ of the Lahore Shuddhi Sabha published between 1896 and 1898.[4]

The first decades of the twentieth century witnessed an upsurge of Sikh journalism. New papers focussed on female education or family life *(Istri Satsang,* a Panjabi weekly from Amritsar, c.1904-10: *Panjabi Bhain,* the Ferozepur Sikh Kanya Mahavidyala's Panjabi monthly, c.1909-20). Others were designed for soliders *(The Sikh Sepoy,* the Ferozepur Sikh Recruiting Committee's monthly journal in Panjabi, 1917-20), reproduced scripture and sermons *(Nirgunyara,* published by the Khalsa Tract Society, 1900-present),

1. Generalization based on police reports on the Punjab press (Home Political and Public, NAI) and research in Sikh periodicals, particularly the *Khalsa Advocate, Khalsa Samachar, Khalsa Akhbar, Khalsa Gazette,* and *Shuddhi Pattar.*
2. Jagjit Singh, "Singh Sabha Lahir," p. 125. Also, Punjab press reports. Detailed information on these papers is in Section 4.
3. Amar Singh, *Ditt Singh,* pp. 75-76, 128. A jagir also supported the Guru Nanak Parkash Press.
4. For background on these papers, see the Punjab press reports and *Bhagat Lakshman Singh Autobiography* (ed. by Ganda Singh, Calcutta, 1966), pp. 105-44.

or spoke for a section of the Sikh community (e.g., the Ramgarhia periodicals *Ramgarhia Patrika* of Lahore and the *Viskarma* of Amritsar). Despite failures, newspapers tended to circulate for longer periods of time—the Urdu *Lyall Gazette,* begun in 1911 by Sardar Amar Singh; the Panjabi *Khalsa Samachar,* begun by Bhais Wazir Singh and Vir Singh at Amritsar in 1899; and the *Khalsa Advocate,* an English weekly beginning in 1901 and running until 1923 when it merged with the *Khalsa* to form the Panjabi *Khalsa Te Khalsa Advocate.*

The lack of a central organization to coordinate activities necessitated informal contacts among leaders and these developments in Sikh journalism. As early as 1880, attempts were made to bring the Lahore and Amritsar Singh Sabhas under one executive body, but the vitality of the Lahore group and the orientation of the Amritsar leadership doomed the project. From 1883 onward there were two Khalsa Diwans, Lahore and Amritsar, with two constellations of associated sabhas. Although Sikhs could cooperate to meet common threats or to establish institutions such as the Khalsa College, Amritsar (1893), much of their energy was devoted to bickering over internal matters and personality conflicts.[1] This had changed by the turn of the century. The almost geometric multiplication of organizations made impossible the maintenance of satisfactory informal contacts among the sabhas. Unnecessary duplication of programmes and large projects requiring united action (such as the virtual bankruptcy of Khalsa College) pointed to the utility of a central agency to coordinate and in a limited sense to guide the smaller units. Too, by 1900 many founding fathers had died, and with them, the acute bitterness and personal feuds. A new generation, headed by Sardar Sunder Singh Majithia, consequently prepared a draft constitution and in 1902 formed the Chief Khalsa Diwan, Amritsar.[2]

The Chief Khalsa Diwan fulfilled several functions for the Singh sabhas. First, it furnished a meeting place and centre of communication for educated Sikhs. Delegates attended monthly sessions and discussed problems with the executive committee. The Diwan's annual conference offered an even greater opportunity for interaction and exchange of ideas. Secondly, the Diwan raised funds for and helped administer central institutions such as the Amritsar Khalsa Orphanage and Khalsa Tract Society. It also provided preachers, singers and tour groups for local religious gatherings. Finally, the Chief Khalsa Diwan took a stand on theological and social issues and if

1. Jagjit Singh, "Singh Sabha Lahir," pp. 126-27; Shamsher Singh Ashok, *Kahan Singh,* pp. 23-31. For the Khalsa College dispute, Ganda Singh, *A History of the Khalsa College, Amritsar* (Amritsar, 1949), pp. 1-23.
2. Jagjit Singh, "Singh Sabha Lahir," pp. 129-30. Item 1006 contains the draft rules.

necessary attempted to mobolize Sikh opinion in support of its position.[1]

The forces giving impetus to the Singh sabhas and the Chief Khalsa Diwan, Amritsar, produced other Sikh institutions, most notably the Sikh Educational Conference. First held in April of 1908, the annual Conference had a constitution and was supervised by an Educational Committee affiliated with the Chief Khalsa Diwan. The Diwan, Singh sabhas, educational institutions and Sikh graduates elected members of the Committee. Besides collecting funds and administering schools, the Conference gave Sikhs an opportunity to air views on education and related topics. Approximately two to three thousand Sikhs attended each session, the location of which rotated annually. During the three-day meetings prominent Sikhs lectured on religion, education and Panjabi, followed by the passing of unanimous resolutions on matters affecting Sikhs such as representation in the education department, examination results, and religious instruction. Large sums were contributed for special programmes and a "national fund" totalling over Rs. 200,000 in 1920.[2]

A second variety of institution also began to appear, Sikh organizations specializing in the publication and distribution of tract material. Pamphlets had been an effective vehicle for conveying ideas and propaganda since the inception of the first Singh sabhas. The earliest tracts depended on the initiative and personal resources of individuals. Bhai Ditt Singh, Bhai Mohan Singh Vaid, and Babu Teja Singh were prominent in this field. They wrote, published, and sold their own essays, generally at a great loss.[3]

The resulting tracts can be sorted into two categories. Some carried a message of *elan* or *benati* (appeal). Tracts commonly were used to request support for an organization, project or idea. Apparently the Sikhs responded to the calls because *benati* items increased after 1900.[4] The most popular variety of tract, however, was the polemic, a short piece attacking enemies or defending a cause. The titles of such tracts often indicate their style and purpose: "a war," "a crushing defeat," "a demolishing attack on fools," "refutation of lies," or Avtar Singh's derisive counter to *Sikh Hindu Hain,* "As the

1. Based on the unpublished minutes of the Chief Khalsa Diwan, 1903-05 (CKD Office, Amritsar) and the correspondence between Kabul Singh and the Diwan, in Kabul Singh's private papers (in the possession of the his son, Sardar Waryam Singh, Chandigarh).
2. Background on the educational conference is contained in two anniversary volumes: *Golden Jubilee Book* (Amritsar, 1958); *Silver Jubilee Book* (Amritsar, n/d.); also, Charan Singh, Darbara Singh, *The Work of the Sikh Educational Conference* (Amritsar, 1944).
3. Illustrated by excerpts from Mohan Singh Vaid's diary, reprinted in Munsha Singh Dukhi, *Mohan Singh Vaid,* p. 319.
4. Examples include Mohan Singh Vaid's two tracts titled *Benati* (items 425-26), an appeal for the improvement of morals and better treatment of Sikh women, and a call for support of Panjabi.

face, so the slap, or a face-breaking reply" (*Jeha Munh Tehi Chaper Arthat Munh Tor Khandan*. Amritsar, 1906). Punjabis were experiencing intense self-examination which generated intellectual turmoil and encounters with rivals. In the late nineteenth century, described as "the time for the drawing of bows," publicists were quick to reach for their pens. Nothing was sacred in the emotional tract wars—scripture, heroes, or family life. Not lagging behind in controversy, a few Sikhs criticized Hindus, Arya Samajists, Muslims, and Christians. Others turned on fellow Sikhs. Lines were sharply drawn and defended on issues such as control of shrines, the nature of Sikh ceremony, and conversion. Panjabi has a store of insult and derogatory terms, and probably these have never been put to more devastating use than when Sikh opponents locked horns.[1]

Although the adventures of individual pamphleteers continued, societies took over the bulk of religious propaganda. Founded in 1894, the Khalsa Tract Society led in the production of small, cheap volumes on theology and social topics. The society financed itself through subscriptions; in 1901, for example, 369 subscribers donated approximately one rupee a month for which they received a copy of publications and the "Sat Sri Akal" of the *Panth*. Statistics from the 1902 report indicate that the Society had published 192 items in eight years and distributed over half a million copies. Guidelines for prospective contributors reflect the aims of the organization. Essays were to be brief and to the point, suitable for both men and women, and in "pure" Panjabi (Gurmukhi script). Authors should support their arguments with scripture and not speak against other religions.[2] The bulk of the Society's works consisted of scripture and prayers, biographies, and didactic tales on morals, society, and religion. It also published dictionaries, glossaries, and two Khalsa directories. The latter are notable because they contain members of Singh sabhas and information on Sikhs employed in government.[3]

Organizations such as the Sikh Book Club of Peshawar soon challenged the monopoly of the Khalsa Tract Society. By 1911 the Club and its successor, the Panch Khalsa Agency, had printed 125 items on ritual, marital relations, "loyalty," the nature of God, and cleansing of "non-Sikh converts."[4] These

1. Shamsher Singh Ashok, *Kahan Singh*, p. 8. Also, descriptions in Amar Singh and Munsha Singh Dukhi. Examples of forceful tracts include Babu Teja Singh, *Man Mat Prahar* (Lahore, 1900, item 674) and Mohan Singh, Nabha, *Fohash Navishan Da Badshah* (Amritsar, n/d.).
2. *Khalsa Tract Society Da Report, 1902* (Amritsar, 1903, item 1123), pp. 33-35. Bhai Vir Singh wrote or edited most of the tracts.
3 *Khalsa Directory* (Amritsar, 1898, item 846; Amritsar, 1900, item 847). Both are in Panjabi.
4. *Punjab Book Catalogue for the Quarter Ending March 31, 1911*, in *Punjab Gazette* (Supplement), pp. 105-06.

in turn were supplemented by Panjabi Prachar societies printing translations or original works in Gurmukhi.[1] A final innovation in the preparation of inexpensive literature came in 1908 with the founding of the Khalsa Handbill Society. The Society published as many as twenty thousand copies of a work for free distribution among villagers untouched by urban meetings or periodicals. A predominately agrarian community, the Sikhs pioneered in programmes to link rural and urban co-religionists with publicity, tracts, and *prachar* (preaching or missionary programmes).[2]

The efforts of these institutions to unite the Sikhs at least initially had an opposite effect, the widening of existing schisms. The supporters of the Chief Khalsa Diwan, frequently referred to as the "Tat Khalsa" ("true" or orthodox Sikh) because of their insistence on separation from Hinduism and attachment to Sikh symbols, were determined to strengthen Sikhism at any cost. To expand the Sikh population, for example, they advocated mass reclamation of low caste Sikh converts to Hinduism, Islam and Christianity. The leaders of this "depressed class movement" assisted in the rebaptism of converts and then ate food from their hands. Too, the Diwan and its affiliates aggressively demanded reform of the gurdwaras. The managers of Sikh shrines showed little respect for distinct Sikh symbols or theology. Flounting their authority and treating the gurdwaras as private property, they permitted Hindu idols, pictures of gods, prostitutes, gambling and pornography in or nearby the temples. When confronted with the demand that they end the practices and pay penance for misconduct, the managers generally responded by refusing Tat Khalsa Sikhs admission to places of worship and rejecting their offerings. Just before the third Sikh Educational Conference at Amritsar in 1910, for example, religious authorities asked the District Commissioner to ban a proposed procession from the Railway Station to the Golden Temple on the grounds that Conference leaders had overridden social norms and had eaten with outcastes. Armed conflict was avoided only because a late train forced the procession to proceed directly to the Khalsa College.[3]

The militant action of the Tat Khalsa party had two significant consequences. First, they became alienated from thc *pujaris*, managers, and their numerous backers. Reformers tended to turn their backs on the priesthood because of its resistance to purification of low castes and other changes. In some cases they quit attending places of worship and abandoned formal reli-

1. Munsha Singh Dukhi, *Mohan Singh Vaid*, pp. 186-89, 222.
2. Munsha Singh Dukhi, *Mohan Singh Vaid*, pp. 132-33. See, for example, *Sidaq De Bere Par* (Lahore, 1910, item 938). The Sikh Handbill Society was begun at approximately the same time.
3. Nahar Singh, "Sikh Politics," pp. 32-33.

gious observances, leaving themselves open to charges of being irreligious :

> So far as is known they have made no efforts to establish gurdwaras which would be administered by priests of their own way of thinking, but they seem on the other hand to have developed an almost complete indifference to their religion and its attendant rites and ceremonies. The freedom of thought and laxity of observances displayed by the Tat Khalsa are looked upon with something like dismay by orthodox Sikhs...[1]

This seeming abandonment of tradition led to a new development, organized resistance to the Chief Khalsa Diwan. By 1910 several organizations (e.g., the Puratan Khalsa Diwan and the Central Khalsa Diwan of Nabha) contested the Chief Khalsa Diwan's claim to represent all Sikhs.[2]

To *pujaris* the Tat Khalsa party was ultra-progressive; to another section of Sikhs the so-called advanced party was too conservative, compromising and equivocating on key issues. From its inception in 1907, the Panch Khalsa Diwan, or Khalsa Parliament, championed almost fanatical alterations in Sikh practice which upset even members of the Chief Khalsa Diwan. The Panch Khalsa faction and its base organization, the Bhasaur Singh Sabha, demanded innovations such as the banning of *ragis* (singers) who had not been properly baptized, complete equality and intermixing of men and women, and cessation of social relations with Hindus (dining, marriage).[3] It further assumed the responsibility of prescribing "correct" Sikh ceremonies and editing the *Adi Granth*. The latter activity caused a particularly bitter controversy. In its edition of scripture, the Diwan omitted the "Rag Mala," a concluding section comprising religious poems of a Muslim, Alim. The resulting screams of "sacrilege" evoked an emotional defence and disdain from the Panch Khalsa Diwan.[4] Babu Teja Singh and his friends also carried the ideological battle into the camp of the Chief Khalsa Diwan with charges that its collection of

1. Nahar Singh, "Sikh Politics," p. 33. Letters in the *Tribune*, 1909-10, support the CID opinion.
2. Nahar Singh, "Sikh Politics," p. 33. Little information is available on these organizations, but research probably will show that they played a key role in internal Sikh politics.
3. Discussed in *Khalsa Dharmik Conference De Tije Salana Report* (Bhasaur, 1923). Also, *Panch Khalsa Diwan Salana Diwan Sabandhi Samachar Da Duja Bhag* (Bhasaur, 1916 item 1130).
4. *Khalsa Dharmik Conference*, pp. 29-30.

Sikh rituals, *Gurmat Prakash Bhag Sanskar,* perpetuated non-Sikh traditions.[1]

Within half a century the forces confronting the Sikhs had produced a wide and bewildering range of institutions. Although involved with the same problems, the institutions and their members came up with varied and often conflicting analyses of the nature of Sikhism and what must be done to insure its survival. Divergent opinion and conflict also characterized another aspect of the Sikh experience under the British *raj*, communal identity and communal politics.

The Sikhs and Communal Politics

Ideological movements in the late nineteenth century furnished much of the impetus for the development of Sikh political consciousness. Although the memory of past glory and attitudes inherited from the Ranjit Singh period probably had some influence, the drive to establish religious and social boundaries, emphasis on symbols and general self-strenghening primarily determined Sikh attitudes and action. As previously noted, this meant that Sikh institutions became fields on which rival groups jockeyed for power, authority, and prestige. Internal developments in turn affected how Sikhs handled a key political problem, communal relations with other Punjabis.

The relationship between Hinduism and Sikhism became an absorbing issue for Sikh leaders. On the one hand, pressure was mounting for disengagement from the Hindu faith, a move felt necessary for the maintenance of Sikh custom and identity. Occasional derogatory remarks by Hindu preachers reinforced Sikh suspicion. On the other hand, Punjabi Hindus and Sikhs shared a history of persecution, social patterns, and religious tradition. They were quite close in 1849, and to break them apart invited trouble. Moreover, Arya Samajists, with whom educated Sikhs initially identified and cooperated, insisted that Sikhs were Hindu. As in the case of the Singh sabhas, Arya Samajists bolstered their community by adapting to changed circumstance and evolving new institutions. One chief Arya goal was to insure that Sikhs be counted as Hindu for the purpose of determining weightage in employment and education.[2]

A decade after the introduction of the Arya Samaj in the Punjab (1877),

1. *Ibid.* Also, *Salana Diwan*, pp. 1-28. The writer, probably Babu Teja Singh, claimed that the Khalsa Diwan overemphasized the role of the Granthi and thus undermined the notion of Sikh equality. Unequal treatment of women and ideas on how much should be donated also came under attack. For a reply, see Man Singh, *Sach Da Parkash* (Amritsar, 1918, item 404).
2. The Samaj activities discussed in Kenneth W. Jones, "Communalism in the Punjab : The Arya Samaj Contribution," *Journal of Asian Studies*, XXVII, 1 (Nov. 1968), pp. 39-54.

however, Sikh cooperation had turned to hostility. Dayanand's remarks about the Gurus were judged offensive, as was Arya reluctance to accept Sikhs as full partners in their institutions. Speeches at annual Samaj functions in 1887 and 1888 drove away most of the remaining Sikh supporters.[1] The Tat Khalsa party increasingly portrayed the Arya Samaj as the number one enemy of Sikhism, with preachers and publicists from both sides crossing swords in journals, debates, and in exchanges of tracts.

Two controversial essays illustrate the themes and innuendo in the Arya-Sikh literature. The first is Radha Kishen Mehta's provocative tract titled "*Prescription for Granthi Phobia.*"[2] The Arya pamphleteer begins with the usual statement that he does not wish to injure the religious feelings of the other sect. The "however" follows, in this case, Radha Kishen claims that he has been forced to comment on Sikhism because of alleged abuses against Dayanand by Bhai Jawahir Singh, secretary of the Lahore Singh Sabha. After charges against Jawahir Singh (including rape and opportunism) comes a defence of Dayanand combined with criticism of Guru Nanak. According to the Arya writer, Nanak pretended to be an *avatar* of God and ordered Guru Angad to commit incest with his own mother. The work closes with these scathing remarks on the *janam-sakhi* accounts of Guru Nanak's travels:

> Listen Bhai Sahib, we have found one more science in your sacred book, and that science is geography. As far as we can tell, your understanding of the subject is complete. How foolish are present and past masters of geography who have not taken into account your knowledge and the geographical wisdom of Guru Nanak. Nanak deserves to be congratulated for having discovered mountains such as Prabhat Parbat, Shraddha Parbat, Kota Parbat, etc., and a number of oceans and ports bearing strange names such as Surat Bunder, Chapta Bunder, etc. It is our view, Bhai Sahib, that you should get new maps prepared spotting out these various holy places, and if you yourself go to one of these ports and preach the *Guru Granth Sahib* there, it is certain that this and all similar branches of knowledge will spread over the

1. For further details, see Ganda Singh, "The Origins of the Hindu-Sikh Tension in the Punjab," *Journal of Indian History*, XXXIX (April 1961), pp. 120-23; Jones, "Communalism" pp. 47-50; *Bhagat Lakshman Singh Autobiography*, pp. 58-60.
2. *Nushkha-i-Granthi Fobia* (Lahore, 1889, item 524).

> universe. We shall raise subscriptions to meet the expenses of your travels in this regard.[1]

The corresponding Sikh tract, "Prescription for the insanity of the followers of Dayanand" matches Radha Kishen's piece in emotion and in an ability to strike at the jugular of the opponent. Ganda Singh, president of the Guru Upkar Parcharini Sabha, Amritsar, wrote this essay to "refute" Lala Sahib Dyal's "Remedy for the whims of Ditt Singh" *(Ilaj-i-Wahmat-i-Ditt Singhia)*. Disclaiming an intention of injuring his "brothers" (Hindus and Aryas) Ganda Singh then proceeds to do so for a hundred pages. First is a character sketch of Sahib Dyal, whom Ganda Singh claims was famous for his spitting out of dirty matter (lit., "feces") on the "true Sikhs and the Gurus." The author surveys Hindu-Sikh relations and deals with the assertions against Sikhism. For example, in reply to Sahib Dyal's insinuation that Sikhs were women because they wore hair, Ganda Singh inquires why "Dayanandis" imitate females and shave their faces ? Do the Vedas insist on men emulating women ? If salvation depends on cut hair, why do Hindu women not shave their heads ? If they are equal to men, why do they not wear the sacred thread ? Turning to Dayanand, Ganda Singh challenges the claim that he saved Hindus and Sikhs from Christianity with the defence that Sikh revitalization had begun prior to the founding of the Arya Samaj. Instead of being a hero, Dayanand is pictured as a foul-mouthed braggart whose existence was built on untruths and calumny. Dayanand supposedly spent his time splitting other Indian communities with "daggers of bad words."[2] The final part of the tract attempts to meet Sahib Dyal's statement that Sikhism and Panjabi are only suitable for rustics, simple and uneducated men. Ganda Singh quotes extensively from foreign scholars (except for Trumpp, on whom Sahib Dyal relies) to show that Panjabi is a viable language and that Sikhism can claim to be a world religion. In fact, Ganda Singh concludes, had it not been for brave Sikhs and the efforts of Guru Gobind Singh, Hinduism and the "weak" Hindu population would have succumbed to Islam. Dayanand might consider the British an enemy, but the new rulers never tried to convert forcibly like the "foes" defeated by the Sikhs. Sikhism remains the only progressive and virile faith for Punjabis.

The neo-Sikh group also encountered the aggressive section of the Hindu community in more concrete political situations. Arya Samajists, for example, backed the Amritsar Singh Sabha in a controversy over the location of Khalsa

1. *Nushkha-i-Granthi Fobia*, p. 39. Author's translation from Panjabi.
2. *Nushkha-i-Khabt-i-Dayanandiyan* (Amritsar, 1904), p. 51.

College (1890-92) and helped shift the site from Lahore to Amritsar. Amazed and upset by this intervention in Sikh affairs, Lahore Sabha members charged that the Samaj joined the discussion only to prevent the creation of a rival to its own Lahore DAV College.[1] Further episodes occurred in 1900. One revolved around the Dyal Singh Will Case in which Dyal Singh's widow attempted to invalidate his transfer of ancestral property to a trust on the grounds that as the wealthy aristocrat had been a Sikh, the Hindu law of inheritance did not apply. Hindus tended to back the trustees in the drawn-out legal proceedings, Sikhs, the Sardarni Dyal Singh. Ruling in favour of the trustees, the Lahore High Court stated that there was no legal difference between Hindus and Sikhs. The decision embittered the Sikhs and strengthened their resolve to demarcate boundaries between their religion and Hinduism.[2] Within a few months Arya Samajists took another step which raised the spectre of Sikhism in danger. In June the Wacchowali or vegetarian faction of the Samaj "purified" thirty low caste Sikhs and shaved their heads. Sikh leaders attempted to dissuade the Rahtias, but failed because they could not guarantee that henceforth Sikhs would treat members of the depressed castes as equals. This direct threat temporarily mobolized the Sikh community. In Lahore, for example, Sardar Mehar Singh and Bhagat Lakshman Singh formed a Khalsa Sudhar Sabha which sent literature and preaching teams to the villages warning against Arya Samaj activities. The Sabha offered to baptize low caste Sikhs and give them certificates so that in theory they would receive fair treatment from their co-religionists.[3] Five years later the Tat Khalsa party won a momentary victory over Hindu opponents by having idols removed from near the Golden Temple, Amritsar. Hindus and their Sikh allies retaliated with mass protest meetings, petitions, and a partially successful campaign to ban Singh sabha leaders from gurdwaras.[4] The Sikh gurdwara victory in 1905 was balanced by a Hindu triumph at the 1910 Hindu Conference, Multan. An important Sikh aristocrat and religious leader, Gurbakhsh Singh Bedi, presided over the conference and publicly proclaimed that Sikhs were Hindu.[5] The next decade was filled with similar skirmishes over issues such as the categories in census reports (were Sikhs to be counted as Hindu ?).

1. Detailed treatment in Bhagat Lakshman Singh, "Controversy on the Location of the Khalsa College Amritsar and After," (unpub. mss., with Dr. Ganda Singh, Patiala). Also, *Bhagat Lakshman Singh Autobiography*, pp. 89-93.
2. Articles by Bhagat Lakshman Singh in *The Khalsa*, June-Aug, 1900.
3. *Bhagat Lakshman Singh Autobiography*, pp. 160-68.
4. Editorials and letters in the *Khalsa Advocate*, July 1905. For a copy of the Hazur Sahib encyclical which expelled Singh Sabha members from gurdwaras, see, *Tribune*, Aug. 1, 1905, p. 5.
5. See, for example, Sewa Ram Singh's letter in the *Khalsa Advocate*, Oct. 28, 1910, pp. 5-6. Also, items 37, 41.

In addition to these specific incidents, throughout the period Sikhs and Hindus contested the key issue of Hindi versus Panjabi. Hindus favoured substituting Hindi for Urdu, the official language of the courts and educational system. Sikhs supported Panjabi in the Gurmukhi script. Each tended to identify its language with religion and communal unity, and each launched sporadic campaigns in the form of meetings and delegations to influence the government. Although the British rejected the appeals and maintained Urdu, the Hindi-Panjabi question remained a factor perpetuating communal discord.[1]

Cleavages between Punjabi Sikhs and Hindus did not preclude temporary political alignment against a common danger or for a mutually beneficial object. At a time when they were quarrelling over language and conversion, for example, Hindus and Sikhs could cooperate in opposing Urdu and in reclaiming converts from Islam. Despite this overlapping of allegiance, however, the intensity of the ideological and social movements within each community, and the institutionalization of differences in symbols and outlook made difficult long-term political alliance. The literature of the nineteenth century suggests that at least one section of Sikhs was on better terms with Muslims and Christians than with Hindus. Riots and cow protection provided two exceptions. Hindus and Sikhs invariably sided in affairs sparked by religious festivals or sacrilege to holy spots. Similarly, they cooperated to prevent the sacrifice or sale of beef. In the upsurge of cow protection in the Punjab (1880-1890), Sikhs joined hands with Sanatan Hindus and Arya Samajists to form cow societies and to agitate on the issue.[2]

This pattern of Sikh relations with Muslims underwent change between the 1890's and 1920. Growing Sikh fascination with martyrdom probably contributed to worsening relations. Sikh writers and societies published hundreds of poems and short accounts on how Sikhs had suffered under Muslim rule (the term generally used was *Muslim,* not Mughal). The detailed and frequently gory accounts must have had a lingering psychological effect on a generation without firsthand contact with pre-British Punjab. In addition, Arya-Muslim conflict spilled over into the Sikh community. Muslim pamphleteers claimed Nanak as a Muslim or played up sections of the *janam-sakhi* accounts which out of context reflected adversely on the Gurus.[3] The revival producing such literature also accelerated Muslim missionary efforts. Muslims

1. The *Tribune* and the *Panjabee,* 1904-1908, contain numerous articles and correspondence on the issues.
2. For the Sikh role in cow protection associations, see the files in For. Secret, 1884, NAI.
3. Discussion in *Tribune,* May 5, 1911. Also, items 272, 418, 578.

would convert a Sikh, cut his hair, and on occasion have him eat beef in public. These Muslim converts sometimes turned out to be the most rabid critics of Sikhism.[1] Similarly, the Sikhs were becoming more aggressive. In 1897, for example, the Lahore Shuddhi Sabha "reconverted" over four hundred Muslims.[2] With fresh emphasis on Sikh symbols and custom, Sikhs began to demand the opening of *jhatka* shops for the sale of meat butchered by a single stroke of the blade. Muslims found *jhatka* repugnant and resisted the innovation.[3] Constitutional developments initiated another phase of Sikh-Muslim conflict. From the 1909 Morley-Minto reforms onward Sikhs felt that transfer of power to the hands of a Muslim majority threatened the welfare of their community. They fought for new patronage and at every turn tried to neutralize Muslim claims.[4]

The mounting spiral of tension erupted more frequently in armed confrontation and rioting. Muslims burned down dharmshalas and interfered with Sikh ceremonies; Sikhs raided mosques and prevented Muslim calls to prayer.[5] More important than actual riots was the increased sensitivity of Sikh and Muslim journalists to incidents which twenty years earlier might have been ignored. The tendency to focus on Sikh-Muslim relations can be traced in the editorial policy and news coverage of prominent Sikh periodicals.[6]

The Sikhs and the British Raj

The introduction of British rule influenced many of these developments among Punjabi Sikhs. Elements accompanying the *raj* such as Christian missions, techniques of organization and journalism, and western concepts accentuated divisions and the spread of communal consciousness. Moreover, the very nature of British government made possible political organization along religious lines. Two institutions transferred to the Punjab, the bureaucracy and municipal committees, became arenas of power and competition in which Sikhs, Hindus and Muslims vied for dominancy. These encounters often took the form of public meetings, petitions, and delegations—activities which would have been futile under earlier administrations. The seeming willingness of the British to take into account Indian sentiment, however,

1. See items 578, 418. Also, for an interesting note on public performances of Sikh and Muslim converts, *Purity Servant*, Nov. 1. 1895 (clippings in Bhagat Lakshman Singh collection, Ganda Singh, Patiala).
2. Statistics drawn from stories on conversions in *Shuddhi Pattar.*
3. One important *jhatka* case discussed in GI Home Poll, May 1914, 37A.
4. See, for example, editorials in the *Khalsa Advocate,* June 1909.
5. CID reports for August 1907, in Home Poll Proceedings (Sept. 1907). Also item 618.
6. In the 1895 issues of the *Khalsa Akhbar,* for example, there are few references to Muslim employment or Sikh-Muslim problems. The *Khalsa Advocate* and the *Khalsa Samachar,* published after 1900, contain such references in virtually every edition.

encouraged mobolization of public opinion. The act of collecting information through commissions of inquiry reinforced the prevalent idea that the rulers responded to the wishes of the people and created a climate conducive to agitation on popular issues.[1]

Specific British policies and tactics played an equally important role in Sikh affairs. First, the government maintained the Sikh aristocracy and gurdwaras as channels for indirect control of Sikhs. Respected families and religious figures were given rent-free land grants, pensions, recognition in durbars, and the privilege of educating sons in an elite school, Aitchison College.[2] Appreciating the significance of Sikh shrines as nodes of power and authority, the British also continued their *dharmurths* (grants) and in some cases, notably the Amritsar Golden Temple, virtually controlled their administration.[3] British support legitimized the position of managers and leading families as well as other groups or organizations attaching themselves to the *raj*. The Lahore Singh Sabha, for example, cooperated with the British during census inquiries and then exhibited correspondence from the government as recognition of its claim to Sikh leadership.[4] Another area of direct involvement lay in employment policy. Although reluctant to reserve bureaucratic posts on religious lines, the authorities did emphasize Sikh recruitment for the military. After the 1857 mutiny Sikhs became a prime element in the provincial police and imperial army. Besides providing a source of income for many Sikh families, recruitment insured that one group of Sikhs maintained their distinct symbols. The British officers believed that the presence of orthodox belief and custom among troops reinforced martial spirit and discipline, and therefore every Sikh recruit was required to undergo baptism, attend services, and obey the tenets of his faith. As previously noted, Sikh troops became a reservoir of ideological and financial support for Singh sabha reformers.[5] Also significant were British attempts to manipulate and play off Sikh factions. For example, informal

1. Detailed treatment in N.G. Barrier, "The Punjab Government and Communal Politics, 1870-1908," *Journal of Asian Studies,* XXVII, 3 (May 1968), 523-39.
2. The Foreign department proceedings contain hundreds of files on the economic and political relations between the British and the landed Sikh families. For example, see For. Secret, Nov. 22, 1850, 117-19A.
3. For a key file on the handling of religious endowments, see GI Home Public, March 1876, 232-69A. Also, confidential minute on the Golden Temple, PG Home Public Aug. 1887, 22-23A (West Pakistan Record Office, Lahore).
4. Nahar Singh, "Sikh Politics," p. 18. Also, editorial in *Khalsa Akhbar,* May 23, 1895, p. 2.
5. Nahar Singh, "Sikh Politics," pp. 14-15; comments in the official recruiting manuals (see items 82, 176).

pressure was exerted on leaders to denounce Dhulip Singh's claim to the throne and property of his father, Maharaja Ranjit Singh.[1]

These tactical manoeuvres reflected a basic British ambiguity toward the Sikhs. On the one hand the rulers admired Sikh virility and bravery, their rejection of Brahmans and idols, and their theology akin in several ways to Christianity. In the army officers studiously reinforced a sense of allegiance to Sikhism. At the same time the British never quite trusted the Sikhs. Constantly on the alert for indications that the Sikhs were about to reclaim their lost kingdom, the government screened troop activities and nervously tracked wandering Sikh preachers. If Sikh nationality did assert itself, the British were aware of the repercussions not only in the Punjab but throughout the Empire. They therefore faced the task of supporting Sikh nationality and trying to keep it within bounds.

In fact the British had little to fear from Sikhs for several decades. Except for brief Kuka outbursts and theab ortive agitation for the return of Dhulip Singh in 1880's, Sikhs tended to be loyal subjects. The instantaneous denunciation of both occasional Sikh misadventures and charges of disloyalty attest to their loyalty to the government.[2] To a large extent "loyalty" typified the style and tone of Sikh politics until 1919. Sikh politicians tended to accept the structure and assumptions of the British administrative system. They occasionally prepared memorials on issues affecting the community (civil service examinations, distribution of patronage, education in Panjabi), but these were couched in respectful language which presumed that the *ma-bap,* the rulers, would right wrongs and care paternally for their subjects.[3]

Exceptions did exist. After 1907 a small group of Sikhs, mostly immigrants to North America and England, joined ultra-nationalist or revolutionary activities. The Hindustan Ghadr Association of San Francisco, for example, received leadership and most of its finances from the Sikhs in America. The Ghadr party produced newspapers and tracts aimed largely at Sikh troops and agriculturists. Its programme and related revolutionary circles in which Sikhs participated had some impact in the form of military risings and dacoities in the Punjab, but

1. Memoranda in "Maharaja Dhuleep Singh, Secret Correspondence," H Book Series, IOL.
2. For example, see the petition from a Sikh deputation in *Punjab Gazette* (supplement), March 28, 1872, pp. 264-65.
3. Illustrated by the evidence and memorials before the Hunter Education Commission. *Report of the Punjab Provincial Committee* (Calcutta, 1884), pp. 301-13, 499-504.

when leaders were imprisoned or executed following the Lahore Conspiracy Trials, the revolutionary tide never regained momentum.[1]

Sikh revolutionists failed to gather widespread sympathy even from their own community. No matter what they might have felt privately, Sikh journalists and leaders publicly denounced the actions of nationalists such as Kartar Singh and re-emphasized Sikh loyalty. The exigencies of war accelerated Sikh assistance to the government. Singh sabha members formed recruitment committees and circulated calls for devotion and service.[2]

This variety of political expression was not atypical of the times. All Punjabis were attempting to win the title of "loyal" and concomitant patronge. Similarly, like members of other Punjab communities the Sikhs tended to shun nationalist or Congress politics. The communal consciousness and hardening of differences occurring since the 1870's accounts largely for the failure of the Congress in the Punjab. Strained communal relations made Hindus, Sikhs, and Muslims reluctant to give commitment to a secular political organization. Sikhs did attend Congress sessions, particularly those in Lahore in 1893 and 1900, but their support was superficial and transitory. As Mohan Singh Vaid has noted, political cooperation across religious lines broke down quickly and usually intensified antagonism.[3] In the final analysis, Punjabis were more concerned with strengthening their communities and interest groups than involvement in nationalist programmes. Punjabis talked of "the nation," but more often than not, they meant the Hindu nation, the Muslim nation, or the Sikh nation.[4]

A renewed sense of separate political identity based on religion eventually brought the Sikhs into conflict with the British. Sensitized to their distinctiveness and acquiring a militant self-assuredness, the Sikhs moved first from a posture of abject loyalty to questioning of British motives and finally toward disrespectful assertion of "just demands." The process was slow and only beginning in the first decades of the twentieth century, but beneath the facade

1. Background in the following: Khushwant Singh, *Ghadar* (New Delhi, 1968); Vidya Sagar Suri, *A Brief Biographical Sketch of Sohan Lal Pathak* (Patiala, 1968); *Gadar Parti Da Itihas.* (Jullundur, 1961); F.C. Isemonger, J. Slattery, *An Account of the Ghadr Conspiracy* (Lahore, 1919).
2. One such Sikh response is reflected in *Khalsa Advocate*, April 25, 1914, p. 2. Some Sikhs silently supported the revolutionists and those imprisoned for political activity. Munsha Singh Dukhi, *Mohan Singh Vaid*, pp. 259-70.
3. Munsha Singh Dukhi, *Mohan Singh Vaid*, pp. 71-73.
4. Such Sikh references can be found in almost any collection of speeches given before the Sikh Educational Conference. On the spread of nationalist sentiment based on religious affiliation, see N.G. Barrier, "The Arya Samaj and Congress Politics in the Punjab." *Journal of Asian Studies*, XXVI, 3 (May 1967), 363-79.

of the threadbare liturgy "Sikhs are loyal," Sikh-British relations were shifting.

The initials signs of unrest involved a central Sikh institution, the Khalsa College at Amritsar. Deterioration in the finances, administration and student conduct of the College led the government to force a revised constitution on the Managing Committee in 1908. The altered arrangements provided for a College Council of 58 members, with 5 official nominees, 25 from Sikh states, 26 from British districts, and 2 elected by graduates. The government dominated the states representatives. A similar change in the Managing Committee brought the College entirely under official supervision. Upset by the move, Sikhs held meetings and threatened boycott. The immediate tension subsided but the College remained a source of irritation for the British.[1] A similar disturbance occurred over a ban on the wearing of turbans in the Indian Medical Service and in the inns of court in London.[2] The Anand Marriage Bill, legalizing a marriage ceremony according to traditional Sikh rites, sparked the largest Sikh political mobolization prior to 1919. Within a year, October 1908-September 1909, the Sikhs conducted over three hundred mass meetings to demand revision of the Bill, particularly the inclusion of *sajhdhari* Sikhs (clean-shaven Sikhs) within its operation. Although only partially successful, the campaign stood as an example of potential Sikh unity, with coordinated petitions signed by almost 700,000 Sikhs.[3] The principle of communal representation in the Morley-Minto constitutional reforms accentuated Sikh efforts to protect themselves. Working through the Chief Khalsa Diwan and new "Sikh Leagues," politicians prepared lists of demands for more Sikh representation—demands based not on population but the intangible value of Sikh military contributions to the Indian Empire. Sikh papers supplemented the petitions with detailed studies of the communal composition of departments which allegedly proved that Sikhs were being ignored. Sikh militancy reached new heights with the Rakabganj Gurdwara affair in the winter of 1912. The British unthinkingly removed a small part of the shrine so that a road could be built to the nearby secretariat. The Sikhs rallied to the defence of the gurdwara, which had special significance because of its association with the ninth Guru, Tegh Bahadur. The British eventually compromised when confronted with threats of violence, but again, British-Sikh relation had been scarred.[4]

1. Ganda Singh, *Khalsa College*, pp. 67-80; Nahar Singh, "Sikh Politics," pp. 21-22, 38-54.
2. For holidays, the turban issue, the following : GI Home Poll, July 1914, 184-98A: GI Home Med., July 1908, 1-12A; Home Jud., March 1909, 126-27A.
3. Meetings and petitions in GI Jud., Dec. 1908, 94-5B; Also, Talwar, "Anand Marriage".
4. Sardul Singh Couveisser, "Gurduara Rakabganj De Jhamal" in Ganda Singh, *Panjab*, pp. 208-13; *Khalsa Advocate*, Jan. 17, 1914, p. 1; May 16, 1914, p. 2. Also, items 246, 792, 793.

Although the government had some notion of the forces involved in the origin and nature of new Sikh aggressiveness, it was unable to sort out the various elements. The British did feel, however, the neo-Sikh movement posed a threat to the loyalty of the Sikhs, a concern reflected in this selection from a C.I.D. note on Sikh politics:

> The most fundamental and immediate of the evils which the present situation seems likely to produce is the dismantling of the fabric of the orthodox Sikh faith, with a consequent disregard of the loyal traditions which have hitherto powerfully affected the character of the Sikh attitude towards the British administration ......There need be no hesitation in predicting that those Sikhs who affect the new faith will inevitably tend to degenerate as regards their loyalty to the Crown. The movement is in any case fatal to the continued existence of the orthodox Sikh as the term is now understood, for it engenders a disregard of the creed and ritual of the tenth Guru which has done so much to raise the Sikh to his present high level of excellence as a man and a soldier. The consequences may be serious if ever the Tat Khalsa party succeeds in obtaining possession of the Golden Temple, and are in a position to abrogate to themselves the leadership in religious affairs which they have already assumed in politics.....The British Government, more particularly the military administration, has put itself in a queer position as regards the Sikhs, who have been fostered and petted and taught to regard themselves as a great nation with great national traditions. This glorification of the Sikhs has been productive of curious results, because, while it has kept the banner of Sikhism flying to the great advantage of the government, it now appears to be likely to be used as an instrument to scourge us by a section of those for whose good it was primarily undertaken. Neo-Sikhism is nonetheless dangerous because it may appear outwardly to be merely an exaggerated form of a cult of the birth of which Government has itself been largely responsible.

> The Chief Khalsa Diwan and the neo-Sikhs generally more particularly adhere to Guru Gobind Singh who welded the Sikhs into a militant race. Though some of the members of the Diwan and Singh Sabhas do no more than endeavour to promote homogeneity and progress, there are others who have become inflated with Guru Gobind Singh's military teachings and try to spread that inflation to the Sikhs generally......The neo-Sikh party is suffering from what may be expressively, if vulgarly, termed "wind in the head," and the advent of what appeared to it a favourable opportunity for action might readily stir it into active rebellion.[1]

Confronting a political problem they helped create, the British ultimately decided to take a "safe" course. They backed elements in Sikh society thought to be reliable and loyal, the *Pujaris* and pro-Hindu section. The shift from tacit approval of Sikh reformers to support for their opponents set the stage for intense conflict. The government was committed to a position that, under the right circumstances, could imbroil the authority of the *raj* with the *izzat*, the pride or self-respect, of the Sikhs. When the circumstances did arise in 1921, the British found themselves facing not the moderate Chief Khalsa Diwan and the Singh sabhas, but new opponents, the Shiromani Gurdwara Parbandak Committee and the Akali Dal.

In less than seventy years the Sikhs had thus travelled a long road. By 1919 their literacy per capita and their rate of population growth were the highest in the Punjab. Battles over theology and custom still raged, but the boundaries and symbols of Sikhism had been demarcated. Too, a range of institutions had evolved which expanded the *Panth* and brought it into collision with other Punjabis and the government. The elements involved in this transition are barely visible, but the publications discussed in the following sections should contribute to our understanding of how the Sikhs once again became a militant people.

1. Nahar Singh, "Sikh Politics," pp. 55-57.

SECTION I

AUTHOR LIST OF SIKH PUBLICATIONS

SECTION 1

AUTHOR LIST OF SIKH PUBLICATIONS

This section contains Sikh books and tracts listed alphabetically by author. Information has been collected from British catalogues and research libraries in England, India and Pakistan.

These comments pertain to problems connected with organization of material. Bibliographical information on each item is arranged according to the following format :

a. Author. Titles or honorifics such as "Bhai" follow the name. If several honorifics are given for one name, the items have been alphabetized by the initial letters of the honorifics. For example, several publications are by authors with the name "Arjan Singh." In the bibliography, "Arjan Singh" comes first, followed by "Arjan Singh, Bhai" and "Arjan Singh, Raja." The compiler has accepted the titles of authors as printed in catalogues or on title pages, and no attempt has been made to sort out individuals on the basis of external evidence.

b. Title and language. Transliteration of titles is discussed in the preface. For abbreviations, consult the list immediately following the preface.

c. Place of publication, publisher, date and pagination. District or princely states in parentheses follow the place of publication in cases of small towns or villages.

d. Locations. Symbols for depositories where items are located have been included in the abbreviations list.

e. Annotation and cross-references. Background on items varies with the nature of material and the source of information. When available information is sparse, or when the title is self-explanatory, only approximate translations of the titles has been provided. Cross-references in parentheses follow the annotation, or if no annotation, the location or pagination. Readers should also refer to the two indexes for related titles.

The preface contains a discussion of sources, methodology and technical problems. Mention should be made, however, on treatment of the *Janam-Sakhi* literature. Generally these traditional biographies have been placed under the individual registered either as author or editor. The exceptions are the *Janam-Sakhis* of Guru Nanak, which are arranged by the manuscript they reproduce—the Bala tradition (Bhai Bala), the Puratan tradition (Colebrooke, Hafizabad) and the Mani Singh tradition (Gyan Ratnavali). A published version of the Puratan manuscript, for example, is found under "Puratan. *Janam-Sakhi.*" Evaluation and background on these sources is in W.H. McLeod, *Gurū Nānak and the Sikh Religion* (Oxford, 1968), pp. 7-33.

Author List of Sikh Publications

1 **AJIT SINGH, Sardar :** The Guru Prescribed Duties of the Sikhs to the British Empire. Lahore, Sardar Ajit Singh, 1914. 6 p. IOL

A pro-British tract by a Lahore Chief Court pleader. Also reprinted in vernacular editions: Government Inglish Ke Mata'liq Khalsa Qaum Ka Dharm. (U) Lahore, Machine Press, 1915. 8 p. BTSL; Angrezi Parti Sikh Kaum Da Dharm (P) Lahore, Washington Press, 1915. 14 p. PPU

2 **AJMER SINGH :** Rehat Parkash. (P) Ludhiana, Khalsa Press, 1911. 40 p. IOL

Debate among Hindus, Muslims, Arya Samajists, Sanatanists, and Sikhs on the best religion. Sikhism wins because all finally agree that it is a universal faith. Appended are comments by foreign doctors on the bad effects of alcohol.

3 **AJMER SINGH, Sardar :** Anand Biwah Par Vichar Ka Khandan. (PN) Patiala, Sardar Ajmer Singh, 1908. 16 p. IOL

Refutation of the pamphlet Anand Biwah Par Vichar (Discussion of Anand marriage) which criticized the Sikhs of the 'new light' (Tat Khalsa) who supposedly did not follow the religion of their ancestors. (731)

4 **AMAR DAS, Bawa :** Sikhan Nu Amar Sikhchha. (P) Ludhiana, American Tract Society, 1912. 44 p. PPU

Immortal education for Sikhs, a Christian missionary tract.

5 **AMAR SINGH :** Chamakda Hira Ya Jiwan Britant Sardar Hari Singh Nalva. (P) Lahore, Anglo-Sanskrit Press, 1904. 176 p. BM/IOL

The shinning jewel or a biographical sketch of Sardar Hari Singh Nalva, Ranjit Singh's famous general.

6 _____ : Chhoti Nunh Ya Lachhmi. (P) Amritsar, Khalsa Agency, 1908. 188 p. BM

Tale of a Sikh heroine, Lachhmi.

7 _____ : Sri Guru Arjan Charittra. (P) Lahore, Sri Akal Press, 1897. 8 p.

Biographical sketch of Guru Arjan.

8 **AMAR SINGH, Bhai :** Arya Samaj Aur Uske Bani Ki Taraf Se Dunya Ke Mukhtalif Hadiyan-i-Mazhab Ke Be'izzati. (U) Lahore, Dev Bidhan Press, 1890. 30 p. BM

The insult of the prophets of different religions of the world by the Arya Samaj and its founder, a condemnation of the language and tactics of the Arya Samajists against other religions, particularly the Sikhs. Appended are excerpts from Arya Samaj publications and Sikh protest meetings.

9 _____ : Daryai Ghore. (P) Amritsar, Bhai Wasawa Singh, 1916. 28 p. IOL

Verses on the theft of two horses from Emperor Shahjahan's stables by Bhai Bidhi Chand. The horses originally were sent from Kabul for Guru Hargobind but Shahjahan's men had seized them.

10 _____ : Dayanandi Firqa Ki Mukrimana Karrawaiyan. (U) Lahore, Dev Bidhan Press, 1890. 43 p.

Subversive activities of the Dayanandi sect.

11 _____ : Dharambir Mandal, Yani Sikh Biran Dian Shahidian. (P) Lahore, Bhai Amar Singh, 1912. 242 p. IOL

Verses on the martyrdom of Sikhs.

12 _____ : Ghar Da Nirbah. (P) 4 Pts. Amritsar, Khalsa Agency, 1905. 221, 25, 173, 25 p. BM/IOL

Looking after the house. The author has written a novel to depict the household affairs of daily life in a Sikh joint family. The necessity of social reform and female education is highlighted.

13 _____ : Hase Da Samundar. (P) 2/e., Amritsar, Khalsa Agency, 1910. 96 p.

Ocean of laughter, a collection of humorous stories on Punjabis and particularly contemporary Sikh life.

14 **AMAR SINGH, Joord :** Farz Khalsa. (P) Ferozepur City, Upper India Printing Works, 1918. 14 p. BTSL/IOL

The duty of the Khalsa, poems by a member of the Ferozepur Recruitment Committee. The author distributed five

AMAR SINGH, Joord (contd)
hundred copies to Sikh soldiers and potential recruits.

15 **AMIR SINGH, Diwan :** Novel Prakash Kaur. (P) Amritsar, Diwan Amir Singh, 1915. 232 p. IOL
Domestic story written to illustrate social evils among Sikhs.

16 **ANAND KISHORE :** Jiwan Charitra Sri Guru Gobind Singhji. (H) Lahore, Anand Kishore, 1914. 298 p. IOL
Life of Guru Gobind Singh.

17 **ARJAN SINGH :** Daswandh Bhandar Arthat Sikh Qaum Lei Ik Uttam Tajwiz. (P) Amritsar, Wazir Hind Press, 1902. 32 p.
The setting aside of tithes, or a fine plan for the consideration of the Sikh community.

18 **ARJAN SINGH, Bhai :** Samachar Bhai Tara Singhji. (P) Haldiwala (Amritsar), Bhai Arjan Singh, 1919. 16 p. BM
Metrical life of Bhai Tara Singh, a well-known philanthropist of Amritsar.

19 _____ : Virtant Baba Pahauri Vala. (P) Amritsar, Bhai Arjan Singh, 1909. 16 p. PPU
Account of a devotee of Guru Angad.

20 **ARJAN SINGH, Raj :** Ath Updesh Ramgarhia Bradari De Sudhar Lai. (P) Maula, Raj Arjan Singh, 1916. 8 p. IOL
Eight rules for the reformation of the Ramgarhia community.

21 **ARUR SINGH :** Amritsar Nivasi Sikhan De Nam Khulha Chittha. (P) Amritsar, Bhai Arur Singh, 1918. 4 p.
An open letter to Amritsar Sikhs asking them to demand separate representation on the local municipal committee.

22 _____ : Athwin Badshahi Ki Janam Sakhi. (U) Lahore, Nawal Kishore Press, 1904. 24 p.
Life of the eighth Guru, Harkishan.

23 _____ : Chauthi Badshahi Ki Janam Sakhi. (U) Lahore, Nawal Kishore Press, 1903. 24 p.
Life of the fourth Guru, Ram Das.

24 _____ : Satwin Badshahi Ki Janam Sakhi. (U) Lahore, Nawal Kishore Press, 1904. 38 p.
Life of the seventh Guru, Har Rai.

25 **ATMA SINGH :** Granth Sakhi Parman. (P) Lahore, Sri Gurmat Press, 1902. 807 p. IOL
Commentary on certain sayings of the Sikh Gurus.

26 **ATMA SINGH, Bhai :** Dharam Rakhsha Yani Sri Guru Tegh Bahadur Sahib Ji Ki Qurbani. (PN) Gujranwala, Narindra Press, 1903. 16 p.
The defender of the faith, or the self-sacrifice of Guru Tegh Bahadur.

27 _____ : Guru Hazar Hai. (P) Amritsar, Bhai Atma Singh, 1919. 39 p. BM
The Guru is present, a story of a Sikh lady whose husband was killed by a Pathan. The Pathan then asked the lady to accompany him as a wife, but she did not consent and called on Guru Gobind Singh for help. Suddenly the Guru appeared on his favourite charger, killed the pathan, and revived her husband.

28 **ATTAR SINGH :** Khalsa Dharm Shastar Sanskar. (P) Amritsar, Amir Chand Press, 1893. 40 p. BTSL
A description of the chief rituals ordained for the Sikhs in their scriptures. The author also discusses the idea that in the Kaliyug, the present iron age, the only means of salvation is the repetition of the holy Name of God.

29 **ATTAR SINGH, Bhai:** Bhaundu Sikhan Da Ilaj Arthat Naqli Sikh Updesh. (PN) Amritsar, Wazir Hind Press, 1902. 16 p. PPU
The cure for deluded Sikhs, or instructions for Sikhs who are imposters.

30 _____ : Bhaundu Sikh Prabodh Arthat Man Mat De Rogian Da Daru. (P) Amritsar, Bhai Buta Singh, 1907. 28 p. IOL
Knowledge of deluded Sikhs, or medicine for patients afflicted with egotistic religion, a condemnation of customs and ideas which the author considers opposed to the teachings of the Gurus.

31 _____ : Brahman Kasauti. (P) Amritsar, Bhai Attar Singh, n/d. 8 p. PPU/IOL
Testing stones for Brahmans, a comparison of Hindu Brahmans and Sikh religious leaders.

32 _____ : Qissa Baran Mah Qaumi. (P) Amritsar, Wazir Hind Press, 1902. 16 p. BTSL
An address to the Sikh community on the necessity of religious reform.

33 **ATTAR SINGH, Sardar (Chief of Bhadour, Translator):** The Rayhit Nama of Prahlad Rai, or the Excellent Conversation of the Duswan Padsha and Nand Lal's Rayhit Nama, or Rules for the Guidance of the Sikhs in Religious Matters. Lahore, 1876, 17 p. BM
Rules of conduct for Sikhs, translated from Panjabi.

34 _____: Sakhi Namah; Sakhee Book, or the Description of Gooroo Gobind Singh's Religion and Doctrines. Benares, Medical Hall Press, 1873. vii, 205 p. BM/ KC/IOL

The British collaborated in publishing this collection of stories and prophecies, a Gurmukhi version of which was popular with the Kuka sect. Attar Singh edited the stories as an "act of sincere loyalty." He attempts to disprove the Kuka contention that Guru Gobind Singh wrote the material; instead he places its origin at 1834, an example of apocryphal writing.

35 _____ : Travels of Guru Tegh Bahadur and Guru Gobind Singh. Lahore, 1876. ix, 137 p. BM/IOL/KC

36 **AUTAR SINGH, Bhai** : Amar Kund Athwa Sar Rahit Nama. (P) Lahore, Sri Akal Press, 1899. 24 p.

Immortal pond, a discourse on the principles of Sikhism.

37 _____ : Chehra Dekhan De Shisha. (P) Rawalpindi, Bhai Autar Singh, 1911. 112 p. IOL

A Mirror for seeing one's face, an examination of the criticism against Baba Gurbakash Singh Bedi's presiding at the Punjab Hindu Conference, 1910.

38 _____ : Chehra Dekhan De Shishe Da Zamima. (P) Rawalpindi, Bhai Autar Singh, 1911. 4 p. IOL

A supplement of the mirror for seeing one's own face, a tract criticizing Bhai Teja Singh of the Chief Khalsa Diwan and suggesting reforms in the constitution of the Diwan.

39 _____ : Khalsa Dharam Shastra. (P) Anandpur, Ram Narain Singh, 1914. 439 p. IOL

A code of social and religious practices for Sikhs.

40 _____ : Khalsa Sudhar Taru. (P) 8 Pts. Lahore, Sri Gurmat Press and Sant Singh Luther Oriental Press, 1900-1. 532 p. PPU

Scheme for the reformation of the Khalsa community.

41 _____ : Kur Na Pujje Sach Nun Sau Gharat Ghariae. (P) Amritsar, Bhai Autar Singh, 1911. 8 p.

The liar may construct a hundred pictures but he will not reach the truth; a tract supporting the views expressed by Baba Gurbakhsh Singh Bedi (that Sikhs are Hindus) in his presidential address at the Hindu Conference held at Multan.

42 _____ : Milaun Lai Akhiri Puchh, Tatha Dharam Dhiya Panchaiti Nirmala Akhare Da Dastur-ul-Amal Wa Akhare Sambandhi Samachar. (P) Lahore, Sri Gurmat Press, 1904. 20 p. IOL

My last appeal for unity, together with a memorandum on the rules and activities of some of the religious organizations of the Nirmalas.

43 _____ : Sikh Khalsa Dharam Siddhant De Dikhan Waste Prakashman Laltain. (P) Lahore, Sri Gurmat Press, 1903. 40 p.

Glowing lamps for looking at the religious principles of the Sikhs.

44 **AVTAR SINGH, Bhai** : Gurdarshan Shastar. (P) Amritsar, Sri Gurmat Press, 1916. 236 p. PPU

Book containing the advice of the Gurus.

45 _____ : Khalsa Dharam Darpan. (P) Lyallpur, Bhai Partap Singh and Bhai Sundar Singh, 1910. 103 p. PPU/IOL

A mirror of the Sikh religion, discussion of the advantages of maintaining distinctive features of Sikhism such as uncut hair.

46 _____ : Khalsa Dharam Shastar. (P) Lahore, Arorbans Press, 1894. 135 p. PPU

Treatise on Sikh social and religious rites.

47 _____Shok Pattar. (P) Lahore, Sri Gurmat Press, 1905. 48 p. IOL

A document of sadness, a tract expressing sorrow at the death of Baba Khem Singh Bedi.

48 _____ : Sikh Dharm Tatdarshan, Arthat Khalsa Dharam Ke Asul. (P) Amritsar, Wazir Hind Press, 1899. 114 p. PPU

A true exhibition of the Sikh religion, or the principles of the Khalsa faith.

49 _____ : Sikhi Dharam. (P) Amritsar, Bhai Mayya Singh, 1894. 24 p. PPU

Narrative on Sikh principles.

50 **AYA SINGH, Sant:** Bibek Uttar Prasan. (P) Lahore, Munshi Gulab Singh, 1898. 14 p.

Wise questions and answers on Sikhism, in verse.

51 **AZIZ UD-DIN, Qazi** : Dalip Singh Ke Halat. (U) Lahore, Koh-i-Nur Press, 1888. 50 p.

An account of Dhulip Singh, the son of Ranjit Singh, who attempted to regain his father's kingdom by negotiations with the British and the Russians.

52 **BACHAN SINGH, Sardar:** Bhai Prem Singh Nabha Vale De Chhape Hoe Sikhmat Bibek De Vivak. (P) Lahore, Anglo-Gurmukhi Press, 1906. 60 p. IOL

The author, a Sikh barrister, wrote this and other pamphlets to counter attacks made by Hindus and the Tribune against removal of idols from the precincts of the Golden Temple. His English comments can be found in the Civil and Military Gazette, August-September 1905.

53 _____ : Jeha Munh Tehi Chaper Arthat Munh Tor Khandan. (P) Amritsar, Punjab Commercial Press, 1906. 80 p. PPU

As the face, so the slap, or a face-breaking reply, criticism of the tract Sikh Hindu Hain. (465, 687)

54 _____ : Nabhe De Ishtihar Da Uttar Ate Khandan. (P) Amritsar, Wazir Hind Press, 1905, 27 p. PPU

Reply and criticism to the pamphlet of Nabha Singh Sabha tract supporting Anand marriage.

55 _____ : Sikh Te But Parasti. (P) Amritsar, Wazir Hind Press, 1905. 8 p. PPU

Sikhs and the worship of idols, a supplement to the Khalsa Samachar (originally published in the Civil and Military Gazette, Lahore, on August 3, 1905).

56 **BADAN SINGH, Sant:** Shri Guru Granth Sahibji Adi Satika. (P) 4 Pts. Faridkot, Maharaja of Faridkot, 1907. app. 5,000 p. IOL

Adi Granth, with commentary. Maharaja Bikram Singh of Faridkot paid all the expenses of preparing this work and subsidized its publication.

57 **BALA**: Janam-Sakhi. (P) Lahore, Diwan Buta Singh, 1871. 589 p. BM/IOL

58 _____ : Janam-Sakhi (P) Lahore, Maulvi Maibub Ahmad, 1890. 780 p. IOL

Editions of Guru Nanak's "biography" based upon the manuscripts attributed to his contemporary, Bhai Bala.

59 **BALDEO SINGH, Dr:** The Trumpet Call, A Short Discourse in Verse about the Religious Aspect of the Khalsa of To-day. Lahore, Victoria Press, 1900. 16 p.

60 **BALWANT SINGH:** Guru Gobind Singh Ji And His Message. Sargodha, Balwant Singh, 1916. 20 p. IOL

61 _____ : Upadarv Hai Ke Anarth? (P) Lahore, Balwant Singh, n/d. 49 p. PPU

Is it confusion or tyranny? A lecture on Sikh religion and martyrs.

62 **BALWANT SINGH, Bhai:** Khalsa Skulan Da Hor Skulan Nalon Wadha Kinan Kinan Galan Wich Ho Sakda Hai? (P) Amritsar, EC, 1915. 8 p.

In what respects can we make Sikh schools better than other schools? A paper on religious training for Sikh teachers read at the Eighth Educational Conference (1915).

63 **BALWANT SINGH, Sardar:** Address. (P) Amritsar, EC, 1914. 20 p. PPU

Presidential speech at the Seventh Educational Conference (1914). The Chief Khalsa Diwan subsequently published an English translation: The Presidential Address Read at the Seventh Sikh Educational Conference. Amritsar, EC, 1915. 15 p. BM/PPU

64 **BARMA SINGH, Bhai:** Jang Chamkaur. (P) Lyallpur, Bhai Barma Singh and Thakur Singh, 1916. 16 p. BM/IOL

Ballad on battle of Chamkaur fought by Guru Gobind Singh against the Mughal army.

65 **BASANT RAM, Sadhu:** Nikkian Jindan Vadde Sake. (P) Amritsar, Chattar Singh, 1917. 48 p. BM

Ballads on Sikh martial bravery and the death of Guru Gobind Singh's sons.

66 **BASANT SINGH:** Sikhan De Guru Kaun Hai? (P) Peshawar, Basant Singh, 1911. 4 p.

Pamphlet endevouring to prove that the Adi Granth has become the only source of truth for the Sikhs since the death of Guru Gobind Singh.

67 **BASANT SINGH, Bhai:** Pakhand Nashak. (P) Lahore, Bhai Basant Singh, 1912. 12 p. IOL

Destruction of imposters, criticism of the teachings of Ram Das against Sikhism.

68 _____ : Sachchi Kurbani. (P) Lahore, Bhai Basant Singh, 1894. 18 p. PPU

True sacrifice, account of martyrdom of Guru Arjan.

69 _____ : Sri Guru Nanak Upkar. (P) Lahore, Punjab Economical Press, 1894. 8 p. BTSL

Discussion of Guru Nanak's mission, in verse.

70 **BELA SINGH, Bhai:** Singhni Parbodh. (P) Lahore, Bhai Bela Singh, 1917. 31 p. IOL

Knowledge for Sikh women, fictitious account of the troubles of a Sikh who married a non-Sikh.

71 **BELL, Evans :** The Annexation of the Punjaub, and the Maharajah Duleep Singh, London, Trubner and Company, 1882. 108 p. BM/IOL/KC

72 **BHAG SINGH, Bhai :** Sankhep Lila Arthat Sri Guru Nanak Dev Ji Da Jiwan Britant. (H) Lahore, Khalsa Press, 1897. 108 p. PPU

Short account of the life of Guru Nanak.

73 **BHAGWAN DAS :** Teghke Dhani Tegh Bahadurji Ka Balidan. (P) Gujranwala, Mckee Press, 1901. 52 p.

Master of the sword : Guru Tegh Bahadur's martyrdom.

74 **BHAGWAN SINGH :** Path Amrit Vidhi Pap Niwarni. (P) Lahore, Anglo-Sanskrit Press, 1896. 16 p.

The way of Sikhism and curing the disease of bad actions, recitations on the nature of Sikhism.

75 **BHAGWAN SINGH, Arif :** Khalsa Deviyan Almaruf Singhaniyan De Sidq. (P) Bhalwal, Bhagwan Singh. 1914. 52 p.

Account of how Sikh women suffered for their religion, written by editor of Hakim, Bhalwal.

76 **BHAGWAN SINGH, Bhai :** Granth Wadda Gur Upkar ? (P) Amritsar, Bhai Labh Singh, 1909. 32 p.

Is the Adi Granth more important than the actions of the Gurus ? A survey of the contributions by the Sikh Gurus in the cause of religion.

77 _____ : Janam Sakhi Sri Guru Arjan Sahibji. (P) Lahore, Khalsa Press, 1898. 123 p.

Biography of Guru Arjan.

78 _____, Khalsa Mat Hulas. (P) Amritsar, Bhai Amar Singh, 1909. 103 p. PPU

Brief histories of the Sikh Gurus.

79 **BHAGVANTI :** Sidak De Bere Par. (P) Amritsar, Amar Press, n/d. 10 p.

Truth always succeeds, dialogue between two women on problems of daily life. In addition to conveying information on Sikh domestic problems, the tract calls for Sikh unity against Arya Samaj pressures.

80 **BHANU DATT, Pandit :** Guru Singh Itihas. (P) Lahore, Panjab University, 1883. 320 p. IOL

History of the Sikhs, based primarily upon the Bala Janam-Sakhi and Santokh Singh's Nanak Prakash and Suraj Prakash.

81 _____ : Guru Singh Sabha Itihas Nawin. (P) Lahore, Anglo-Sanskrit Press, 1892. 76 p. PPU

History of Sikhism, with notes on Singh Sabhas.

82 **BINGLEY, A.H. :** Sikhs. Simla, Government Central Printing Office, 1899. 112, ix p. IOL/KC

Handbook for army recruiters, with details on Sikh customs and demography. Appendices include lists of tribes and principle fairs; a large map locates Jat and Rajput gotras in the Punjab.

83 **BIR SINGH :** Baramasa Guru Gobind Singh. (P) Lahore, Montgomery Press, 1874. 12 p. IOL

Sketches of battles between Guru Gobind Singh and the Mughal army.

84 **BISHAN DAS PURI, Bhai :** Larai Ate Sikh. (P) Gurdaspur, Sardar Jawahir Singh, 1915. 16 p. BTSL/IOL

The war and Sikhs, an appeal for Sikhs to fight for the British, published by the Secretary of the Gurdaspur Singh Sabha.

85 _____ : Panjabi Ate Hindi. (P) Amritsar, EC, 1913. 22 p. PPU/IOL

Essay on the use of Hindi and Panjabi in Sikh institutions, read at the Sixth Educational Conference (1913).

86 _____ : Panjabi Ate Urdu Da Takara.(P) Amritsar, EC, 1914. 16 p. IOL

Panjabi versus Urdu, a paper read at the Seventh Educational Conference (1914).

87 _____ : Panjabi Da Bhandar Bharo. (P) Amritsar, EC, 1912. 36 p.

Fill the storehouse of Panjabi, a paper presented to the Fifth Educational Conference (1912) by the Headmaster of the Jullundur Normal School.

88 **BISHAN SINGH :** Baba Banda Bahadur Da Britant. (P) Lahore, 1914. 265 p. KC

Life of Banda Bahadur.

89 _____ : Shahid Khalsa. (P) Amritsar, Wazir Hind Press, 1916. 223 p. KC/IOL

History of Sikh martyrs.

90 **BISHAN SINGH, Bhai:** Sur Bir Khalsa Ya Baran Mislan. (P) Amritsar, Master Bhagwan Singh, 1917. 109 p.

Background on the Sikh misals and the Phulkian States.

91 **BISHAN SINGH, Gyani :** Nawin Durga Parbodh. (P) Amritsar, Bhai Chattar Singh, 1910. 158 p. BTSL/PPU/IOL

New revelations about Durga, essay on idol-worship and the nature of Sikhism.

92 **BISHAN SINGH, Gyani :** Sher Khalsa. (P) Amritsar, Bhai Dhian Singh, 1917. 186 p.

Stories of Sikh martyrs and their fight against Muslims.

93 **BRIJ NARAIN VARMA, RAI :** Phul Namah Tawarikh. (U) Lahore, Murid-i-Am Press, 1914. 224 p. IOL

History of Phulkian states and their Sikh rulers.

94 **BUDH SINGH, Bawa,** Koel Koo. (P) Sargodha, Bhai Budh Singh, 1917. 199p. BM

Echo of the Cuckoo, history of famous Punjab secular poets with extracts from their works.

95 _____ : Subut-i-Fawaid-i-Keshan. (U) Lahore, Guru Gobind Press, 1897. 32 p. BTSL

Proofs of the advantages of wearing long hair.

96 **BUDH SINGH, Bhai :** Dharamsalan Te Gurdwarian Di Rahin Mudhli Vidya Da Parchar Karan Partha Lekh. (P) Amritsar, EC, 1915. 7 p.

A paper on the advancement of elementary education among the Sikh masses through instruction in Sikh temples, read at the Eighth Educational Conference (1915).

97 _____ : Ik Lekchur. (P) Lahore, Sri Gurmat Press, 1904. 48 p. IOL

Lecture on Guru Gobind Singh.

98 _____ : Jagra Karan Di Than Vichar Kolon Kam Lao. (P) Amritsar, Bhai Budh Singh, 1912. 4 p. BTSL

In place of squabbling, take up your work thoughtfully, an open letter to Sikhs on the Educational Conference.

99 _____ : Jiwan Charittra Sri Guru Gobind Singh Sahibji. (P) Lahore, Caxton Press, 1895. 48 p.

Life of Guru Gobind Singh.

100 _____ : Kal Taran. (P) Dalcheki (Sialkot), Panjabi Agency, 1912. 15 p.

Beautiful verses, poetry on the birth and mission of Guru Nanak.

101 _____ : Munshi Ram Da Kukrughun. (P) Dalcheki (Sialkot), Bhai Budh Singh, 1914. 15 p.

Bad actions of Munshi Ram, criticism of Pandit Munshi Ram's pamphlet against Sikhs. (454)

102 _____ : Panjabi Boli De Prachar Te Sawar Lai Panjabi Vidvan Istriyan Te Purkhan Age Apil. (P) Hissar, Bhai Budh Singh, 1910. 25 p.

Address on the diffusion of Panjabi presented at the Third Educational Conference (1910).

103 _____ : Pakhand Vinash. (P) Amritsar, Bhai Sewa Singh, 1914. 32 p.

Destruction of show, against idol worship.

104 _____ : Sikhi De Purne. (P) Sargodha, Khalsa Brothers, 1916. 306 p. PPU

Accomplishments of Sikhs, instances of devotion to Sikhism in trying times.

105 _____ : Sri Amritsar Darshan. (P) Amritsar, Bhai Budh Singh, 1907. 16 p.

History of the Golden Temple.

106 _____ : Upkar Namuna. (P) Dalcheki (Sialkot), Bhai Budh Singh, 1914. 16 p.

Example of good actions, discussion of Guru Gobind Singh's assistance to Hindus.

107 _____ : Vedan Da Gyan. (P) Tung (Amritsar), Bhai Budh Singh, 1913. 272 p. IOL

Knowledge of the Vedas, Sikh denunciation of practices in the Vedas such as Niyog, fire worship and animal sacrifice.

108 _____ : Vedan Da Pol. (P) Amritsar, Bhai Budh Singh, 1912. 247 p. PPU/IOL

The hollowness of the Vedas, comparison of the Hindu scriptures and the Adi Granth.

109 **BUDH SINGH, Gurdaspuri :** Granth Timmar Nas. (P) Gurdaspur, Budh Singh, 1912. 247 p. BM

Attempt to prove Sikh superiority over Hinduism by critical discussion of Hindu rites and legends.

110 **BURTON, R.G. :** The First and Second Sikh Wars. Simla, Government Central Branch Press, 1911. IOL

Survey of military operations, with maps and information on the role of political agents in precipitating the conflicts. An official interpretation.

111 **BUTA MAL CHAVALA, Bhai :** Gurmatan Te Manmattan Da Sanbadu. (P) Lahore, Bhai Amar Singh, 1912. 32 p. BTSL

The relation between true and false religion, a discussion between a lady who believes in Sikhism and another who adheres to Hindu mythology.

112 **BUTA RAM KHANNA :** Zulam Ka Pahla Hissa. (U) Amritsar, Buta Ram Khanna, 1892. 8 p. BM/IOL

First part of tyranny, narrative on Sikh and Hindu martyrs by an Arya updeshak.

113 **CHANDA SINGH :** Sri Guru Granth Ji Ke Madh Se Paryai Farsi Padon Ke. (P) Amritsar, Amar Press, 1888. 76 p.

Synonyms of Persian words occuring in the Adi Granth.

114 **CHANDA SINGH, Bhai :** Granth Sri Dukh Bhajan Gatha. (P) Bewal (Rawalpindi), Bhai Chanda Singh, 1916. 24 p. BM

Metrical life of Thakur Nihal Singh, a devoted Sikh of Ashram Dukh-bhajani, Thoha Khalsa (Rawalpindi).

115 _____ : Ustati Swami Sri 6 Guru Ratan Harji Ki. (H) Amritsar, Chashma-i-Nur Press, 1894. 16 p.

Verses praising Bhai Ratan Singh, a poet and saint of Amritsar.

116 **CHANDAN GIR, Baba :** Sat Guru Baba Nanakji Ki Ardas. (PN) Rawalpindi, Gulshan-i-Panjab Press, 1898. 4 p. BTSL

Biographical sketch of Guru Nanak.

117 **CHARAN SINGH, Bhai :** Chanchal Murti. (P) Amritsar, Bhai Charan Singh, 1912. 192 p.

Adventures of a Sikh hero who escaped from Muslim captors with three Hindu ladies and a Muslim girl, who were also under arrest and who subsequently converted to Sikhism.

118 **CHATUR SINGH :** Puran Mashi Di Vaddi Katha. (P) Amritsar, Wazir Hind Press, 1901. 36 p.

Religious discourse on the significance of the night of the full moon for Sikhs.

119 _____ : Sri Kalghidhar Upkar. (P) Amritsar, Wazir Hind Press, 1900. 16 p.

Good deeds of Guru Gobind Singh, in verse.

120 **CHHAJJU SINGH, Bawa (Trans.) :** Japji Sahib. (P, E) Lahore, Arorbans Press, 1894. 94 p. IOL

Japji, with interpretation in English.

121 _____ : The Ten Gurus and Their Teachings. Lahore, Punjab Printing Works, 1903. 432 p. BM

A reinterpretation of Sikh history and theology by an Arya Samaj publicist.

122 **CHHANGA SINGH, Bhai :** Shahid Bilas. (P) Amritsar, Bhai Chhanga Singh, 1910. 46 p. KC

Verses on the martyrdom of the sons of Guru Gobind Singh.

123 **CHUHAR SINGH, Bhai :** Sikh Bachche Da Sikhi Sidaq. (P) Amritsar, Bhai Chuhar Singh, 1914. 14 p.

Story of the religious faith of a Sikh child who was captured with Sikh troops by the Mughal army.

124 **COURT, Henry:** History of the Sikhs: or, Translation of the Sikhan De Raj Di Vikhia ..Together with a Short Gurmukhi Grammar. Lahore, Civil and Military Gazette Press, 1888. lxxxiv, 239 p. BM/IOL

History of the Sikhs prior to British annexation in 1849, with notes on Sikh customs, songs and proverbs, and a translation of portions of the Bala Janam-Sakhi. A translation of Sarda Ram's Punjabi work. (584)

125 **CUNNINGHAM, Joseph Davy :** A History of the Sikhs from the Origin of the Nation to the Battles of the Sutlej. London, John Murray, 1849. BM/BTSL/IOL/KC/PPU

Cunningham's survey of Sikh religion and history remains perhaps the best available source on the Ranjit Singh period and on the Sikh Wars. His sympathy for the Sikhs and interpretation of British intentions toward the Punjab destroyed Cunningham's career as a Political agent.

126 **CUTT, Robert Needham:** The Country of Baba Nanak or Sikhland. London, Trubner and Company, 1880. 47p. KC

127 **DALEL SINGH:** Ak Nun Milni. (P) Hoshiarpur, Bhai Dalel Singh, 1909. 16 p.

Essay directed against the custom of embracing the ak plant by Sikh women on festivals and special occasions.

128 **DALJIT SINGH, Sardar :** The Presidential Speech by Sardar Daljit Singh at the Third Sikh Conference. Amritsar, EC, n/d. 32p. PPU

129 _____ : Shahid Bilas. (P) Amritsar, Akal Press, n/d. 8p. PPU

Narrative of Guru Tegh Bahadur's martyrdom.

130 _____ : Sikh Mat Ki Ta'lim Par Risalon Ka Silsila. (P,E) Lahore, Christian Knowledge Society, 1908, 190p.

The teachings of Sikhism discussed under five headings: morality, disattachment, good works, love of God and love for fellow man.

131 _____ : Sikhism or the Higher Religious Synthesis. Jullundur, New Albion Press, n/d. 29p. KC/PPU

Lecture before the Jullundur City Singh Sabha, November 5, 1903.

132 _____ : Some Aspects of Sikhism. Simla, Thacker, Spink and Company, 1906. 39p. KC/PPU

Lecture on the higher synthesis of

DALJIT SINGH, Sardar (contd)
Sikhism, comparing Sikh ideas of spiritualism with other world philosophies.

133 **DARBARA SINGH, Bhai** : Ramgarhia. (P) Simla, Ramgarhia Sabha, 1913. 70p. BM/IOL
Account of the rise and decline of Ramgarhia Sikhs.

134 _____ : Siharfi. (P) Simla, Sardar Kishan Singh, 1914. 16p. IOL
On the necessity of spreading general and industrial education among Ramgarhia Sikhs.

135 **DARSHANA NAND SARASWATI** : Kya Sikh Hindu Nahin ? (U) Rawalpindi, Chaudhri Balak Ram Anand, 1911. 8 p.
Are the Sikhs not Hindus? Controversial tract which attempts to prove that all Sikhs are Hindus.

136 **DASANDA SINGH** : Rahit Nama Rahtian Singhan Da. (P) Amritsar, Akal Yantar Press, 1884. 42 p.
Rules and observances for the orthodox Sikh.

137 **DAULAT RAI, Lala** : Bharat Ke Maha Purshon Ka Silsila Nambar 2, Ya'ni Mahan Bali Guru Gobind Singh Ji Ka Jiwan Charittra. (U) Lahore, Rifah-i-Am Press, 1901. 296 p. KC/PPU
The great men of India series, number 2 : life of Guru Gobind Singh.

138 **DAYA RAM** : Wain Hamari Guru Nanak Dev Ji. (U) Lahore, Munshi Ram Agarwal, 1908. 146 p. PPU/IOL
Life and teachings of Guru Nanak.

139 **DAYA SINGH, Bhai** : Parya Granth Sahib. (P) Amritsar, Dabir-i-Hind Press, 1887. 336 p.
Notes and commentary on the Adi Granth.

140 _____ : Sau Sakhi Pathshai 10. (UG) Amritsar, Wazir Hind Press, 1907. 192 p.
Traditions and prophecies concerning Guru Gobind Singh.

141 **DEVA SINGH, Bhai** : Angrezi Raj De Sukh Ate Wartman Kal Wich Parja Ka Dharm. (P) Talagang (Attock), Kanwar Charanjit Singh, 1917. 13 p. IOL
The blessings of the British raj and our duties toward the government in the present period.

142 _____ : Jiwan Sudhar. (P) Roorkee, Bhai Deva Singh, 1909. 40 p.
Improvement of life, essays on Sikh religious concepts.

143 _____ : Nam Adhar. (P) Amritsar, Wazir Hind Press, 1905. 120 p.
Commentary on Sikhism and its place in the Iron Age.

144 **DEVA SINGH, Sant** : Sugam Jap Pradip. (P) Amritsar, Wazir Hind Press, 1902. 133 p. BTSL
Commentary on the Jap Sahib.

145 **DHANNA RAM, Pandit** : Ved Prachar Sri Guru Nanakji Di Sikhya. (P) Lau (Jhang), Pandit Dhanna Ram, 1908. 28 p. IOL
Attempt to show that the Sikh Gurus professed the Vedic religion.

146 **DHARA SINGH, Bhai** : Sri Guru Vanshkul Dipka. (P) Lahore, Khalsa Press, 1905. 8 p.
Genealogy of the Gurus.

147 **DHARM DEV, Pandit** : Istri Sudhar. (P) Lahore, Lala Mohan Lal, 1905. 23 p. PPU
Reform of women, ideas on how and what to preach to women by a Sikh updeshak.

148 **DHARM SINGH** : Dharm Parkash. (P) Amritsar, Riaz-i-Hind Press, 1886. 48 p.
Sikh theology.

149 **DHARM SINGH, Bhai** : Singhan Di Bahaduri. (P) Amritsar, Bhai Chattar Singh, 1918. 8 p.
Heroic deeds of Sikhs during the First World War.

150 **DIDAR SINGH, Bedi** : Akas Bani Parmarath Jap Sahib. (SI) Mufid-i-Am Press, 1897. 80 p.
A voice from heaven, or an exgesis of the Jap Sahib.

151 **DITT SINGH, Gyani** : Bhai Bota Singh Ji Shahid. (P) Lahore, Khalsa Press, 1901. 43 p.
Verses on the martyrdom of Bhai Bota Singh.

152 _____ : Dambh Vidaran Arthat Sadhu Dayanandji De San 1875 Isawi De Sattyarth Parkash Par Vichar. (P) Lahore, Punjab Economical Press, 1902. 210 p.
The exposure of haughtiness, or an examination of Dayanand's Satyarth Parkash of 1875.

153 _____ : Darpoke Singh. (P) Lahore, Anglo-Sanskrit Press, 1895. 68 p.
The cowardly Sikh, a dialogue between two Sikhs on the links between Sikhism and Hinduism. Ditt Singh gave the copyright of this controversial tract to

the Lahore Shuddhi Sabha. For background, see the editorials and letters in Khalsa Akhbar, 1895.

154 _____ : Dharam Darpan. (P) Lahore, Khalsa Press, 1900. 33 p. BTSL

A mirror of religion.

155 _____ : Durga Prabodh. (P) Lahore, Dr. Baldev Singh, 1899. 512 p. BTSL/KC

Discussion of Guru Gobind Singh's significance for Sikhs. The author also tries to prove that the Gurus did not worship idols.

156 _____ : Gurmat Arti Prabodh. (P) Lahore, Khalsa Press, 1900. 56 p. IOL

Condemnation of the popular mode of saying morning and evening prayers among Hindus, with a call for Sikhs to remain true to the concepts of prayer preached by the Gurus.

157 _____ : Guru Arjan Charittra. Lahore, (P) Khalsa Press, 1896. 16 p.

Account of Guru Arjan.

158 _____ : Kalgidhar Upkar. (P) Lahore, Khalsa Press, 1899. 8p. PPU

Verses on life and message of Guru Gobind Singh.

159 _____ : Mera Ate Sadhu Dayanand Da Sambhand. (P) Lahore, Khalsa Press, 1900. 56 p. BTSL/PPU

Religious discussions between myself and Sadhu Dayanand, an account of a series of debates in which Ditt Singh allegedly humiliated the founder of the Arya Samaj. Also printed in Urdu : Mera Ate Sadhu Dayanand Ka Mabahis. Lahore, 1900. 34 p. PPU. For background on the debates, see Giani Amar Singh, Jivan Charitar Giani Ditt Singh. (Amritsar, 1962), pp. 28-54. (182)

160 _____ : Miran Kotie Mahtab Singh Di Bahaduri. (P) Lahore, Khalsa Press, 1900. 32 p. BM

The bravery of Mahtab Singh of Miran Kot.

161 _____ : Miran Manaut. (P) Lahore, Bhai Baldev Singh, 1902. 29 p. PPU

Essay on differences between worshipping a Muslim saint and the Sikh Gurus.

162 _____ : Nakli Sikh Prabodh. (P) Lahore, Khalsa Press. 1895. 196 p. BM/BTSL/PPU/IOL

Knowledge of the false Sikh, a Singh Sabha tract calling for reforms within the Sikh community.

163 _____ : Pamma Prabodh. (P) 2/e., Lahore, Bhai Baldev Singh, 1906. BTSL/IOL

Verses directed against Brahmans.

164 _____ : Sabeg Singh Di Shahidi. (P) Lahore, Khalsa Press, 1900. 53 p.

Martyrdom of Sabeg Singh.

165 _____ : Shahidian (P) 2/e., Lahore, Baldev Singh, 1911. 192 p. BM/KC/IOL

Poems on the martyrdom of Guru Arjan, Taru Singh, Bota Singh and some women and children.

166 _____ : Sikh Bachche Di Sachchi Shahidi. (P) Lahore, Khalsa Press, 1898. 19 p. PPU/IOL

Martyrdom of a Sikh boy.

167 _____ : Singhanian. De Sadiq. (P) Lahore, Khalsa Press, 29 p. IOL

Fortitude of Sikh women, a story of tortures that Sikh women had to endure because they refused to convert to Islam.

168 _____ : Sri Guru Nanak Prabodh. (HG) Lahore, Vidya Prakashak Press, 1890. 68 p. BM

Account of the life and religious discussions of Guru Nanak, with explanatory notes.

169 _____ : Sultan Poara. (P) Lahore, Khalsa Press, 1896. 65 p. PPU

Religious dialogue between a Sikh and a Hindu who worships Sakhi Sarwar, a Muslim Saint. The Sikh tries to bring the Hindu into the Sikh faith.

170 _____ : Ta'lim Satyarth Prakash Ka Asli Foto. (U) Lyallpur, Hari Chand, 1910. 202 p. KC/PPU

Real picture of the Arya Samaj, criticism of Samajists with particular references to their intervention in Sikh affairs.

171 _____ : Tara Singh Vain Di Shahidi. (P) Lahore, Khalsa Press, 1899. 74 p. BM

Verses on martyrdom of Tara Singh.

172 **DIYAL SINGH, Sant:** Bijli Bhagat Prabodh. (P) Lahore, Khalsa Press, 1898. 32 p.

Criticism of the efforts to electrify the Golden Temple.

173 **DUNI CHAND :** War Sri Guru Tegh Bahadurji Di. (P) Amritsar, Chashma-i-Nur Press, 1903. 24 p.

Verses on the life of Guru Teg Bahadur.

174 **FAKIR CHAND, Lala:** Ath Jang Sri Chamkaur Sahib Da. (P) Lyallpur, Lala Fakir Chand, 1917. 14 p.

Verses on the battle of Chamkaur.

175 _____ : Maharaja Guru Gobind Singh. (U) Lahore, Nawal Kishore Press, 1903. 16 p. IOL

176 **FALCON, F.W. :** Handbook on Sikhs. Allahabad, Pioneer Press, 1896. 142 p. BM/BTSL/IOL

Recruitment manual, with information on Sikh religion and society.

177 **FATEH SINGH, Bhai :** Holiyan Ki Kartut. (P) Toba Tek Singh (Lyallpur), Khalsa Jatha, Bar, 1910. 14 p.

Verses condemning the Holi festival as celebrated by Hindus and pointing out the correct manner of celebration from the Sikh viewpoint.

178 **FIELD, Dorothy :** The Religion of the Sikhs. London, John Murray, 1914. 114 p. BM/IOL/KC/PPU

Western interpretation of Sikhism, with excerpts from Sikh scriptures.

179 **GAHL SINGH, Sardar :** Panjab Dhandora. (P) Narnol (Patiala), Sardar Gahl Singh, 1918. 33 p.

Appeal for Sikhs to enlist, with war poems and selections from scriptures.

180 **GANDA SINGH :** Vigyan Kosh. (U) Lahore, Aftab-i-Panjab Press, 1885. 420 p.

Collection of new things, life of Guru Nanak.

181 **GANDA SINGH, Bhai :** Manmattan Di Kartut. (P) Gujranwala, Bhai Ganda Singh, 1916. 8 p.

Opposition to self-styled religion, an account of the troubles experienced by a Sikh family in marrying non-Sikh girls.

182 _____ **:** Nushkha-i-Khabt-i-Dayanandiyan. (PN) Amritsar, Amar Press, 1904. 256 p. BTSL/IOL

Prescriptions for the insanity of the followers of Dayanand, a refutation of Lala Sahib Dyal's Ilaj-i-Wahmat-i-Ditt Singhia (Remedy for the whims of Ditt Singh). (159, 396)

183 **GANEM SINGH :** Sri Guru Dasam Lila. (P) Amritsar, Wazir Hind Press, 1898. 25 p.

History of early Sikhism and Guru Gobind Singh.

184 **GANESH SINGH, Baba :** Sri Guru Dasam Lila Prashnu Uttri. (P) Amritsar, Wazir Hind Press, 1902. 32 p. IOL

Biography of Guru Gobind Singh in the form of questions and answers.

185 _____ : Sri Guru Nanak Suryodaya Janam Sakhi. (P) Amritsar, Chashma-i-Nur Press, 1895. 560 p. BTSL

Life of Guru Nanak.

186 **GANESH SINGH, Bedi :** Baran Mislan. (P) Amritsar, Anand Parkash Press, 1893. 8 p.

The Twelve Sikh misals.

187 **GANESH SINGH, Sant :** Istri Amrit Nikhed. (P) Lahore, Sri Gurmat Press, 1902. 8 p.

Refusal of Amrit to Sikh women, criticism of efforts by reforming groups such as the Panch Khalsa Diwan to give initiatory rites to Sikh ladies.

188 _____ : Khalsa Biwah Paddhat. (P) Lahore, Sri Gurmat Press, 1901. 328 p.

Marriage rites of the Sikhs.

189 **GANGA SINGH, Bhai :** Dharma Kasoti. (U) Delhi, Sardar Mangal Singh, n/d., 46 p.

Testing stone of religion, an evaluation of world religions calculated to prove that Sikhism is superior.

190 _____:Isai Prabodh. (P) Amritsar, Wazir Hind Press, 1903. 36 p. PPU/IOL

Exposition of Christianity, criticism of Christianity in the form of a dialogue between a Christian and a Sikh.

191 **GHANAYA LAL SHARMA, Lala :** Tat Khalsa Mat Pariksha. (U) Amritsar, Sanatan Dharm Press, 1905. 80 p. IOL

A Test of the religious views of the Tat Khalsa Sikhs.

192 **GHASITA MAL, Bawa :** Kashif-ul-Asliyat-i-Khalsa. (U) Hoshiarpur, Khatri Press, 1899. 8 p.

A description of the true condition of the Sikhs.

193 **GHULAM ALI KHAN :** Sher-i-Panjab Maharaja Ranjit Singh. (U) Lahore, J.S. Sant Singh and Sons, 1909.

Life of Ranjit Singh.

194 **GHULAM QADIR, Faqir :** Tarikhi Qisson Ka Silsila Nambar Ek, Baba Nanak Sahib. (U) Sialkot, Punjab Press, 1893. 16 p.

Short life of Guru Nanak.

195 **GOBIND SAHAI (ed.) :** Jap Parmarth. (U) Lahore, Mufid-i-Am Press, 1879. 142 p.

Japji Sahib translated into Urdu, with a life of Guru Nanak and a short account of the other Gurus.

196 **GOKUL CHAND NARANG :** Transformation of Sikhism, Or How the Sikhs Became a Political Power. Lahore, Tribune Press, 1912. xxiv, 197 p. BM/IOL

Narrative of the stages through which Sikhs passed before becoming sovereign

in the Punjab, stopping at 1768 with the occupation of Lahore. Appendices include a statement on Sikh scriptures, an essay (Is Sikhism a Mixture ?), and a note on the chief features on the Sikh religion.

197 **GOPAL DAS, Pandit :** Navin Parnali Jiwan Sudha, Tisri Pustak. (H) Lahore, Punjab Economical Press, 1894. 70 p.

Biographical reader, with sketches on the first five Gurus.

198 **GOPAL SINGH :** Risalai Chechak Wah Jangi Singhan. (PN) Amritsar, Chashma-i-Nur Press, 1878. 12 p.

Lines on vaccination, followed by a poem on Sikh intrigues preceding the First and Second Sikh Wars.

199 **GOPAL SINGH, Mahant :** Sachcha Bali Dan. (U) Amritsar, Anand Parkash Press, 1895. 36 p. IOL

The true sacrifice. on martyrdom of Guru Tegh Bahadur. Subsequently republished in English : True Sacrifice, Or the Martyrdom of Siri Guru Teg Bahadur. Lahore, Punjab Patriot Press, 1898. 18 p. BM

200 **GORDON, John J.H. (General) :** The Sikhs. Edinburgh, William Blackwood and Sons, 1904. 236 p. BM/IOL/KC/PPU

"A sympathetic short sketch of this warlike race, and of their rise through much tribulation to power as a nation, and transformation by the fortune of war into loyal and hearty subjects" (p. 1) by a soldier who served many years with Sikh troops.

201 **GOUGH, Charles and Arthur D. Innes :** The Sikhs and the Sikh Wars. London, Arthur D. Innes, 1897. xiv, 304p. BM/IOL/KC

Survey of the Ranjit Singh period and British annexation, with discussion of post-1849 policy toward the Sikhs. Numerous maps and battle plans illustrate the Second Sikh War.

202 **GRIFFIN, Lepel :** The Law of Inheritance to Chiefships As Observed by the Sikhs Previous to the Annexation of the Panjab. Lahore, Punjab Printing Company, 1869. 109p. BM/BTSL/IOL

Survey of inheritance rules, with background on individual chiefs and families. The last sections deal with changes initiated by the British.

203 _____ : Ranjit Singh. Oxford, Clarendon Press, 1905. BM/IOL/KC

204 **GUILFORD, E :** Sikhism. Westminister, Lay Reader's Headquarters, 1915. 39p. BM/IOL/PPU

Interpretation of Sikhism by a missionary at Tarn Taran.

205 **GULAB SINGH, Bakhshi :** Gurmat Vikhyan Nashon Ka Khandan. (P) Amritsar, Bakhshi Gulab Singh, 1914. 39 p.

Explanation of the Gurus' teachings against intoxicants.

206 **GULAB SINGH, Bhai :** Jiwan Britant Sri Guru Arjan Devji. (P) Lahore, Khalsa Press, 1898. 16 p.

Life of Guru Arjan.

207 **GULAB SINGH, Munshi :** Bhagton Di Bari. (P) Lahore, Mufid-i-Am Press, 1896. 224 p. PPU

Account of devotees, background on Sikh saints.

208 **GURBAKHSH SINGH :** Ganj Gurbakhsh Singh. (P) Lahore, Arjan Parkash Press, 1880. 8 p.

Sikh marriage songs.

209 **GURBAKHSH SINGH, Bhai :** Guru Kaun Hai ? (P) Baghbanpura, Guru Nanak Agency, 1913. 46 p. PPU/IOL

Who is the Guru ? Dialogue between a true Sikh and an unfaithful Sikh on the present state of their religion.

210 _____ : Parhe Likhe Sikhan De Apil Qaum Wal Farz. (P) Amritsar, EC, 1914. 16 p. PPU

Duties of educated Sikhs toward their community, a paper read at the Seventh Educational Conference (1914).

211 _____ : Sachchi Shahidi. (P) Henzada (Burma), Bhai Gurbakhsh Singh, 1913. 42 p. IOL

Verses on the martyrdom of Guru Gobind Singh's sons, written by a police officer.

212 _____ : Sadhe Panthak Git. (P) Manewa (Burma), Subedar Major Anoth Singh, 1915. 34 p.

Moral and social songs for Sikhs.

213 **GURBAKHSH SINGH, Granthi :** Yag Prabodh. (P) Rupar (Ambala), Gurbakhsh Singh, 1908. 30 p.

Account of Sikh religious meetings in the Malay state.

214 **GURDAS, Bhai :** Waran Bhai Gurdasji Dian. (P) Lahore, Vidya Prakashak Press, 1893. 304 p. BM

The celebrated poems of Bhai Gurdas, a contemporary of the fourth, fifth and sixth Gurus. These verses deal with Sikh history and religion and have been accorded the title of the key to the Guru Granth Sahib.

215 **GURDIAL SINGH, Bhai** : Pandit Ji Kehri Gurmat Karaunde Ho ? (P) Rajajang (Lahore), Bhai Gurdial Singh, 1914. 8 p. PPU/IOL

Oh Pandit, what religion are you practicing ? Criticism of the assertion that Sikhs are Hindus.

216 _____ : Pisne Ka Rangraw Ka Rangraw. (P) Rajajang (Lahore), Gurdial Singh, 1914. 48 p. BTSL/IOL

Criticism of Sikhs accepting the Hindu caste system.

217 _____ : Sadi Maya Da Vehn. (P) Rajajang (Lahore), Bhai Gurdial Singh, 1914. 15 p.

The flow of our wealth, an appeal for funds to educate Sikh youths.

218 _____ : Viyakhyan Sri Guru Nanakji. (P) Tarn Taran, Bhai Gurdial Singh, 1912. 27 p.

Account of Guru Nanak's visit to Mecca and his teachings there, in the form of a dialogue.

219 **GURDIT SINGH, Bhai** : Bachchi Da Varlap. (P) Lyallpur, Bhai Gurdit Singh, 1915. 24 p.

The cry of a girl, verses on the problems of a Sikh girl married into a non-Sikh family.

220 _____ : Professor Harkishan Singhji De Lekh Par Vichar. (P) Amritsar, Bhai Gurdit Singh, 1915. 4 p.

Criticism of Professor Harkishan Singh's note supporting the claims of Sant Lakhbir Singh as a spiritual leader.

221 _____ : Sachcha Updesh. (P) Lyallpur, Bhai Gurdit Singh, 1907. 16 p.

Exposition of Sikh theology, with emphasis on the nature of worship.

222 _____ : Siri Guru Nanak Upkar. (P) Manauli (Ambala), Bhai Gurdit Singh, 1906. 16 p.

The teachings of Guru Nanak.

223 **GURDIT SINGH, Kavi** : Jhagra Nunh Sauhara. (P) Lahore, Mohammad Abdal Aziz, 1917. 24 p. PPU

Verses on a dispute between a Sikh woman and her father-in-law.

224 **GURDIT SINGH, Vaid** : Gurbani Da Virlap. (P) Amritsar, Bhai Gurdit Singh, 1917. 27 p. IOL

Criticism of the wrong pronunciation and spelling of Gurbani and of improper methods adopted to sing it.

225 **GURMUKH SINGH, Bhai** : A Brief History of the Golden Temple. Amritsar, Lahore, Gurmukh Singh, 1892.

226 _____ : Gutt Hai Ke Sundaka ? (P) Ludhiana, Managing Committee, Sikh Kanya Pathshala, 1913. 16 p.

Is it a lock of hair or a heap ? Criticism of different forms of hair plaiting and wearing ornaments by Sikh women.

227 _____ : Jiwan Charitra Bhai Mati Das. (P) Lahore, Bhai Ram Das, 1913.

Life of Bhai Mati Das, a Sikh saint during the time of Guru Tegh Bahadur, and an account of his ancestors.

228 _____ : Kritghan Te Kritagya. (P) Barundi (Ludhiana), Bhai Gurmukh Singh, 1919. 16 p.

Loyal and disloyal, verses describing the debt that Hindus owe Sikhs for protection in Muslim times, also praising the Sikh Gurus and hailing the advent of British rule.

229 _____ : Lasani Kramat. (P) Lahore, Gurmukh Singh, 1895. 8 p. PPU

The incomparable miracle, account of Guru Gobind Singh's career.

230 _____ : Sudhararak. (P) Lahore, 1888. 84 p. BM

A lecture on social and religious reform.

231 _____ : Wihar Sudhar. (P) Bhasaur, Panch Khalsa Diwan, 1910. 338 p. IOL

Marriage reform, verses against the betrothal and marriage ceremonies performed by Hindus.

232 **GURMUKH SINGH, Pandit** : Gur Gira Ragmala Mandan Parbodh Granth. (P) Lahore, Sant Taihal Singh, 1908. 120 p. PPU

History of Sikhism and Sikh gurdwaras.

233 _____ : Vedic Sanatan Gurmat Martund. (P) Lahore, Machine Press, 1913. 70 p. IOL

Attempt to prove that the Sikh Gurus believed in the Vedas.

234 **GURMUKH SINGH, Pardesi** : Chandal Chaukri Da Kaccha Chiththa. (P) Amritsar, Gurmukh Singh, 1919. 29 p. PPU

The wicked gang's spurious letter, a reply to criticism of Sikhism and reform efforts.

235 **GURMUKH SINGH, Sardar** : Guru Nanak Parkash. (U) 2/e., Lahore, Aftab Punjab Press, 1891. 302 p. KC

Lithographed life of Guru Nanak, with commentary on Sikh theology.

236 **GYAN SINGH, Bhai** : Baba Atal Hulas. (P) 3/e., Amritsar, Bhai Buta Singh,

1908. 28 p.

Verses on life of Baba Atal, son of Guru Hargobind.

237 _____ : Nirmal Panth Par Dipaka. (P) Sialkot, Guru Gobind Press, 1891. 100 p. BTSL/IOL

A commentary on the Nirmala sect, which supports the claim that its members are true followers of the Sikh Gurus.

238 **GYAN SINGH, Gyani :** Amrit Parkash. (HG) Lahore, Arorbans Press, 1898. 154 p.

Discussion of the significance of Sikh baptism.

239 _____ : Khalsa Dharam Patit Pawan. (P) Lahore, Anglo-Sanskrit Press, 1895 156p.

Regeneration of the fallen Sikhs. Urges that persons who have renounced the Sikh faith can be brought back to it and purified by a Shudhi ceremony.

240 _____ : Pothi Sri Guru Panth Prakash. (HG) Lahore, Husaini Press, 1880. 796 p.

Verses on the lives and adventures of the Sikh Gurus. Later enlarged editions, with information on religious observances, include the following : Guru Panth Prakash. (P) Lahore, 1889. 559 p. IOL; Guru Panth Prakash (P) Amritsar, Dabir-i-Hind Press, 1899. 1088 p. IOL

241 _____ : Ripduman Prakash. (P) Patiala, Bhupinder State Press, 1919. 190 p. KC/PPU

Commentary on life of Guru Nanak.

242 _____ : Sri Bhupendra Nanad. (P) Patiala, Bhai Gyan Singh Gyani, 1917. 110 p.

A book of social rites for Sikhs.

243 _____ : Tawarikh-i-Guru Khalsa. (U) 3 Vols. Sialkot, Guru Gobind Singh Press, 1892. 182, 360, 528 p. IOL/KC/PPU

History of the Sikh Gurus and Sikh religion. Volume one and two contain a detailed account of the early Gurus, Banda, and Mughal persecution. Volume three gives background on the Sikh misals, Ranjit Singh, and the Phulkian princes. Subsequent editions generally were in Panjabi.

244 **HAKIM SINGH, Bhai :** Parsang Babe Attal Rai (P) Amritşar Pustak Parcharni Sabha, 1912. 55 p. BM

Life of Baba Atal, eldest son of Guru Hargobind

245 **HARBANS SINGH, Sardar :** Address. (P) Amritsar, EC, n/d. 27 p. BTSL

Presidential address, Tenth Educational Conference (1917).

246 **HARCHAND SINGH :** Pamphlat Mutaliq Gurduara Rakabganj. (U) Lahore, Brahman Steam Press, 1914. 4 p. BTSL

Call for Sikh action to defend the Delhi Rakabganj Gurdwara against demolition by British engineers.

247 **HARCHARAN SINGH, Sodhi :** Jarmani Nun Jittana. (P) Ferozepur, Sodhi Harcharan Singh, n/d. 16 p. BTSL

To conquer Germany, a collection of verses on the First World War and the benefits of the British raj.

248 **HAR GOPAL, Pandit :** Sawanih-i-Umri Baba Nanak. (U) Lahore, Arya Press, 1884. 16 p.

Life of Guru Nanak.

249 **HARIBHAJAN SINGH, Sant:** Savitari Natik. (P) Amritsar, Sardar Dan Singh, n.d. 72 p. BTSL

Drama on the education of women and the Sikh religion.

250 _____ : Sri Tarn Taran Mahatam. (P) Amritsar, Bhai Arur Singh, 1913. 8 p.

Verses on the history of Tarn Taran.

251 **HARI SINGH:** Bijai Mukht Dharam Shaster. (P) Lahore, Victoria Press, 1896. 452 p. BM/PPU

Religious teachings of Guru Gobind Singh in the form of dialogues between himself and his followers on social and religious subjects.

252 **HARI SINGH, Bhai:** Katha Puranmashi. (P) Amritsar, Hari Singh. 1908. 32 p.

Religious discourse on the night of the full moon, a story relating how the Sikh fair, held at full moon each month 160 miles west of Apchalnagar, was founded by Guru Gobind Singh.

253 **HARNAM SINGH :** Tankhwah Nama. (P) Amritsar, 1885. 18 p. BM

Verses on the fines paid by Sikhs as penalties for irregularities in ceremonial observances.

254 **HARNAM SINGH :** Bharam Niwaran. (P) Lahore, Bhai Harnam Singh, 1910. 30 p.

Removing of doubts, quotations from Adi Granth and discussion on the subjects of superstitions introduced by Brahmans.

255 _____ : Bijli Bidaran. (P) Lahore, Khalsa Press, 1897, 63 p.

Discarding electricity, condemnation of the proposal to introduce electric lights in the Golden Temple.

256 _____ : Gur Upkar. (HG) Lahore, Arorbans Press, 1896. 30 p. PPU

Philanthropic deeds of the Gurus.

257 _____ : Khalsa Dharam Dipak. (P) Amritsar, National Press, 1903. 16 p.

The lamp of the Khalsa religion.

258 _____ : Khalsaji Hun Dhokha Na Khana. (P) Amritsar, Wazir Hind Press, 1903. 16 p.

Oh Khalsa, do not be deceived any more.

259 _____ : Khalsa Panth Vich Vidiya Prachar Ate Bradari Da Sambandh. (P) Sargodha, Nihang Bahadur Agency, 1914. 24 p.

The extension of education and the establishment of brotherhood among Sikhs.

260 _____ : Nihang Bahadur. (P) Sargodha, Nihang Bahadur Agency, 1914. 191 p.

Account of the battles fought by the Nihangs.

261 _____ : Pakhand Khandan. (P) Amritsar, Bhai Harnam Singh, 1907. 16 p.

Refutation of hypocrisy, condemnation of Hindu elements in the Sikh religion.

262 _____ : Pamian Di Kartut. (P) Amritsar, Wazir Hind Press, 1903. 16 p.

Actions of the Hindu Brahmans.

263 _____ : Panchal Desh Di Fariyad Khalsaji Agge. (P) Amritsar., Bhai Harnam Singh, 1910. 42 p. IOL

Verses urging social reform among Sikhs.

264 _____ : Sachcha Hoka. (P) Amritsar, Wazir Hind Press, 1902. 16 p.

The true proclamation, discussion on the significance of Sikhism for the contemporary world.

265 _____ : Shahidi Guru Bans Baba Wadbhag Singhji, Sodhi, Kartarpur Walian Di. (P) Amritsar, Bhai Harnam Singh, 1916. 24 p. IOL

Life of Baba Wadbhag Singh, one of the ancestors of the Sodhi family of Kartarpur.

266 _____ : Sri Guru Gobind Singhji Daswen Patshahi Di Sachchi Muhabbat To Hinduan Murdian Nal Kiti. (P) Amritsar, Wazir Hind Press, 1903. 16 p.

Guru Gobind Singh's true love for the fallen Hindus.

267 _____ : Shri Guru Nanak Sahibji Ke Darshan Wa Daswen Badshahji Ke Sahibzadon. (U) Amritsar, National Press, 1903. 8 p.

Commentary on the work of Guru Nanak and an account of the death of Guru Gobind Singh's sons.

268 **HARNAM SINGH, Doctor :** Khalsa Skulan De Vidyarthian Di Arogta De Sadhan. (P) Amritsar, EC, 1915. 16 p. PPU

The means of maintaining the health of students in Sikh schools, a paper read at the Eighth Educational Conference (1915).

269 _____**, Doctor:** Sarirak Bal (P) Amritsar, EC, 1914. 16 p. PPU

Physical energy, a paper on the physical training of Sikhs, read at the Seventh Educational Conference (1914).

270 **HARNAM SINGH, Munshi:** Keson Ki Azmat. (U) Jullundur, Aftab-i-Hind Press, 1891. 16 p.

Respect for hair, discourse favouring the maintenance of hair.

271 **HARNAM SINGH, Sardar :** Imperative Necessity of Bread-Earning Education. Amritsar, EC, 1915. 8 p PPU

Paper delivered at the Eigth Educational Conference (1915) by the Assistant District Inspector of Schools, Lyallpur district.

272 **HASAN NIZAMI, Khawaza:** Sikh Qaum Aur Uske Bani Ki Nishat Musalmanun Ki Muhabbat Amez Rae. (U) Batala, Nizamia Book Depot, 1919. 52 p. IOL

Muslim opinion, full of love, concerning the Sikh community and its message, attempt to prove that the words Syed and Sikh are synonyms.

273 **HAYAT ALI, Mian:** Bang Di Khul. (PN) Lyallpur, Mian Hayat Ali. 1914. 8p.

Permission for the call to prayer, account of an incident in Lyallpur district where Sikhs stopped Muslims from praying in public.

274 **HAZARA SINGH, Bhai:** Bharmi Sikh Prabodh. (P) Amritsar, Bhai Hazara Singh, 1918. 16 p.

Guidance for an erring Sikh, a dialogue in verse on superstitious practices among sections of the Sikh community.

275 _____ : Janam Sakhi Sri Guru Harkishan ji Di. (P) Lahore, Khalsa Press, 1897. 64 p. KC/PPU

Traditional biography of Guru Harkishan.

276 _____ : Janam Sakhi Sri Guru Har Raiji Di. (P) Lahore, Khalsa Press, 1897. 128 p. BTSL

Traditional biography of Guru Har Rai.

277 _____ : Manmatian Di Irkha (P) Amritsar, Bhai Hazara Singh, 1917. 13 p.

Jealousy of non-believers, criticism of Hindus and an appeal for Sikhs not to associate with them.

278 **HIRA DAS, Sant** : Gurmat Samanya. (P) Bapara-i-Kalan (Ludhiana), Singh Sabha, 1907. 230 p. IOL

Verses on Sikh rituals.

279 **HIRA SINGH, Bhai** : Ratan Amolak (PN) Amritsar, Anand Prakash Press, 1898. 146 p. BTSL

The priceless gem, commentary on Sikhism.

280 _____ : Shahidi Baba Gurbakhsh Singhji. (P) Amritsar, Bhai Hira Singh, n/d. 19 p. PPU

Martyrdom of Baba Gurbakhsh Singh.

281 _____ : Sri Gurmat Mandan. (P) Amritsar, Wazir Hind Press, 1898. 48 p. PPU

Establishment of the Sikh religion, survey of Sikh history and theology.

282 **HIRA SINGH, Maharaja of Nabha** : English Translation of the Lecture Read at theGeneral Khalsa Conference, Amritsar. Lahore, Mufid-i-Am Press, 1904. 10 p. IOL

283 **HUKAM SINGH** : Parsang Dasan Guran De Avtar Dharne Da (P) Amritsar, Nanak Press, 1894. 16 p.

References to the incarnations of the ten Gurus, sketch of Sikh history with emphasis on the mystical experiences of the Gurus and their achievement of salvation.

284 **HUKAM SINGH, Sardar** : Panth Pukar. (P) Amritsar, Wazir Hind Press, 1918. 208 p. PPU/IOL

Cry of the Panth, suggestions for reform of Sikhism and the Sikh community.

285 _____ : Vivah Sanskar De Labh. (P) Lahore, Lahore Machine Press, 1914. 43 p. PPU/IOL

The value of the marriage ceremony.

286 **INDAR SINGH, Bhai** : Dhur Ki Jot. (P) Rasin (Ludhiana), Bhai Indar Singh, 1914. 32 p.

Light from the beginning, a dialogue attempting to establish that Baba Ram Singh, the founder of the Namdhari sect, was an incarnation of the Guru.

287 _____ : Ideals of the Sikh Educational Conference. Amritsar, EC, 1914. 16 p.BM

Paper read by Headmaster Khalsa, High School, Ambala, at the Seventh Educational Conference (1914).

288 **INDAR SINGH, Munshi** : Akhiri Peshwa. (U) Sialkot, Guru Gobind Singh Press, 1894. 54 p. IOL

The last prophet, an effort to show that Guru Gobind Singh was the last messenger of God. The author also discusses the origin and current state of Sikhism and suggests reforms.

289 **INSHAULLAH KHAN, Maulvi** : Sikh Aur Musalmanon Ke Ruhani Ta'alluqat. (U) Lahore, Maulvi Inshaullah Khan, 1909. 80 p.

The spiritual relations of Muslims and Sikhs. A series of letters published in the Lahore paper Watan in which the contributors have tried to show that the spiritual leaders of Islam were always on the most friendly terms with the Sikh Gurus.

290 **ISHAR SINGH, Bhai**: Yatra Sri Darbar Sahib Amritsarji. (P) Lahore, Bhai Ishar Singh, 1908. 32 p.

A trip to the Darbar Sahib. a description of the mismanagement of the Golden Temple and other holy spots of the Sikhs.

291 **ISHAR SINGH, Pandit** : Sri Gurmat Digvijai (P) Lahore, Pandit Ishar Singh, 1905. 155 p. IOL

Conquests of the Sikh religion, survey of Sikh religion and history.

292 **JAGAT SINGH, Bhai**: Dayanand, Yat Lala Sukh Lall Mat Khandan. (P) Chima (Amritsar), Bhai Jagat Singh, 1909, 27 p. IOL

Criticism of the doctrines of Dayanand and Sukh Lal concerning Sikh beliefs.

293 _____ : Gurmat Parkash (P) Amritsar, National Press, 1904. 108 p. PPU/IOL

The light of the Sikh religion.

294 _____ : Jiwan Bhai Gur Das Ji Da. (P) Amritsar, Khalsa Hitkari Jatha, 1912. 32 p. IOL

Life of Bhai Gurdas, well-known Sikh saint and contemporary of Guru Arjan and Guru Hargobind.

295 _____ : Risala-i-Sat Parkash. (U) Lahore, Rifah-i-Am Press, 1898. 220 p.

Attempt to show by quotations from the Adi Granth that the teachings of the Guru and those of the Arya Samaj have one common end, to bring people back to the Vedic faith.

296 **JAGAT SINGH, Pandit** : Gurmat Parkash. (P) Eminabad (Gujranwala).

JAGAT SINGH, Pandit (contd)
Pandit Jagat Singh, 1912. 152 p.
Commentary on the Adi Granth by an Arya Samaj Updeshak, who tries to prove that all the Sikh Gurus were followers of the Vedas and Shastras.

297 **JAGJIT SINGH, Bhai:** Vidiya Sambandhi Natak. (P) Amritsar, EC, 1914. 14 p. PPU
A paper, in the form of a drama depicting how self-help, mutual love and education can be promoted among Sikhs, presented at the Seventh Educational Conference (1914).

298 **JAI CHAND SHARMA, Pandit:** Khalsa Hindu Aur Murti Pujak Hain. (H) Amritsar, Sanatan Dharm Press, 1905. 8 p. BTSL/IOL
The Sikhs are Hindus and image-worshippers.

299 **JANG SINGH:** Jang Jarman Men Singh Bahadur. (P) Dhilwan (Patiala), 1918. 18 p. BM
Sikh bravery in the war with Germany.

300 **JASWANT SINGH, Bakhshi:** Sikhkhi Prakash. (P) Lahore, Sri Gurmat Press, 1902. 12 p.
Verses on the Sikh faith.

301 **JAWAHIR SINGH :** Amal-i-Arya. (U) Lahore, Islamia Press, 1889. 120 p.
The actions of the Aryas, an anti-Arya Samaj tract by one of its former members.

302 **JAWAHIR SINGH, Bhai:** Git Jawariye Di Istri Da Virlap. (P) Lyallpur, Bhai Jawahir Singh, 1913. 8 p.
Cry of the gambler's wife, didactic verses on the evils of gambling.

303 _____ : Jhok Sharabian Di (P) Lyallpur, Bhai Jawahir Singh, 1913. 8 p.
The song of the drunkard, verses on the consequences of drinking.

304 _____ : Kaya Ved Ishvuri Bani Hai ? (E, P) Lahore, Punjab Sewak Agency, 1912. 20 p.
Are the Vedas divine scriptures ? Attempt to disprove the Arya Samaj contention that the Vedas Were divinely inspired.

305 _____ : Lasani Peshwa Urf Fazilat-i-Khalsa. (U) Lahore, Bhai Jawahir Singh, 1912. 70 p.
The incomparable prophet, or the greatness of the Sikh religion.

306 _____ : Sri Amritsarji De Darbar Sahab De Gujhe Bhed (P) Amritsar, Bhai Jawahir Singh, 1908. 16 p. IOL
Secrets of the Darbar Sahib, criticism of the institution's management.

307 **JAWALA SINGH, Bhai:** Khalsa De Bole. (P) Lahore, Khalsa Press, 1901. 21 p. BM
Glossary of words and expressions in the Panjabi language (generally used by the Nihang Singhs).

308 _____ : Sain Mianmirji Di Viyakulta Unhan Nun Panjwen Sat Guran De Khed Paun Samaen Wairag Wich A Ke Hoi. Se (P) 2/e., Lahore, Bhai Jawala Singh, 1911. 8 p.
Verses describing the emotions of the Muslim saint Mianmir as he witnessed the persecution of Guru Arjan and five of his disciples.

309 **JAWALA SINGH, Sardar :** Biwah Sanskar Bhag. (P) Amritsar, Wazir Hind Press, 1899. 120 p.
Portions of the marriage ceremonies.

310 _____ : Roshani Bijli Birodhak Akhkhian Da Surma. (P) Amritsar, Wazir Hind Press, 1898. 48 p.
An eye-opening powder for the opponents of electric lights for the Golden Temple.

311 _____**, Sardar:** Sri Guru Granth Sahibji De Akhand Pathan Di Bidhi (P) Amritsar, Wazir Hind Press, 1899. 52 p.
Directions for reading the Adi Granth from one end to the other without a break.

312 **JHANDA SINGH, Sant:** Pahul Ki Miryada Ka Granth (P) Lahore Viddiya Press, 1895. 42p.
A book on the ceremony of Sikh baptism.

313 **JHANDU SINGH:** Junj Guru Nanak (H) Lahore, Aftab Press, 1874. 32p. IOL
An Account of the marriage of Guru Nanak

314 **JIWAN SINGH:** Panth Sewak Ya Panth Ghatak (P) Amritsar, Coronation Printing Works, n.d. 4p. BTSL
Server of the Panth or murderer of the Panth, criticism of the editorial policy of the Panth Sewak, Lahore.

315 _____ : Siri Kalgi Dhar Upkar (P) Lahore, Guru Nanak Agency, 1906. 104 p.
The blessings conferred by Guru Gobind Singh.

316 **JODH SINGH, Bhai :** Bharosa. (P) Lahore, Sri Gurmat Press, 1906. 16 p.
Verses on how Sikh women should conduct their lives.

317 _____: Dharam Palan. (P) Lahore, Anglo-Sanskrit Press, 1896. 16 p. IOL
Obedience to religion, biographical sketch of Guru Tegh Bahadur.

318 _____: Guru Sahib Ate Ved. (P) Amritsar, Khalsa National Agency, n/d. 128 p. PPU
Reply to the book "Gurus were the worshippers of the Vedas".

319 _____: Jathe Bandi. (P) Amritsar, Khalsa National Agency, 1910. 42 p. PPU
A system of organization, a discussion of the nature of institutions and their value, with particular reference to the needs of the Sikh community.

320 _____: Lekh Sikhi Asulan Par. (P) Amritsar, Khalsa National Agency, 1910. 16 p. PPU
Articles on the principles of Sikhism. Explanations why Sikhs do not cut their hair and maintain other visible signs of their faith.

321 _____: Life of Shri Guru Amar Dasji. Lahore, Sikh Tract Society, 1918. 24 p. KC

322 _____: A Paper on Sikhism, Read Before the Calcutta Religious Convention Held in April 1909. 2/e., Amritsar, Khalsa National Agency, 1910. 16 p. IOL

323 _____: Sachcha Dharmi. (P) Lahore, Balmukand Press, 1900. BM/IOL
"A true man of religion," a tract on the controversy as to whether Sikhs are Hindus. Following a dialogue between two Sikhs on the issue, a worshipper at the Golden Temple quotes from the Adi Granth to show that Sikhism is an independent religion. Appended is an account of Subheg Singh and his son, Shahbaz Singh, who gave their lives for Sikhism.

324 _____: Saukhi Vidya Parthaye Lekh. (P) Amritsar, EC, 1912. 16 p. PPU/IOL
Paper on extension of Panjabi, read at the Fifth Educational Conference (1912).

325 _____: Shahid Hulas. (P) Amritsar, Bhai Jodh Singh, 1906. 84 p.
Description of martyrs, account of the death of Guru Gobind Singh's sons.

326 _____: Sikhi Ki Hai ? (P) Amritsar, Khalsa National Agency, 1911. 160 p. IOL
Collection of selected Vars of Bhai Gurdas, with a brief commentary on their meaning.

327 _____: Sri Guru Arjan Bilas. (P) Amritsar, Wazir Hind Press, 1902. 84 p. KC/IOL
Verses on the life and martyrdom of Guru Arjan.

328 _____: Sri Guru Gobind Singh. (P) Amritsar, Wazir Hind Press, 1898. 16 p.
Account of Guru Gobind Singh's warfare and the sacrifice of his sons at Sirhind.

329 _____: Sri Kalgi Dhar Hulas. (P) Lahore, Anglo-Sanskrit Press, 1899. 292 p. KC/PPU/IOL
Verses on the life of Guru Gobind Singh.

330 _____: Vadda Shahid Hulas. (P) Lahore, Guru Gobind Singh Press, 1900. 100 p.
Description of the great martyrs, verses on the death of Guru Gobind Singh's sons.

331 _____: Vyakhyan Sikh Dharm Par. (H) Amritsar, Khalsa National Agency, 1911. 20 p.
A lecture on the Sikh religion.

332 **KAHAN SINGH, Sardar :** Gurmat Prabhakar. (P) Lahore, Khalsa Press, 1893. 373 p. PPU/IOL
The radiance of the Gurus' teachings, an alphabetically arranged collection of the teachings of the Gurus with explanatory notes. The author tries to show that Sikhism is an independent religion and not a branch of Hinduism.

333 _____: Gurmat Sudhakar. (P) 2/e., Amritsar, Wazir Hind Press, 1901. 641 p. PPU/IOL
Background on the Sikh faith and rituals, with supporting evidence from the Adi Granth, Suraj Prakash and various Rahit Namas. Bhai Arjan Singh Bagrian published the first edition (1898), in Hindi.

334 _____: Gurmukhi Nawal Ka Tisra Hissa. (P) Ludhiana, K.K. Bahadar, 1911. 179 p. PPU
Third part of a Gurmukhi novel and the life of Sardar Bahadur Ram Pal Singh.

335 _____: Ham Hindu Nahin. (P) Amritsar, Khalsa Press, 1899. 109 p. BM/PPU/IOL
We are not Hindus, the most famous of a series of tracts which attempted to

KAHAN SINGH, Sardar (contd)
differentiate Sikhism and Hinduism. (37, 41, 52, 53, 135, 196, 215, 298, 318, 323, 333, 396, 465, 484).

336 _____: Mad Mana Khandan. (P) Amritsar, Chashma-i-Nur Press, 1893. 50p.
Rejection of meat and liquor.

337 _____: Sankhep Jivan Sri Guru Gobind Singh Ji. (P) Amritsar, Punjab Translating and Publishing House, 1913. 120 p.
Life of Guru Gobind Singh.

338 **KAHLA SINGH KAVI** : Qissa Mavan Dhian. (P) Amritsar, Bhai Hardit Singh, 1919. 32 p. PPU
Verses on Sikh family relations.

339 **KALA SINGH, Bhai** : Singhan Namdharian Da Shahid Bilas. (P) Nanagal Wadda (Ludhiana), Bhai Kala Singh, 1913. 56 p. BM/IOL
Description of the incidents connected with the execution of Kuka Sikhs for murders in Raikot and Amritsar. Pro-Kuka.

340 **KAPUR SINGH** : Lahori Handbill, Conference Te Guru Granth Ji Par Vichar. (P) Lahore, Kapur Singh, 1915. 7 p. BTSL
A handbill from Lahore—discussion on the exhibition of the Adi Granth at a a conference, pros and cons on the subject written in the form of a dialogue by the Secretary of the Lahore Sikh Youngmen's Association.

341 **KARAM SINGH** : Kattak Ki Visakh? (P) Amritsar, Wazir Hind Press, 1913. ii, 237 p. BM
In addition to examining whether Guru Nanak was born in the month of Kattak or Baisakh, the author discusses the use of the Bala Janam-Sakhi as a fundamental source on the life of Guru Nanak.

342 **KARAM SINGH, Bhai:** Banda Bahadur. (P) Amritsar, Bhai Karam Singh, 1907. 270 p. PPU/IOL
Life of Banda Bahadur.

343 _____: Shrimati Bibi Harnam Kaur. (P) Amritsar, Manager, Khalsa Advocate, 1907. 136 p. BTSL
Biographical sketch of the wife of Bhai Takht Singh, Bibi Harnam Kaur. The couple ran the Sikh Kanya Mahavidyala at Ferozepur and were active in Sikh religious and educational reforms.

344 **KARAM SINGH, Sabar** : Sada Te Angrezi Sarkar Da Sambandh. (P) Lahore, Punjab Steam Press, n/d. 12 p. BTSL
Our relations with the British government, a tract for distribution at the Eighth Educational Conference (1915). The author highlights the benefits of British rule and the necessity of Sikh loyalty.

345 **KARTAR SINGH, Bhai** : Baba Banda Bahadur. (P) Lahore, Bhai Laddha Singh, 1910. 320 p. BM/PPU/IOL
Life of Banda Bahadur.

346 **KARTAR SINGH, Granthi:** Bir Saputar. (P) Lahore, Bhai Laddha Singh, 1913. 64 p. PPU
Verses on the martyrdom of the sons of Guru Gobind Singh.

347 _____: Khalsa Tattva Prakash. (P) Ferozepur, Bhai Kartar Singh, 1910. 24p.
Light on the true Sikh religion, proceedings of a debate beween members of the Arya Samaj and the Singh Sabha at Ferozepur.

348 _____: Kharag Khalsa. (P) Ludhiana, Sikh Sewak Jatha, 1914. 174 p. BM/PPU
Sword of the Khalsa, an attempted refutation of an anti-Sikh pamphlet by Pandit Bishambar Datta entitled Khalsa Mat Prakash (Light on the Sikh religion).

349 _____: Kissa Niyog. (P) Peshawar, Panch Khalsa Agency, 1910. 28 p. BTSL
Verses condemning the doctrine of Niyog as expounded by the Arya Samaj.

350 _____: Raj Khalsa. (P) Lahore, Laddha Singh and Sons, 1913. 286 p. BM
Verses on the career of Ranjit Singh and his generals.

351 _____: Sidaq Khalsa. (P) Lahore, Laddha Singh, 1911. 252 p. IOL
The faith of the Khalsa, verses on Sikh martyrs.

352 _____: Sri Guru Dasmesh Prakash. (P) Lahore, Bhai Laddha Singh, 1915. 568 p.
Life of Guru Gobind Singh.

353 _____: Tegh Khalsa. (P) Lahore, Bhai Laddha Singh, 1912. 289 p. BM
Survey of the various battles fought by the Sikhs.

354 **KARTAR SINGH, Pandit** : Challenge. (P) Lahore, Sri Guru Bakhsh Press, 1910. 22 p. PPU/IOL/BTSL
Study of Hindu-Sikh relations. The author, a philosopher, associated with the Ferozepur Sikh Kanya Mahavidyala, criticizes the thesis of a Sanatanist, Pandit

Keshwa Nand, that the Gurus loved the Vedas and followed Hindu rituals. Kartar Singh then raises ten questions concerning Hinduism and calls for a religious debate.

355 **KASHMIRA SINGH, Sant :** Mazhab Prakash. (P) Lahore, Sant Kashmira Singh, 1912. 16 p.

Verses on the establishment of the Sikh religion.

356 **KESAR SINGH, Bhai :** Jiwan Charitra Maharaja Ranjit Singh. (P) Peshawar, Sikh Book Agency, 1915. 28 p. BTSL

Life of Ranjit Singh with a brief sketch of his court and chief agents.

357 _____ ; Sankshipt Jiwan Charitra Shri Bhai Taru Singh. (H) Lahore, Sri Guru Arjan Club, 1917. 8 p.

Brief life of a famous martyr, Bhai Taru Singh.

358 **KHARAK SINGH, Sardar :** Address. (P) Amritsar, EC, n/d. 32 p. PPU

Presidential address, Ninth Educational Conference (1916).

359 **KHAZAN SINGH :** History and Philosophy of the Sikh Religion. 2 Vols. Lahore, Nawal Kishore Press, 1914. ix, 699 p. BM/IOL/KC

The first volume discusses Sikh history; the second, the author's interpretation of Sikh philosophy.

360 **KHAZAN SINGH, Bhai :** Janam Sakhi Brahmgyani Sri Nam Dev Ji Maharaj. (P) Lahore, Bhai Khazan Singh, 1914. 332 p.

Life of the saint Namdev by the editor of the Nam Dev Pattra, Lahore.

361 **KHAZAN SINGH, Giani :** Guru Khalsa Diwan Shahinshah Sri Guru Nanak Hai Parliament Sach Khand Valon Panth Sewak Dian Do Galan De Utar. (P) Amritsar, Coronation Printing Works, 1918. 16 p. BTSL

Essay supporting Teja Singh and the Sach Khand Sri Guru Nanak High Parliament against criticism in Panth Sewak.

362 **KIRPA SINGH, Bhai :** Khalsa Ji Da Janam Din. (P) Lahore, Khalsa Press, 1903. 16 p.

Verses on the foundation of the Khalsa.

363 _____ : Lai Lao Laltainan. (P) Amritsar, Wazir Hind Press, 1903. 14 p.

Buy the lamps, or pamphlets issued for the use of the Sikh community.

364 _____ : Sikhan Da Sikhan Nal Vair. (P) Sargodha, Nihang Bahadur Agency, 1914. 36 p.

Enmity between Sikhs, a dialogue on the necessity of Sikhs mixing freely with converts from other religions.

365 _____ : Sikh Dharm Di Bar. (P) Lahore, Khalsa Press, 1904. 8 p. BTSL

Account of the Gurus' philanthropic acts.

366 **KISHAN DAS, Bhai :** Updesh. (P) Lahore, Pandit Kishan Gopal Balram, 1906. 16 p.

A sermon on Sikhism.

367 **KISHAN SINGH ARIF :** Mela-i-Goindwal Ma'i Dohrajat Suthre Shahi. (PN) Amritsar, Chashma-i-Nur Press, 1892, 48 p.

Description of the annual fair at Goindwal, a sacred spot for Sikhs, where cholera broke out in the large gathering. The author attributed the calamity to divine displeasure over the sins of the congregation.

368 **KISHAN SINGH, Bhai :** Pamphlet Char. (U) Amritsar, Bhai Kishan Singh, 1909. 16 p.

Account of the Bedi Young Men's Association, Dera Baba Nanak (Gurdaspur), and suggestion for social reform among the Bedis.

369 _____ : Varat Siyapa.(P) Amritsar, Bhai Labh Singh, 1914. 24 p.

Fasting and wailing, criticism of Sikhs participating in Hindu rituals and an interpretation of the true meaning of fasts for Sikhs.

370 **KOSHAR CHAND, Pandit :** Sri Guru Dasmesh Hulas. (P) Lahore, Bhai Sant Singh, 1918. 26 p. PPU

Verses on the wars of Guru Gobind Singh.

371 **KRISHAN GOPAL, Pandit :** Jangnama Guru Gobind Singh Ji. (P) Lahore, Balmukand Press, 1905. 16 p. IOL

The battles of Guru Gobind Singh.

372 **LABH SINGH, Bhai :** Chief Khalsa Diwan De Central Khalsa Yatimkhana Da Majuda Halat De Asli Photo. (P) Jhelum, Bhai Labh Singh, 1909. 16 p. PPU

The real picture of the present conditions of the Central Khalsa Orphanage, a history of the institution with criticism of its executive board.

373 _____ : Gur Bharosa Arthat Naqli Sikkhan Prati Updesh. (P) Lahore, Sri Gurmat Press, 1905. 16 p.

The Sikh faith, or advice to false Sikhs.

374 _____ : Gurmat Itihas Guru Khalsa. (P) Amritsar, Bhai Labh Singh, 1911. 360 p. PPU/IOL

LABH SINGH, Bhai (contd)
History of the Gurus and evolution of the Sikh faith.

375 _____ : Janam Lila Sri Guru Nanak Ji. (P) Bhikhi (Gujranwala), Bhai Labh Singh, 1912. 37 p.
Verses on the life of Guru Nanak.

376 **LACHMAN SINGH, Bhai :** Desh Kuchal. (P) Sharakpur (Lahore), Bhai Lachman Singh, 1910. 16 p.
The serious condition of the country, a story on the contribution of Singh Sabha to the cause of Sikhism.

377 _____ : Ki Panjabi Nal Sada Piar Hai ? (P) Amritsar, Bhai Lachman Singh, 1914. 8p. PPU
Do we love Panjabi ? Background on the development of Panjabi and an appeal for its widespread use among Sikhs.

378 **LACHMAN SINGH, Sardar :** Address. (P) Amritsar, EC, n/d. 16 p. BTSL
Presidential address, Sixth Educational Conference (1913).

379 **LADDHA Singh, Bhai :** Ad Sri Guru Granth Sahib Di Bani Ka Tika. (P) Lahore, Vidya Press, 1897. 96 p.
Commentary on the Adi Granth.

380 **LAHNA SINGH, Bhai :** Jiwan Charittra Sri Guru Arjan Devi Ji. (P) Lahore, Sri Gurmat Press, 1901. 96 p. PPU
Life of Guru Arjan.

381 **LAKSHMAN SINGH, Bhagat :** The Foundations and Management of Khalsa Schools. Amritsar, EC, 1913. 8 p.
Programme for developing Sikh educational institutions. Background on the author and the evolution of educational programmes among Punjabi Sikhs is found in Bhagat Lakshman Singh Autobiography (ed. by Ganda Singh). Calcutta, Sikh Cultural Centre, 1965.

382 _____ : Principles and Teachings of the Arya Samaj, Lecture Seven : Some Aspects of the Samaj. Lahore, Caxton Printing Works, 1890. 28 p. BM/IOL
Criticism of the Arya Samaj. The author's ideas on the subject are also reflected in his autobiography and the newspaper which he edited, KHALSA (1899-1901).

383 _____ : Panth Age Prarthna. (P) Lahore, Bhagat Lakshman Singh, 1900. 7 p .BTSL
A call for Sikhs to sever relations with Arya Samajists and their sympathizers within the Sikh community because the Samaj converted Rahtia Sikhs to Hinduism and shaved their heads.

384 _____ : A Short Sketch of the Life and Work of Guru Gobind Singh. Lahore, Tribune Steam Press, 1909. 186 p. PPU/IOL
Reinterpretation of Guru Gobind Singh, with a concluding chapter on Hindu-Sikh relations and the problems confronting Sikhs in 1909. Example of Tat Khalsa literature.

385 _____ : The Sikh and His New Critics. Amritsar, Sikh Tract Society, 1918. 82 p. KC/PPU/IOL
Correspondence on the Sikh Gurus, reprinted from the Khalsa Advocate, the Modern Review and the Sikh Review.

386 **LAL SINGH, Bhai :** Singhan Di Bahaduri Ate Masse Di Att. (P) Bhangali (Amritsar), Sant Atma Singh, 1916. 16p. BM
Verses on how Mahtab Singh of Mirkot killed Masse Rangar who had taken possession of Darbar Sahib in Amritsar.

387 _____ : Updeshak De Das Hazari Paran Amdan Di Riport. (P) Amritsar, Sri Gurmat Press, 1912. 26 p. BTSL
Report on the income and expenditures of a Sikh preacher, 1912.

388 **LAL SINGH, Gyani :** Sikh Ih Hai. (P) Amritsar, Coronation Printing Works, 1913 144 p. PPU
This is a Sikh, exposition of Sikh principles.

389 _____ : Sindhi Bachcha. (P) Amritsar, Coronation Printing Works, 1915. 51 p.
Life of a young Sindhi Sikh.

390 **MACAULIFFE, Max Arthur :** Asa Di War. (P) Bombay, 1902. 16 p. KC
Morning prayer of the Sikhs, with commentary.

391 _____: How the Sikhs Became a Militant People. Paris, 1905. 27 p. KC

392 _____**(Translator):** The Japji. Amritsar, New Anglo-Gurmukhi Press, 1897. 17 p. IOL
English translation, with commentary.

393 _____: Lekchar. (P) Amritsar, Chashma-i-Nur Press, 1899. 16 p. BTSL
Lecture on Sikhism presented to the Amritsar Singh Sabha at its twenty-sixth anniversary meeting.

394 _____ : The life of Guru Teg Bahadur. Lahore, Max Arthur Macauliffe, 1903. 66 p. IOL

A primary object of the short sketch is to "set fourth one of the causes that have existed of the loyalty and devotion of the Sikhs to the British," the tyranny of the Muslims, and by contrast, the favourable conditions for the spread of Sikhism under the British raj (foreward).

395 ______:The Sikh Religion. 6 Vols. Oxford, Oxford University, 1909. lxxxviii, 383, 351, 444, 420, 351, 453 p. BM/KC/PPU/IOL

The lives of the ten Gurus and the bhagats of the Adi Granth according to tradition, with translations of selections from their works.

396 **MAHAN SINGH OMKARI:** Sahib Dyal Ke Paragrandah Khayalon Ki Partal. (U) Amritsar, Wazir Hind Press, 1904. 80 p.

A check to the dirty ideas of Sahib Dyal (an Arya writer who had tried to prove that Sikhs were Hindus). (182).

397 **MAHTAB SINGH, Bhai:** Qaumi Unnati. (P) Amritsar, Bhai Mahtab Singh, 1910. 24 p.

Progress of the nation, a lecture on the advancement of Sikhs through religious devotion and reform.

398 ______ : Sukh Suneha. (P) Amritsar, EC, 1914. 8 p. PPU

Paper on the necessity of religious education as well as secular training in Sikh schools, read at the Seventh Educational Conference (1914).

399 **MAHTAB SINGH, Sardar :** Sikhmat Bibek Da Gurmat Anusar Khandan. (P) Amritsar, Anglo and Urdu-Gurmukhi Press, 1905. 44 p. PPU

Criticism of an anti-Sikh pamphlet, Sikhmat Vivek. (Confusion in the Sikh religion).

400 **MAIYA SINGH:** Kalgi Dhar Prakash. (P) Lahore, Khalsa Press, 1903. 16 p. PPU

Life of Guru Gobind Singh.

401 **MAIYA SINGH, Bhai :** Khalsa Dharm. (U) Lahore, 1889. PPU

An interpretation of Sikh religion.

402 **MAKHAN SINGH, Bhai :** Shahidi. (U) Lahore, Islamia Press, 1905. 28 p. BTSL

Verses on the martyrdom of Guru Gobind Singh's sons.

403 **MALAK RAJ :** Nanak Charitra. (U) Lahore, Dev Badhan Press, 1888. 280 p. IOL

Life of Guru Nanak.

404 **MAN SINGH :** Sach Da Parkash. (P) Amritsar, Coronation Printing Works, 1918. 58 p. PPU

Supplement to the Khalsa Advocate of September 17, 1918, in reply to Sambodh Patra published by the Bhasaur Singh Sabha. The Singh Sabha charged the Chief Khalsa Diwan with laziness and trying to end the work of the Panch Khalsa Diwan. Man Singh attempts to answer these charges and in turn raises questions concerning the personal life of Babu Teja Singh and his associates. (919)

405 **MANGAL SINGH :** Angrezi Raj De Sukh Sadhan. (P) Amritsar, Wazir Hind Press, n/d. 8 p. BTSL

The blessings of the British government, written during the First World War. The author (manager of the Public Library, secretary of the Temperance Society, and member of the Singh Sabha, Dholeta, Jullundur) requests that the tract be read aloud in all Sikh public meetings.

406 **MANGAL SINGH, Bhai :** Sikhi Di Bhiyanak Dasha Da Virlap. (P) Amritsar, Bhai Kesar Singh, 1909. 16 p. PPU

Verses on the terrible conditions in the Sikh community.

407 ______ : Tukr Gulami. (P) Mamupur (Patiala), Bhai Mangal Singh, 1908. 20 p.

Condemnation of Sikhs who read Sikh hymns without understanding the true meaning of the Guru's message.

408 **MANGAL SINGH, Munshi :** Zafar Nama. (P) Amritsar, Munshi Mangal Singh, 1909. 222 p. PPU

Life of Guru Gobind Singh.

409 **MANGAL SINGH, Sardar :** Address. (P) Amritsar, Wazir Hind Press, n/d. 28 p. BTSL/PPU

Address by the President of the Reception Committee, Eleventh Educational Conference (1918).

410 **MANI SINGH:** Janam-Sakhi. (P) Lahore, Charag Din and Saraj Din. 1891. 592 p. BM/IOL

This Janam-Sakhi, or traditional biography of Guru Nanak, has been associated with Bhai Mani Singh, a contemporary of Guru Gobind Singh. It is also referred to as the Gyan-Ratanavali.

411 **MANI SINGH, Bhai :** Shahid Sencha. (P) Lahore, Bhai Mani Singh, 1910. 8 p.

Love for the martyrs, an essay drawing attention to the early martyrs of Sikhism and calling on the present generation to uplift their fallen brothers.

412 **MANNA SINGH :** Khalsa Dharam Sanskar Vidhi, Vivah Bhag. (P) Amritsar, Wazir Hind Press, 1901. 48 p.

The religious rites of the Sikh—the chapter on marriage.

413 **MANSA SINGH, Bhai** : Upkar Khalsa. (P) Kuchesar (Bulandshahr, United Provinces), Bhai Mansa Singh, 1915. 46p. BTSL

Verses on the benefits and good works generated by the Khalsa community.

414 **MATHRA SINGH SHAFIQ** : Talism-i-Qudrat al Ma'ruf Dasam Gur Charitra. (U) Gujranwala, McKee Press, 1902. 32 p.

The magic of nature, or the life of Guru Gobind Singh.

415 **MEHAR CHAND, Lala**: Parsansapatar. (P) Lahore, Lala Mehar Chand, 1893. 59 p. BTSL

Recommendation letters, correspondence on the necessity for a correct and attractive edition of the Adi Granth.

416 **MEHAR SINGH** : Je Ehi Hal Riha Tan Asi Dubbe. (P) Lahore, Anglo-Sanskrit Press, 1896. 24 p.

If this condition persists, we shall drown, criticism of Sikh social and religious practices.

417 **MEHAR SINGH, Sardar** : Address. (P) Lahore, Lahore Machine Press, 1917. 16 p. BTSL/PPU

Address by President of Reception Committee, Tenth Educational Conference (1917).

418 _____ : Sardar Mehar Singh Nau Muslim Ka Lektur I, Ya Bawa Nanak Sahib Ka Musalman Hona. (PN) Ludhiana, Master Abdur Rahman, 1906. 24 p. IOL

Guru Nanak was a Muslim, a lecture by a convert to Islam.

419 **MELA SINGH, Bhai** : Jang Nama. (PN) Amritsar, Anand Prakash Press, 1895. 16 p.

Verses on a battle between Guru Gobind Singh and the Mughal armies.

420 **MIT SINGH, Bhai** : Laghu Shahid Prakash. (P) Churchak (Ferozepur), Bhai Palsotam Singh, 1911. 63 p. BTSL

Verses on the martyrdom of Guru Gobind Singh's sons at Sirhind.

421 **MOHAN SINGH, Bhai** : Do Dhara Khanda. (P) Hansaro (Jullundur), Bhai Mohan Singh, 1913. 30 p.

Double-edged sword, reply to ten questions of the Lucknow Singh Sabha regarding the principles of Sikhism.

422 **MOHAN SINGH VAID, Bhai** : Abla Vilap. (P) Tarn Taran, Bhai Mohan Singh Vaid, 1918. 24 p. PPU

Cry of the helpless woman, commentary on the social conditions of Sikh wives and daughters.

423 _____ : Arian De Dhol Da Phol. (U) Amritsar, n/d. 24 p. BTSL

An exposure of the hollowness of the Arya Samajists.

424 _____ : Arya Samaj Bhaiyan De Sikhhan Par Bejan Hamlyan De Uttar. (P) Lahore, Sri Gurmat Press, n/d. 112 p. PPU

Reply to the lifeless attack on Sikhism by our Arya Samaj brothers.

425 _____, **Bhai:** Benati. (P) Lahore, Khalsa Press, 1903. 8 p. BTSL

A request to priests, Singh Sabhas, and all Sikhs to support the Panjabi language. An appeal is also made to the government for aid to Gurmukhi schools.

426 _____ : Benati. (P) Tarn Taran, Bhai Mohan Singh Vaid, 1912. 30 p. PPU

A treatise on morals and social life for Sikh women.

427 _____ : Bridh Vivah Durdasha Natak. (P) Lahore, Anglo-Sanskrit Press, 1904. 50p.

A drama on the evils of marriage in old age.

428 _____ : Dayanandi Dharam Ka Namuna. (P) Amritsar, Chashma-i-Nur, 1900. 8 p. IOL

An example of the religion of Dayanand, an anti-Arya Samaj tract.

429 _____ : Dayanand Mat Darpan. (P) Amritsar, Wazir Hind Press, 1914. 16 p.

A translation and edited version of ninety couplets against Dayanand originally written by Pandit Jagannath Das, Moradabad. Mohan Singh Vaid supplemented the poems with his own ideas and criticism of Dayanand's Satyarth Prakash.

430 _____ : Gurmat Gaurwata. (P) Tarn Taran, Bhai Mohan Singh Vaid, 1907. 96 p.

The greatness of the Sikh message, a note on the advantages of performing marriage ceremonies according to the Sikh religion in contrast to Vedic rites.

431 _____ : Gurmat Virodh Binash. (P) Tarn Taran, Bhai Mohan Singh Vaid, 1908. 83p. PPU/IOL

Destruction of opponents to Sikhism, a defence of Anand marriage in reply to Anand Biwah Par Vichar (Discussion on Anand marriages). (731)

432 _____ : Man Mati Prahar Arthat Sharadh Prabodh. (P) Lahore, Sri Gurmat Press, 1903. 44 p. IOL

Criticism of the Shraddha ceremony prevalent among Sikhs.

433 _____ : Panjabi Di Unnati Di Lor Te Sadhan Parthi Lekh. (P) Amritsar, EC, 1915. 15 p. PPU

Paper on how to popularize Panjabi, read at the Eighth Educational Conference (1915).

434 _____ : Panth Khalsa Pustak. (P) Amritsar, Chashma-i-Nur Press, 1901. 4 p.

An appeal to the Sikhs to return to the teachings of the Gurus and raise Sikhism once again to a prominent position.

435 _____ : Par Upkar Hi Dharam De Mul Hai. (P) Amritsar, Bhai Bahadur Singh, 1919. 8 p. BTSL

To serve others is the main principle of religion, a discussion of the application of Sikhism to everyday life.

436 _____: Sachcha Parkash. (P) Tarn Taran, Bhai Mohan Singh Vaid, 1914. 48 p. PPU

The true light, a discourse on Sikh religion.

437 _____ : Sade Desh Di Muddho Kamzori. (P) Amritsar, Chashma-i-Nur Press, 1900. 4 p.

The cause of the weakness of our country, a call for improvement of indigenous arts, science and medicine.

438 _____ : Sharnagat Hon De Lachchan. (P) Tarn Taran, Bhai Mohan Singh Vaid, 1919. 8 p.

Prerequisites for being sheltered, a tract on the relationship of God and man. Qualifications for salvation include truthfulness, contributions to charity and religious institutions, prayer, and meditation on the nature of the Guru.

439 _____ : Subhag Kaur. (P) Tarn Taran, Bhai Mohan Singh Vaid, 1912. 72 p.

Story illustrating the advantages of female education and the disadvantages of early marriage.

440 _____ : Tika Jap Ji. (P) Lahore, Sri Gurmat Press, 1902. 160 p.

Commentary on the Japji Sahib.

441 _____:Vidhva Vilap. (P) Amritsar, Wazir Hind Press, 1918. 32 p. PPU

Cry of the widow, commentary on the condition of widows in Sikh society.

442 **MOHINDER SINGH, Gyani :** Ajib Kiran. (P) Ghataur (Ambala), Mohinder Singh, 1919. 36 p.

Verses on the martyrdom of Guru Gobind Singh's sons at Chamkaur, written with a view to induce people to subscribe to the funds of a school begun in their memory.

443 **MOTA SINGH, Bhai :** Sri Gur Mihma Prakash. (HN) Amritsar, Chashma-i-Nur Press, 1897. 196 p. PPU

Treatise on Sikh theology.

444 **MUHAMMAD ABDUL GHANI, Mirza:** Jauhar-i-Tegh. (U) Sialkot, Guru Gobind Press, 1894. 14 p.

Miracles of the sword, an account of the martyrdom of Guru Gobind Singh's sons written at the request of a Sikh gentleman who wished to show his love for the Guru.

445 **MUHAMMAD ALI, Maulvi :** The Founder of Sikhism. Lahore, Anjumen-i-Paigham-i-Sulh, 1913. 20 p. BM

Attempt to prove that Guru Nanak was a Muslim saint.

446 **MUHAMMAD HASAN KHAN, Khalifa :** Tarikh-i-Patiala. (U) Amritsar, Safir-i-Hind Press, 1878. 788 p. BM

History of Patiala state, with background on its Sikh rulers.

447 **MUHAMMAD YUSUF, Sheikh :** Bawa Nanak Ka Mazhab. (U) Qadian, Sheikh Muhammad Yusuf, 1919. 168 p.

Attempt to show that Guru Nanak was a Muslim by the editor of an Ahmadiya newspaper, Nur.

448 **MUKH LAL, Pandit :** Nawin Singh Sikhya. (P) Amritsar, Bhagat Bishen Das, 1906. 480 p. IOL

Lessons for new Sikhs, a theological discourse.

449 **MULKH RAJ BHALLA :** Ek Sikh Ki Chitthi. (U) Rawalpindi, Egerton Press, 1891. 15 p.

Letter of a Sikh, on the location of the Khalsa College.

450 **MUL SINGH, Bhai :** Upkar Khalsa. (P) Lahore, Sri Gurmat Press, 1905. 30 p. PPU/IOL

Services of the Khalsa. Account of the rescue of Hindu slaves by Sikh cavalry.

451 **MUNNA SINGH, Hakim :** Khalsa Dharam Sanskar. (P) Lahore, Mufid-i-Am Press, 1899. 48 p.

Rites and ceremonies of Sikhism.

452 _____ : Mai De Jama Nun Amrit Chhakawane Di Vidhi. (P) Amritsar, Wazir Hind Press, 1900. 16 p.

Dialogue on the propriety of serving Amrit to women.

453 **MUNSHI RAM, Pandit:** Guru Putr Asin Nahin Marwai. (P) Doda Kauni (Ferozepur), Pandit Munshi Ram, 1915. 18 p.

We are not responsible for the death of the Guru's sons, an effort to prove that Brahmans did not turn over the boys to Muslim authorities.

454 _____ : Hai Hai Yeh Kaisa Anand. (U) 2/e., Lahore, Lahore Commercial House, 1914. 32 p.

Alas ! Alas !, what is this Anand marriage ? Criticism of the Sikh marriage rites. (101)

455 **NAGINA SINGH:** Sikhism and Its Relation to Hinduism, Lahore 1900. 12 p. KC

456 **NAHAR SINGH, Bhai:** Qissa Kalu Kal Du Puara. (P) Amritsar, Bhai Chattar Singh, 1917. 22 p.

Verses against idol and tomb worship, the wearing of ornaments and other "evils of the day".

457 **NAND KUMAR:** Sikhon Ka Utsthan Aur Patan. (H) Benares, Kashi Nagri Pracharini Sabha, 1915. 227 p. PPU

The rise and fall of the Sikhs, history of Sikhism and assessment of its contemporary state.

458 **NAND LAL:** Tankhwah Nama. (P) Amritsar, Akal Yantar Press, 1884. 16 p. BTSL

Penances imposed by the Sikh religion.

459 **NAND SINGH:** Canada Des Wich Rahna Wale Hindustanian De Dukhra.(P) Lahore, Nand Singh, 1913. 31 p.

Grievances of the Indians (particularly Sikhs) in Canada.

460 _____ : The Philosophic Aspect of Sikhism. Lahore, Sikh Tract Society, 1919. 84 p. BM/IOL

Address delivered at a Congress of World Religions at the Panama Exhibition in 1915.

461 **NARAIN DAS, Sant:** Kachchan Waliyan Di Kartut. (P) Rupar (Ambala), Swami Bishan Das, 1908. 34 p.

Discussion among Hindu and Sikh sects concerning the nature of Sikh orthodoxy.

462 **NARAIN SINGH:** Acharaj Sawapana. (P) Amritsar, Wazir Hind Press, n/d. 8 p. BTSL

A strange dream, a lecture on Guru Gobind Singh and the establishment of the Sikh Panth.

463 **NARAIN SINGH, Bawa:** Jatra Sri Harmandir Amritsar. (P) Amritsar, Vakil-i-Hindustan Press, 1877. 8 p. IOL

Guide to the Golden Temple for pilgrims.

464 _____ : Mazbi Sikhan Ton Chhoh Dur Karan Da Varnan. (P) Amritsar, Chashma-i-Nur Press, 1884. 8 p.

The removal of the idea that contact with outcaste Sikhs means pollution.

465 _____ : Sikh Hindu Hain. (P) Amritsar, Matbakanuni Press, 1899. 32 p. PPU/IOL

The Sikhs are Hindus. (53)

466 **NARAIN SINGH, Bhai:** Ath Qissa Fauji Bhartinama. (P) Rupar (Ambala), Bawa Bhagwan Das, 1917. 8 p. BTSL

Enlist now in the army.

467 _____ : Janam Sakhi Sri Guru Tegh Bahadur Ji. (P) Lahore, Khalsa Press, 1901. 136 p. KC

Traditional biography of Guru Tegh Bahadur.

468 _____ : Khalsa Mat Istri Amrit Mandan. (P) Amritsar, Wazir Hind Press, 1904. 24 p. PPU

Discussion on the baptism of Sikh women. Reprinted by the Khalsa Tract society, 1905.

469 _____ : Ram Das Di Katabri Da Munh Tor Uttar. (P) Muzaffarabad, Bhai Reja Singh, 1916. 16 p.

A face-breaking reply to a pamphlet of Pandit Ram Das (against Sikhism). (532)

470 _____ : Siharfi Ghara Panth.(P) Hoshiarpur, Doaba Khalsa Diwan, 1913. 16 p.

Verses on the superiority of Sikhism and against the worship of popular saints in the Punjab.

471 _____ : Sri Guru Amar Das Ji Da Jiwan Britant. (P) Lahore, Bhai Daya Singh, 1912. 93 p.

Life and teachings of Guru Amar Das.

472 _____ : Tisra Panth Sri Guru Gobind Singh Ji Da Khalsa Panth Sajna. (P) Lahore, Bhai Narain Singh, 1907. 16 p.

The third dispensation, or an account of the establishment of the Khalsa.

473 _____ : Zafarnama. (P) Amritsar, Bhai Chattar Singh, 1889. 144 p. PPU

Life of Guru Gobind Singh.

474 **NARAIN SINGH, Doctor:** Singhani Darpan. (P) Lyallpur, Doctor Narain Singh, 1910. 2 p.

A geneological tree of the Sikh Gurus, with verses on the importance of female education.

475 **NARAIN SINGH, Faridkoti:** Nai Khush Khabari. (P) Amritsar, Anglo-Urdu and Gurmukhi Press, 1906. 8 p.

The new gospel, a life of Guru Nanak in verse. The author, Honorary Magistrate and Updeshak, Khalsa Diwan, Faridkot, wrote these songs so that Sikh children could sing them and improve their character.

476 **NARAIN SINGH, Sardar:** Istri Viddya Utte Laikchar. (P) Amritsar, Sardar, Narain Singh, 1912. 16 p. BTSL

Essay on female education presented at the fifth session of Khalsa Diwan, Shahpur.

477 _____: Majhe Da Mewa. (P) Amritsar, KTS, 1916. 47 p. PPU

The fruit of Majha, an address read by the President of the reception committee of the Sikh Educational Conference held at Tarn Taran (1916).

478 **NARINJAN KAUR, Bibi:** Sur Bir Bhainan. (P) Kairon, Khalsa Bhujangan Conference, 1916. 16 p. PPU

Verses on brave Sikh women.

479 **NARINJAN SINGH, Bhai:** Pakhand Prabodh. (P) Amritsar, Narinjan Singh, 1915. 63 p.

A warning against falseness, directed against Sikhs who do not follow the teachings of the Gurus, with suggestions concerning their reform.

480 **NATHA SINGH:** Junj Nattha Singh. (P) Lahore, Arjun Prakash Press, 1880. 16 p.

Marriage songs of the Sikhs.

481 **NATHA SINGH, Bhai:** Huqqe Di Vichar. (P) Kauli (Patiala), Sadhu Hari Das Mahant, 1913. 16 p.

Discussion on smoking, a call for Sikhs to abandon tobacco and other drugs.

482 _____: Mazmun Dar Barah Azmat-i-Kesan. (U) Lahore, Anglo-Sanskrit Press, 1893. 12 p. BTSL

Essay on the retention of hair.

483 **NATHA SINGH, Gyani:** Our Duty or What We Ought To Do. Ludhiana, Gyani Natha Singh, 1917. 47 p. BTSL/IOL

Appeal to the Sikhs to help the British in the war, written by a teacher at the Malwa Khalsa High School, Ludhiana.

484 **NAURANG SINGH, Sardar:** Sikh Hindu Nahin. (P) Lahore, Sardar Bhaga Singh, 1905. 66 p. PPU

Sikhs are not Hindus. (335)

485 **NIDHAN SINGH, Bhai:** Khalsa Rahit Prakash Ya Khandan Mandan. (P) Gujarwal (Ludhiana), Bhai Nidhan Singh, 1908. 45 p. KC/IOL

Debate on Sikh customs, discussion of controversy among the old and new parties of Sikhs.

486 **NIHAL SINGH:** Khalsa Dharm Judh Prakash. (P) Amritsar, Khalsa Mittra Press, 1885. 8 p.

Verses on Sikh militarism and chivalry.

487 _____: Khurshid-i-Khalsa. (U) Jullundur, Aftab-i-Hind Press, 1885. 146 p. KC

The sun of the Khalsa, survey of Sikh history. The author subsequently collaborated with Bhai Gurmukh Singh in producing an expanded version which treated in detail the evolution of Sikhism from Guru Nanak to the repression of the Namdhari Kuka Sikhs in 1872. Khurshid Khalsa. (P) 12 Pts. Lahore and Jullundur, 1891-? Information cited from Ganda Singh, A Bibliography of the Punjab. Patiala, Punjabi University, 1966, 185 p.

488 _____: Mahatam Gurdwarian Tirthian Wa Panjkosi. (P) Amritsar, Gobind Press, 1887. 16 p.

The merits of visiting Sikh temples and sacred bathing spots.

489 **NIHAL SINGH, Bhai:** Asa Di War Satik. (P) Lahore, Akal Press, 1899. 100 p.

Commentary on the Asa Di Var of Guru Nanak.

490 _____: Gur Darshan. (PN) Hoshiarpur, Hira Lal, 1907. 24 p.

Brief verses on the ten Gurus.

491 _____: Hindu Sikhkhan Da Nabera. (P) Amritsar, Anglo-Urdu and Gurmukhi Press, 1905. 96 p. PPU/IOL

The last word on the Hindu-Sikh controversy.

492 **NIHAL SINGH, Sardar:** Gur Mat Sikhia. (P) Lahore, Sardar Nihal Singh, 1908. 46 p.

Sermons on the doctrines and duties of Sikhs, particularly in the time of adversity.

493 **NIHAL SINGH, Thakur:** Tika Sri Jap Ji. (P) Lahore, Anglo-Sanskrit Press, 1898. 1,134 p. BTSL/PPU

Commentary on the Japji, with an account of Guru Gobind Singh.

494 **PARDUMAN SINGH, Bhai:** Anand Jhok. (P) Baddon (Hoshiarpur), Bhai Parduman Singh, 1911. 8 p. IOL

Verses on the importance of female education and the rights of women.

495 **PARDUMAN SINGH, Bhai :** Hindu Akrtighan. (H) Baddon (Hoshiarpur), Bhai Parduman Singh, 1911. 14 p. IOL

Ungrateful Hindus, description of the martyrdom of Guru Tegh Bahadur and the plight of Hindus at the time of his death.

496 ______, **Bhai :** Khalsa Skulan Wich Dharmak Vidya Puran Dhang Te Hon Parthai Lekh. (P) Amritsar, EC, 1915. 6 p. PPU

A paper on the prime necessity of religious instruction in Sikh schools, read at the Eighth Educational Conference (1915).

497 **PARMANANDA, Swami :** Sher-i-Panjab Maharajah Ranjit Singh Bahadur. (U) Lahore, Daya Singh, 1911.

Life and times of Ranjit Singh.

498 **PARTAP SINGH, Bhai :** Chauthi Sikh Educational Conference Di Sangat. (P) Rasul (Gujarat), Bhai Partap Singh, 1911. 16 p. IOL

Welcome to the Fourth Sikh Educational Conference, verses on educational reform among Sikhs.

499 ______ : Dusht Chawkri Prahar. (P) Rupar (Ambala), Swami Bishan Das, 1909. 96 p.

Attacks on a group of wicked men, a controversial tract written to counter Sikh criticism of Hindu sadhus.

500 ______ : Khalsa Dharm Sanskar Bidhi. (PN) Lahore, Khalsa Press, 1900. 64 p. PPU

Procedures for Sikh religious ceremonies.

501 ______ : Man Putar Di Shahidi. (P) Amritsar, Bhai Labh Singh, 1912. 16 p.

Great respect for the martyrs, the story of the heroic death of a Sikh lady and her child.

502 ______ : Swapan Sidhan Nirniya. (P) Simla, Ramgarhia Sabha, 1912. 16 p.

Judgement of false traditions, criticism of the distinction of caste and creed among Sikhs.

503 **PAYNE, C.H. :** A Short History of the Sikhs. London, Thomas Nelson and Sons, n/d. 248 p. BM/PPU/IOL

Survey of Sikh history, with chronological tables and selections from writings on and by Sikhs.

504 **PESHAWAR SINGH :** A Tragic Poem or the Martyrdom of Sri Guru Teg Bahadur. Lahore, Economical Press, 1896. 18 p. BM/IOL

505 **PHUMAN SINGH, Bhai :** Kandhin Vasa. (P) Amritsar, Bhai Phuman Singh, 1909. 130 p. IOL

Abode in the wall, description of the tragic end of Guru Gobind Singh's sons who were walled up alive.

506 **POTHOHARI, A :** Amritsar Versus Lahore, Or the Controversy about the Location of the Khalsa College. Rawalpindi, Egerton Press, 1891. 12 p.

Summary of the agitation over the location of the Khalsa College by an Arya Samajist and member of the Dayanand Anglo-Vedic College Committee. A detailed account of the controversy is in an unpublished note by Bhagat Lakshman Singh, dated December 4, 1932. (in possession of Dr. Ganda Singh, Patiala)

507 **PREM SINGH, Bhai :** Akali Hukam. (P) Amritsar, Bhai Prem Singh, 1913. 4 p. BTSL

Appeal for the formation of a committee to print and publish the Adi Granth.

508 ______ : Nawan Zahar. (P) Amritsar, KTS, n/d. 35 p. BTSL

New poison, a drama about how education affects the life of a Sikh family.

509 **PREM SINGH, Granthi ;** Zarur Paran Yog. (P) Amritsar, Wazir Hind Press, 1904. 4 p.

Very important to read, accolades to the British for supporting Sikhism. Also a description of the marriage ceremony of Sardar Sundar Singh, Kabul. The author tried to show how Sikhs outside India have been progressive.

510 **PRITAM SINGH ;** Maharaja Ranjit Singh, the Lion of the Punjab. Lahore, Anglo-Sanskrit Press, 1906. 42 p. BM/KC

511 **PRITAM SINGH, BHAI :** Kair Sudhar. (P) Lahore, Sri Gurmat Press, 1905. 40 p.

Unreformed, a Sikh reply to the pamphlet Ikhtiar-ul-Islam (Why I became a Muslim).

512 **PURAN DAS, Bhai :** Janam Sakhi Swami Nam Dev Ji. (P) Lahore, Albion Press, 1898. 433 p. PPU

A traditional life of Namdev.

513 **PURAN SINGH, Bhai :** The Life and Teachings of Guru Gobind Singh. Amritsar, Khalsa Agency, n/d. IOL

514 ______ : Life and Teachings of Sri Guru Tegh Bahadur. Amritsar, Khalsa Agency 1908. 79 p. BM/KC/PPU/IOL

515 _____ : Life of Sri Guru Arjan Dev. Amritsar, Khalsa Agency, n/d.

516 _____ : Sketches from Sikh History. Amritsar, Khalsa Agency, 1908. 137 p. BM/IOL/KC/PPU

Introductory essays on the nature of Sikhism and true martyrdom, followed by life sketches of Bhai Mani Singh, Bhai Taru Singh, Bhai Mahan Singh, Bhai Subeg Singh and other martyrs.

517 _____ : Thoughts on the Life and Teachings of Guru Nanak. Amritsar, Khalsa Agency, n/d.

518 _____ : The Victory of Faith. Amritsar, Khalsa Agency, 1908. 66 p. BM/BTSL/PPU/IOL

Description of the martyrdom of Guru Gobind Singh's four sons.

519 **PURATAN** : Janam-Sakhi. (P) Lahore, Singh Sabha, 1884. 279 p. IOL/KC

520 _____ : Janam-Sakhi. (P) Dehra Dun, 1885. iv,461 p. BM/IOL

521 _____ : Janam-Sakhi. (P) Rawalpindi, Max Arthur Macauliffe, 1885. 288 p. BM/KC

The first two traditional biographies of Guru Nanak are reproduction of the manuscript which H T. Colebrooke deposited in the India Office Library in 1815 or 1816. After Dr. Ernest Trumpp publicized the manuscript, in 1883 the Lieutenant Governor of the Punjab made arrangements for having it sent temporarily to Lahore. The Lahore Singh Sabha published its lithographed version in 1884, followed by a government-financed, photo-zincograph edition in 1885. The third Janam-Sakhi reproduces a related but slightly different manuscript obtained by Professor Gurmukh Singh from Hafizabad and published by M.A. Macauliffe.

522 **PURNA CHAND, Bawa** : Jiwan Charittra Guru Nanak. (P) Lahore, Balmukand Press, 1903. 32 p. BTSL/IOL

Life of Guru Nanak.

523 **QADIR YAR** : Bait Hari Singh Nalva. (P) Amritsar, Chashma-i-Nur Press, 1880. 8 p. IOL

Verses on the exploits of Hari Singh Nalua, a favourite general of Ranjit Singh.

524 **RADHA KISHEN MEHTA** : Nushkha-i-Granthi Fobia. (U) Lahore, Arorbans Press, 1889. 40 p. BM

Prescription for Granthi-phobia, a provocative attack on Sikhism and the Gurus by an Arya Samajist.

525 **RAGHBIR SINGH, Sardar** : Address. (P) Amritsar, EC, 1916. 27 p. BTSL

Address by President of Reception Committee, Ninth Educational Conference (1916).

526 _____ : Dasvandh Kithon Ditta Jave ? (P) Amritsar, EC, 1912. 34 p. BTSL

From where should we pay our tithe ? Essay on tithing and how to save money for the Sikh Educational Conference.

527 **RAJINDAR SINGH, Sardar** : Khabt-i-Qadiayani Ka Ilaj. (U) Lahore, Guru Gobind Singh Press, 1897. 142 p.

Sikh tract on a cure for the madness of the Mirza of Qadian.

528 **RALA SINGH, Bhai** : Satwanti. (P) Amritsar, Wazir Hind Press, 1905. 205 p. IOL

Novel on early Sikh times.

529 **RAM CHAND** : Jiwan Britant Baba Banda Bahadur. (P) Lahore, Anglo-Sanskrit Press, 1898. 80 p.

Life of Banda Bahadur.

530 _____ : Jiwan Charittra Sri Guru Gobind Singh Ji. (P) Lahore, Anglo-Sanskrit Press, 1897. 50 p.

Life of Guru Gobind Singh.

531 _____ : Shri Guru Tegh Bahadur Ji Da Jiwan Charittra. (P) Lahore, Anglo-Sanskrit Press, 1896. 56p.

Life of Guru Tegh Bahadur.

532 **RAM DAS, Pandit** : Murakh Singh Siapa. (P) Kohala (Murree), Pandit Ram Das, 1914. 32 p.

The mourning of foolish Sikhs, a call for Sikhs to quit slandering Hindus. (469)

533 **RAM DITTA MAL** : Dusri Badshahi Ki Janam Sakhi. (U) Lahore, Nawal Kishore Press, 1903. 24 p.

Life of Guru Angad.

534 _____ : Guru Nanak Maharaj Ki Sawanih Umri. (U) Lahore, 1903. 120 p. PPU

Life of Guru Nanak.

535 _____ : Panchvin Badshahi Ki Janam Sakhi. (U) Lahore, Nawal Kishore Press, 1907. 38 p.

Life of Guru Arjan.

536 _____ : Tisri Badshahi Ki Janam Sakhi. (U) Lahore, Nawal Kishore Press, 1903. 46 p.

Life of Guru Amar Das.

537 **RAM KISHAN SINGH, Bhai** : Jiwan Charittra Bhai Nand Lal Sahib. (U) Lahore, Bhai Daya Singh, 1912. 11 p.

Life of Bhai Nand Lal, one of Guru

RAM KISHAN SINGH, Bhai (contd)
Gobind Singh's famous disciples who was a poet also.

538 _____: Khalsa Jubili. (P,U) Lahore, Sewa Press, 1899. 32 p. BM/IOL
Survey of Sikh history, with apologetics on aspects of the Sikh faith such as preservation of hair.

539 _____: Sikh Istrian De Prasang. (P) Amritsar, Wazir Hind Press, 1914. 24 p. PPU
Verses on the heroic deeds of Sikh women.

540 **RAM NARAIN SINGH, Sodhi :** Kharag Khalsa Dharm Shastar. (P) Amritsar, Sri Gurmat Press, 1908. 182 p. BTSL/IOL
History of Sikh religion, and a code for daily conduct.

541 **RAM NATH, Lala :** Waqya-i-Baba Nanak. (U) Amritsar, Anand Prakash Press, 1894. 48 p.
Life of Guru Nanak.

542 **RAM SINGH, Bhai :** Kes Rakkhan De Gun. (P) Sialkot, Guru Gobind Singh Press, 1894. 52 p.
The virtue of keeping the hair uncut.

543 _____: Kitab Rasman Wa Lag Chag. (P) Amritsar, Chashma-i-Nur Press, 1899. 16 p. BTSL
A book on ceremonies and conduct, proposals for curtailing extravagance among Sikhs in rites relating to birth, marriages and death.

544 _____: Subut-i-Fadi-i Kesan. (U) Sialkot, Guru Gobind Singh Press, 1894. 38 p.
Statement on the benefits of uncut hair.

545 **RAM SINGH, Gyani :** Gurbani Di Viakhia—Param Viddia. (P) Amritsar, Bhai Budh Singh, 1909. 20 p. BTSL
Commentary on the Adi Granth and Sikh religion.

546 _____: Guru Param Anusar Param Jotak. (H) Bundala (Jullundur), Bhai Ram Singh Gyani, 1909. 20 p.
The supreme light according to the supreme Guru, a study of the true astronomy given by the Gurus—a man can derive no good by knowing about the sun and stars if he does not worship God and know the secrets of his own soul.

547 _____: Kala. (P) Bundala (Jullundur), Bhai Ram Singh Gyani, 1919. 32 p.
A tract on the power of God and the Gurus, with an account of the author's educational activities.

548 _____: Param Parsad. (P) Amritsar, Sri Gurmat Press, 1910. 78 p. PPU
The greatest offering, discussion of the Gurus and their teachings.

549 _____: Punnian Di Katha. (P) Bundala (Jullundur), Bhai Ram Singh Gyani, 1908. 16 p.
Commentary on Sikh rituals during the occasion of eclipses.

550 **RAM SINGH, Sardar :** Paltan No. 15 Sikh Di Shurbirta Ate Kadardani. (P) Lahore, Khalsa Press, 1897. 16 p.
Survey of a battle fought by a Sikh platoon on the frontier, reprinted with slight alterations from Khalsa Akhbar, December 14, 1897.

551 **RANBIR SINGH :** Je Iho Ravish Rahi, Tan Din Diwi Kaum Lut Javegi. (P) Lahore, Ranbir Singh, 1910. 12 p. PPU
If this situation continues, then in two days the Sikh nation will be devastated, discussion of the religious and social condition of Punjabi Sikhs.

552 **RANBIR SINGH, Raja of Patiala :** Speech. (P) Amritsar, EC, n/d. 15 p. PPU
Presidential speech, Eighth Educational Conference (1915).

553 **RATTAN SINGH SHAHID :** Prachin Panth Prakash. (P) Amritsar, Wazir Hind Press, 1914. 586 p. PPU
Account of the Gurus and Sikh history up to the establishment of Sikh supremacy in the Punjab.

554 **RAUNAQ RAM, Munshi :** Khalsa Panth Ki Haqiqat. (U) Bhadaur (Patiala), Munshi Raunaq Ram, 1914. 118 p.
The truth about the Sikh Panth, controversial attack on Sikhism. (974)

555 **RUP SINGH, Bhai :** Sikhism : A Universal Religion. Amritsar, Coronation Printing Works, 1913. 37 p. BM/PPU/IOL
Evaluation of Sikhism as a world religion. Also published in Panjabi : Sikhi Alamgiri Mazhab Hai. Amritsar, Coronation Printing Works, 1913. 36 p. BTSL

556 **SADHU SINGH, Bawa :** Sri Guru Bans Tarwar. (HG) Rawalpindi, Egerton Press, 1899. 62 p.
Family tree of the Gurus, survey of early Sikh history.

557 **SADHU SINGH, Bhai :** Gur Sikhan Da Sidak Bharose Ate Radha Swami De Jhuthe Hath Da Pol. (P) Sheron (Amritsar), Bhai Sadhu Singh, 1912. 8 p.
The true faith of the Sikhs and the hollowness of the false hands of the Radha Swamis.

558 _____ : Istriyan Lai Gurmat Vidiya. (P) Dharowali (Gujranwala), Sri Guru Gobind Singh Kanya Pathshala, 1916. 12 p. BTSL
Religious education for women.

559 _____ : Khalsa Panth. (P) Amritsar, Bhai Sadhu Singh, 1915. 16 p. PPU
Verses on the history of Sikhism.

560 _____ : Qissa Sabat Surat. (P) Amritsar, Bhai Chattar Singh, 1911. 8 p.
Verses condemning the cutting of the beard. The same publisher also printed an enlarged edition in 1917. 48 p. PPU.

561 _____ : Sada Te Sarkar Angrezi Da Piyar. (P) Dharowali (Gujranwala), Sri Guru Gobind Singh Kanya Pathshala, 1916. 8 p.
Our love for the British government.

562 **SADHU SINGH, Mahant :** Uthanka Sri Guru Granth Sahib Ji. (P) Lahore, Sri Akal Press, 1899. 514 p.
An introduction to the Granth Sahib.

563 **SADHU SINGH, Rai Bahadur :** Dharamsalan Da Prabandh. (P) Tarn Taran, Khalsa Dharm Pracharak Vidyala, 1915. 208 p.
Note on the management of Sikh temples.

564 _____ : Sikhan Wich Modh Di Vidiya Kikun Wadhe. (P) Amritsar, EC, 1912. 14 p.
Paper on Sikh primary education, read at the Fifth Educational Conference (1912).

565 _____ : Sikh Vidyarthian Nun Apni Parhai Ton Uprant Hor Ki Sikhna Lorida Hai Parthai Lekh. (P) Amritsar, EC, 1915. 8 p. BTSL/PPU
What is needed now is for Sikh students to spend time on their studies, an essay on the value of commercial and industrial education for Sikhs, read at the Eighth Educational Conference (1915).

566 **SAIN LOK, Bhai :** Radha Swami Adarsh. (P) Abbotabad, Singh Sabha, 1913. 192 p.
Controversy between a follower of Radha Swami teachings and a Sikh, on the superiority of Sikhism.

567 **SALIG RAM :** Sri Nanak Mat Nirna. (H) Amritsar, Chashma-i-Nur Press, 1877. 8 p.
Exposition of the religion of Guru Nanak, an attempt to show that Sikhism as preached by Guru Nanak was the same as the religion of the Vedas.

568 _____ : Udasin Mat Pardipika Pritham Sikha. (HG) Amritsar, Gyan Updesh, Press, 1877. 8 p. IOL
A brief account of the Udasis, a sect of faqirs supposedly founded by a son of Guru Nanak.

569 **SAMPURAN SINGH, Sant :** Gurmat Sidhant Biyora. (P) Lahore, Gurmat Pracharak Agency, 1913. 128 p. PPU
Description of the Sikh principles.

570 _____ : Ki Sikh Butprasat Han ? (P) Lahore, Mehr Singh Chawala, 1919. 31 p. PPU
Are the Sikhs idol-worshippers ? Lecture at a meeting of the Lahore Singh Sabha.

571 _____ : Sikh Kis Nun Akhde Han ? (P) Tarn Taran, Bhai Mohan Singh Vaid, 1919. 55 p. PPU
Whom can we call a Sikh? Discussion of the true nature of Sikhism and the requirements it places upon followers of the Gurus.

572 **SANTOKH SINGH, Bhai :** Gur Upkar. (P) Amritsar, Bhai Partap Singh, 1906. 16 p.
Verses on the martyrdom of Guru Gobind Singh's sons.

573 _____ : Qudrat Da Sirdar Khalsa. (P) Amritsar, EC, 1914. 8 p.
A paper on the necessity of union and education among Sikhs, read at the Seventh Educational Conference (1914).

574 _____ : Sachchi Sikhya. (P) Amritsar, Wazir Hind Press, 1900. 8 p. BTSL
True instructions, suggestions concerning religion and personal conduct addressed to Sikhs.

575 _____ : Sri Granth Gur Partap Suraj Ras. (P) 4 Vols. Lahore, Aftab-i-Panjab Press, 1883-84. app. 3,000p. IOL
Biographies of Gurus based on the Bala Janam-Sakhi and other traditional sources, popularly known as the Suraj Prakash. Originally published in 1844. Background on Santokh Singh is in M.A. Macauliffe, The Sikh Religion (Oxford, 1909), I, lxxvi-lxxvii.

576 _____ : Vidya Nal Manevan. (P) Amritsar, EC, 1912. 16 p.
Verses on Sikh education, read at the Fifth Educational Conference (1912).

577 **SANT RAM ASHUFTA :** Hindu Jati Aur Sikh Gur. (P) Lahore, Sant Ram Ashufta, 1915. 14 p.
The Hindu community and the Sikh Gurus, an attempt to prove that the troubles suffered by the Gurus were not for the sake of Hindus, and that the Gurus showed no special favour to the Hindus.

578 **SANT RAM ASHUFTA :** Nau Muslim Ko Nasihat. (U) Amritsar, General Agency Akhbarat, 1911. 8 p.

Advice to a new Muslim, reply to a Sikh convert to Islam which argued that the Guru was a Muslim.

579 **SANT RAM, Pandit :** Kya Brahman Guru Ghar De Drohi Hain ? (H) Lahore, Pandit Sant Ram, 1909. 84 p. IOL

Are Brahmans traitors to the house of the Guru ? Defence of Brahmans against the Sikh accusation that they were implicated in the death of Guru Arjan.

580 **SANT SINGH :** Sri Guru Charitra Prabhakar. (H) Amritsar, Chashma-i-Nur Press, 1877. 50 p.

Verses on the lives of the Sikh Gurus.

581 **SANT SINGH, Bhai :** Gutka Guru Sikhya. (P) Amritsar, Bhai Sant Singh, 1906. 34p. BTSL

Booklet on the teachings of the Gurus.

582 _____ : Panjabi Kavita Wich Tin Vyakhyan. (P) Bishandaur (Jhelum), Bhai Sant Singh, 1915. 48 p. IOL

Three lectures in Panjabi verse on the good deeds of the Gurus and the need for reform among Sikhs.

583 _____ : Tawarikh Dason Guru Sahiban Ki (U) Amritsar, Bhai Chattar Singh, 1911. 200 p. IOL

Life of the Gurus, with comments on the present state of Sikhism.

584 **SARDA RAM, Pandit :** Sikhan Di Raj Di Vithiya. (P) Ludhiana, Rev. A. Rudolph, 1868. 500 p. BM/KC/PPU/IOL

History of the rise and progress of the Sikhs, with selections from Janam Sakhis, and an account of Panjabi rites and folklore. (124)

585 **SARDUL SINGH :** Gur Parnali. (P) Amritsar, Amir Chand Press, 1893. 20 p. IOL

Genealogy of the Gurus, with list of essential rules of conduct for Sikhs.

586 _____ : Parmeshwarji Di Prarthana. (HG) Amritsar, Chashma-i-Nur Press, 1880. 16 p.

Prayers and hymns for use by the Amritsar Singh Sabha.

587 _____ : Prashanotari. (P) Amritsar, Khalsa Sat Sangat Sabha, 1900. 16 p. PPU

Questions and answers on Sikh religion.

588 _____ : Sardha Puran. (P) Amritsar, Chashma-i-Nur Press, 1891. 290 p. IOL

Fulfilment of respect, treatise on Sikh theology and daily life.

589 **SARDUL SINGH, Bhai :** Janam Sakhi Sri Guru Amar Das Ji Di. (P) Lahore, Khalsa Press, 1897. 228 p.

Life of Guru Amar Das.

590 _____ : Janam Sakhi Sri Guru Angad Sahib Ji Di. (P) Lahore, Khalsa Press, 1895. 92 p. BTSL

Life of Guru Angad.

591 _____ : Sri Guru Granth Ji De Path Di Vidhi. (P) Lahore, Khalsa Press, 1895. 56 p.

The method of reading the Granth Sahib, a history of the compilation of the Sikh scriptures and how they should be read.

592 **SARDUL SINGH, Caveeshar :** The Battle of Life. How Guru Gobind Singh Fought It. The Military Aspect of Sikhism. Lahore, Ranjit Press, 1919. 28 p. PPU

593 _____ : Your Duty. Lahore, Sikh Tract Society, 1919. 14 p. KC

Assessment of the present state of Sikhism and an appeal to educated Sikhs to reform the community.

594 **SARDUL SINGH, Chawla :** Gutka Nit Nem. (P) Lahore, Sri Gurmat Press, 1904. 188 p.

Discussion of Sikh daily ceremonies and religious duties.

595 **SARDUL SINGH, Gyani :** Gur Purb Di Vidhi. (P) Amritsar, Wazir Hind Press, 1898. 16 p. BTSL

Methods of celebrating the Gurus' birthdays.

596 _____ : Gurmat Sambandi Vayakhan. (P) Amritsar, Wazir Hind Press, 1904. 251 p. BTSL/PPU/IOL

Lectures on Sikh theology.

597 **SARUP DAS, Bawa :** Sakhian Padshahin Tin Kian. (P) Ferozepur, Siddiqi Press, 1889. 368 p.

Lives of the first three Gurus.

598 **SARUP RANDHIR SINGH, Bhai :** Ki Sri Guru Granth Ji But Prasti Hai ? (P) Lahore, Khushhal Singh, 1911. 133p. PPU

Is the worship of idols sanctioned in the Granth Sahib ? A dialogue between a Sikh and a doctor to show that the Adi Granth does not support idolatry.

599 **SAVITRI DEVI :** Sikh Education. Amritsar, EC, 1914. 6 p. BM/PPU

Paper read at the Seventh Educational Conference (1914).

600 _____ : Sikh Education. Lahore, Savitri Devi, 1917. 14 p. BM

Paper presented at the Tenth Educational Conference (1917).

601 _____: Sikhi Vidya. (P) Lahore, Lahore Machine Press, 1917. 21 p. PPU

Essay on the nature of Sikhism.

602 **SAYAM SINGH, Gyani :** Mari Mat Puja Khandan. (P) Amritsar, Gyani Sayam Singh, 1907. 16 p.

Condemnation of the worship of tombs.

603 **SEWA DAS PAHIRI :** Lilha Bhagtni Bhilni. (P) Amritsar, Chattar Singh, 1918. 40 p. BM

Story of a Bhil devotee, ballad on a Bhil woman who converted to Sikhism.

604 **SEWA RAM SINGH, Bhai :** A Critical Study of the Life and Teachings of Sri Guru Nanak Dev, the Founder of Sikhism. Rawalpindi, Commercial Union Press, 1904. 183 p. BM/BTSL/IOL

A later version was published as the Divine Master.

605 _____: Qaumi Viddiya Parthaye Lekh. (P) Amritsar, EC, 1912. 15 p. BTSL

Lecture on national education among Sikhs, read at the Fifth Educational Conference (1912).

606 _____: Amrit. (P) Amritsar, Amar Prakash Agency, 1913. 34 p.

Treatise on Sikh baptism.

607 _____: Sikh Mrit Karam Vichar Ate Vasihat. (P) Amritsar, Lahaura Singh, 1890. 24 p. PPU

Sikh ceremonies at the time of death, and a will. A discussion of death, transmigration and funerals. The author suggests that if Sikhs want a particular type of ceremony, they should write instructions into their wills.

608 **SHAH MUHAMMAD :** Bait Shah Muhammad. (PN) Lahore, Muhammadi Press, 1870. 16 p. BM/IOL/PPU

Popular verses on Sikh rule, coming of the British, and annexation. Reprinted in all Punjab languages, with new editions almost every year.

609 **SHAMSHER SINGH, Bhai :** Parsang Bhai Lachhman Singh Ji Shahid. (P) Gujranwala, Bhai Shamsher Singh, 1915. 16 p. PPU

Verses on the martyrdom of Bhai Lachman Singh.

610 **SHANKAR DAYAL :** A translation of Japuji Saheb, or the Morning Prayer of the Sikhs. Fyzabad, C. Smith and Company, 1901. 120 p. BM

Translation of the Japji Sahib, with commentary and a brief assessment of Sikh religion,

611 **SHEO SHAM SINGH :** Dastur-ul-Amal. (U) Amritsar, Sheo Sham Singh, 1910. 12 p.

The rules and regulations regarding death and marriage ceremonies among Jat Sikhs in the Ferozepur District.

612 **SHER SINGH, Gyani :** Arya Samaj Aur Shudhi. (U) Peshawar, Gyani Sher Singh, 1913. 111 p. PPU

Criticism of the Shuddhi (purification) programme introduced by the Arya Samaj.

613 _____: Guru Granth Sahib Te Panth. (P) Peshawar, Gyani Sher Singh, 1919. 105 p. PPU

The Granth Sahib and the Sikh community, an attempt to prove that no human being can be the Guru of the Sikhs, the Guru nominated by Guru Gobind Singh being the Adi Granth. The author calls on the Sikhs to view themselves as the Panth and not recognize any one person as their sole leader.

614 _____: Sikh Te Dayanandi Ved. (P) Peshawar, Sikh Book Agency, 1911. 48 p. IOL

Refutation of the remarks made against the Sikh religion in Khalsa Dharm Aur Ved, which argued that Sikhism was only a restatement of the Vedic faith. (845)

615 **SHIV BRAT LAL :** Panjabi Surma. (P) Lahore, Bharat Literature Company, 1910. 415 p. PPU/IOL

Lives of the Gurus and subsequent Sikh history.

616 **SHIV RAM SINGH :** Gian Dipak. (P) Amritsar, Shiv Ram Singh, 1911. 23 p.

Light of knowledge, advice to the Sihks on reform.

617 **SHIVSHAM SINGH JHUMBAI, Bhai:** English Translation of the Speech Delivered by Bhai Shivsham Singh, President, Reception Committee of the Eighth Session of the Sikh Educational Conference. Amritsar, 1915. 10 p. BTSL

618 **SITA RAM :** Jattan Te Musalmanan Di Larai. (P) Amritsar, Chattar Singh, 1911. 50 p. BM/IOL

Ballads on rioting between Jat Sikhs and Muslims in the tehsil of Batala.

619 **SOHAN SINGH, Bhai :** Anand Jhok. (P) Nila (Jhelum), Bhai Sohan Singh, 1912. 13 p. BTSL

Verses in praise of the Sikh Anand marriage ceremony.

620 **SOHAN SINGH, Bhai** : Banda The Brave. Lahore, Empire Press, 1915. 152 p. BM/KC

One in a series on Sikh Martyrology by the former editor of the Khalsa Advocate in the Sikh and Sikhism.

621 _____ : Dayanandi Dharm Ka Namuna. (P) 2/e.,Lahore, Khalsa Press, 1905. 12 p.

An example of Dayanand's religion, anti-Arya Samaj tract.

622 _____ : Dharam Shahidi Bhai Mani Singh (P) Amritsar, Bhai Sohan Singh, 1918. 16 p. PPU

Verses on the martyrdom of Bhai Mani Singh, a famous contemporary of Guru Gobind Singh.

623 _____ : Exploits of Bhai Sukha Singh, the Khalsa Hercules. Amritsar, Khalsa Agency, 1904. 32 p. BM/KC/IOL

624 _____ : Natak Rup Kaur. (P) Simla, Khalsa Youngmens' Association, 1916. 145 p. BTSL

Drama on the unsuccessful attempt of two docoits to violate the modesty of a devote Sikh woman, Rup Kaur.

625 _____ : Painti Manmat Khandan. (P) Amritsar, Bhai Sohan Singh, 1912. 15 p.

Verses on the superiority of Sikhism and criticism of its Hindu and Muslim opponents.

626 _____ : Prasang Srimati Bibi Saran Kaur. (P) Amritsar, Bhai Chattar Singh, 1919. 8 p.

Verses describing how a Sikh girl, Bibi Saran Kaur, collected and burnt the bodies of forty Sikh martyrs at Muktsar and herself became a martyr when she was detected after completing the task.

627 _____ : Saka Sirhand. (P) Amritsar, Bhai Chattar Singh, 1918. 30 p. PPU

Account of the martyrdom of Guru Gobind Singh's sons.

628 _____ : Sikh Vidya Ute Lekh. (P) Lahore, Sardar Sant Singh, 1910. 24 p. PPU

Lecture on Sikh education read at the Third Educational Conference (1910).

629 _____ : A Tale of Woe, Or the Martyrdom of the Four Sons of Siri Guru Gobind Singhji at Sirhind and Chamkaur. Lahore, Mercantile Press, 1904. 32 p. BM/IOL

630 **SUCHET SINGH** : Kya Dasmen Guru Ji Ne Devi Puji Hai ? (HG) Amritsar, Wazir Hind Press, 1899. 20 p. PPU

Did Guru Gobind Singh worship Devi ?

631 _____ : Sarbadhar Prabhakar. (P) Amritsar, Dabir-i-Hind Press, 1885. 16 p.

The all-supporting sun, principles of Sikhism.

632 **SUCHET SINGH, Bhai**: Deputation.(P) Amritsar, Bhai Suchet Singh, 1912. 7 p.

Account of a deputation to the Manager of the Golden Temple regarding the construction of buildings in Guru Ka Bagh.

633 _____ : Sikhi Ka Namuna. (U) Amritsar, Bhai Suchet Singh, 1910. 23 p.

The proceedings of a libel case against Bhai Suchet Singh, Sikh editor.

634 _____ : Sri Guru Dharam Dhuja. (P) Lahore, Anglo-Sanskrit Press, 1902. 208 p. BTSL

Poems commemorating the heroic deeds of Sikhs for their religion.

635 **SUKH LAL, Pandit** : Nawin Singh Sikh. (P) Amritsar, National Press, 1908. 480 p. PPU

Life of Guru Gobind Singh.

636 **SUMER SINGH, Bawa** : Raihat Nama Sri Bawa Sumer Singh. (P) Lahore, Arjan Prakash Press, 1879. 8 p.

Instructions to Sikhs on how to lead a virtuous life.

637 **SUNDER SINGH, Bhai** : Guru Ki Si ? (P) 2/e., Lyallpur, Bhai Ishar Singh, 1913. 16 p. BTSL/PPU

Who was the Guru ? Praise of the founders of Sikhism, with a general account of the services rendered by them for Hindus.

638 _____ : Ki Khalsa Kalaj Sikhan Hai ? (P) Lyallpur, Bhai Sunder Singh, 1909. 39 p. BTSL/PPU/IOL

Does the Khalsa College, Amritsar, belong to the Sikhs ? The author (teacher at the Khalsa School, Lyallpur) surveys the history of the College, states the circumstances in which it allegedly fell under British control, and suggests means by which it could be transferred to the Sikhs. The essay particularly criticizes Sardar Sundar Singh Majithia and the Chief Khalsa Diwan for their association with the British. Background on the pamphlet and history of the College is in Nahar Singh (ed), "Developments in Sikh Politics, 1900-1911," Gurduara Gazette, April 1969, English section, p. 39.

639 _____ : Ki Konference Which Siri Guru Granth Sahib Ji Da Prakash Zaruri Nahin ? (P) Lyallpur, Bhai Sunder Singh, 1910. 31 p. IOL

Is it necessary to exhibit the Granth

Sahib in a conference ? Essay on religious education among Sikhs.

640 _____ : Short History of the Hari Mandar. Amritsar, Bhai Buta Singh, 1902. 15 p. BM/IOL

641 _____ : Upkari Jiwan. (P) Amritsar, Sat Bivharak Agency, 1910. 80 p.

Life of doing good deeds, story of a Sikh lady who taught her female friends and converted them to Sikhism.

642 **SUNDER SINGH Chavla :** Khuli Chithi. (U) Lahore, Sunder Singh Chavla, 1919. 1 p.

An open letter addressed to the officials of the Tenth Sikh Educational Conference, asking them for accounts and action on the resolutions.

643 **SUNDER SINGH, Ramgarhia :** Annals of the Ramgarhia Sardars. Amritsar, Sunder Singh Ramgarhia, 1902. 62 p. BM

Genealogy and history of the Ramgarhia misal, including information on the founding family after annexation in 1849.

644 **SUNDER SINGH, Sardar :** The History of the Golden Temple, Amritsar, and Shrines Around. Amritsar, Bhai Buta Singh, 1908. 39 p.

645 **SURAJ SINGH, Bhai ;** Adbhut Jiwan. (P) Amritsar, Wazir Hind Press, 1908. 356 p. PPU

Life of Bibi Harnam Kaur and history of the Sikh Kanya Mahavidyala. Ferozepur.

646 _____ : Barhman Da Sair. (P) Amritsar, Wazir Hind Press, 1908. 80 p. IOL

A trip to Burma, a tale based on the theme of tensions between old and new ideas in Sikhism. The book concerns a trip by an old priest and a young boy. During their journey, they discuss issues such as the nature of baptism, offerings, drinking, women, and care for orphans.

647 _____ : Chamakde Lal. (P) Amritsar, Bhai Chattar Singh, 1912, 126 p. BM

Life of Sardar Hari Singh Nalua, the Commander-in-Chief of Ranjit Singh's forces.

648 _____ : Ghamsan Khalsa, Bhaundu Khalsa. (P) Lahore, Bhai Raia Singh, 1902. 26 p. PPU

Warrier Sikhs, Foolish Sikhs, criticism of Sikhs who do not follow the author's interpretation of Guru's religious teachings.

649 _____ : Gur Mati Anand Karauna. (P) Amritsar, Bhai Suraj Singh, 1906. 44p. IOL

Marriages performed according to the Sikh religion, discussion of the Anand ceremony.

650 _____ : Gurmat Kaj Bivhar. (P) Sansarpur (Jullundur), Sardar Maluk Singh, 1912. 101 p. BM

A collection of various rites and ceremonies relating to birth, marriage and death.

651 _____ : Jagrit Khalsa. Jullundur, Khalsa National Press, n/d. 321 p. PPU

Awakening of the Khalsa.

652 _____ : Khalsa Vivah Bhag Vidhi. (P) Amritsar, Bhai Chattar Singh, 1912. 44 p. BTSL

The performance of Sikh marriages.

653 _____ : Lawan Kiththon Challian ? (P) Amritsar, Wazir Hind Press, 1903. 16 p.

From where did the Lewan ceremony (marriage ritual of walking around the sacrifical fire) originate ?

654 _____ : Pukar Gurmat Priya Khalsa. (P) Amritsar, Wazir Hind Press, 1900. 16 p.

Verses appealing to Sikhs to follow only the Gurus, and pointing out the undesirability of maintaining Hindu rites and worshipping Muhammadan saints.

655 _____ : Qaumi Didar. (P) Simla, Bhai Suraj Singh, 1914. 44 p. BM

Poetic and prose account of the history of the Ramgarhia Sikhs.

656 **SURAJ SINGH, Sant :** Anand Ki Rasam Kab Chali Hai ? (P) Amritsar, Wazir Hind Press, 1904. 16 p. IOL

When did the ceremony of Anand marriage come into existence ?

657 _____ : Angrezi Raj Ton Labh. (P) Lahore, Punjab Steam Press, 1916. 16 p. BTSL

Benefits from the British government.

658 _____ : Itihas Ramgarhia. (P) Simla, Ramgarhia Sabha, 1915. 430 p. PPU

History of the Ramgarhia Sikhs.

659 _____ : Tawarikh Sri Guru Khalsa. (P) Amritsar, Bhai Bhagat Singh, 1914. 964 p.

History of the ten Gurus.

660 **SURAJ SINGH, Updeshak :** Pukar Tat Khalsa. (P) Amritsar, Wazir Hind Press, n/d. 16 p. BTSL

An appeal on the essence of Sikhism, a discussion in verses of the injurious

SURAJ SINGH, Updeshak (contd)
ideas and practices affecting Sikhism such as oblations to priests and Hindu ceremonies.

661 **TAHL SINGH :** Gurmat Riti Anusar Vivah Bidhi. (H) Lahore, Sri Gurmat Press, 1903. 96 p. IOL
marriage ceremonies according to the ritual prescribed by the Gurus.

662 _____ : Ramgarhian Di Asliat. (P) Lahore, Sri Gurmat Press, 1904. 19 p. PPU/IOL
Origins of the Ramgarhia Sikhs.

663 **TARA CHAND, Lala :** Khalsa Dharam. (P) Lahore, Anglo-Sanskrit Press, 1897. 60 p.
The Sikh Religion.

664 **TARA SINGH :** Sri Akal Murat Pardarshan. (P) Amritsar, Akaljantra Press, 1882. 28 p.
Description of the Eternal Being, an attempt to reconcile the Sikh concept of God with the Puranic pantheon.

665 _____ : Wah Guru Nam. (P) Lahore, 1878. 63 p. IOL
Explanation of Sikh religious phrases.

666 **TARA SINGH, Pandit** : Sri Gurmat Nirnaya Sagar. (HG) Lahore, Anglo-Sanskrit Press, 1899. 662 p. BTSL/PPU/IOL
A treatise on the religion of the Gurus.

667 **TEJA SINGH :** Rani Jhala Kaur. (P) Amritsar, Bhai Bahadur Singh, 1910. 20 p. BTSL
Verses on the sacrifice of Rani Jhala Kaur after the death of her husband in a battle.

668 **TEJA SINGH, Babu :** Bhuleme. (P) Amritsar, Wazir Hind Press, n/d. 13 p. PPU
Suggestions for the improvement of the Sikh community, including an end to Holi celebrations, use of a Sikh calendar and abolition of caste distinctions.

669 _____ : Dasahira Bhav Panth Jagawa Arthat Panth Dasawa. (P) Lahore, Punjab Steam Press, 1916. 39 p. PPU
A description of the awakening of the Panth, history of the Panch Khalsa Diwan, Bhasaur, and comments on the current state of Sikhism.

670 _____ : Dasam Granth Sar. (P) Bhasaur, Teja Singh, n/d. 15 p. BTSL
The meaning of the Dasam Granth, a commentary.

761 _____ : Dhokha Nivar Pattra. (P) Patiala, Patiala Printing Press, 1912. 24 p. BTSL/PPU
A letter removing doubts, reply to correspondence from Bhai Deva Singh, Secretary of the Amritsar Singh Sabha, which contained charges against Kartar Singh, a controversial Sikh philosopher. Kartar Singh was accused of calling the Adi Granth a pile of papers, using rude language, and attacking the Chief Khalsa Diwan. The collection of documents consists of refutations and notes by members of the Panch Khalsa Diwan, Bhasaur.

672 _____ : Hindu Dharam Shastra Par Vichar. (P) Bhasaur, Teja Singh, 1907. 56 p. BTSL
Thoughts on Hindu religious books, criticism of Hinduism and a declaration of Sikh superiority.

673 _____ : Khalsa Panth. (P) Amritsar, Wazir Hind Press, 1903. 64 p. PPU
Verses on the nature of Sikhism and the Sikh community.

674 _____ : Man Mat Prahar. (P) Lahore, Khalsa Press, 1900. 4 p. BTSL
Attack on self centred religion, reprint of a supplement to the Khalsa Akhbar, July 1900, criticizing a book by Bhai Manna Singh, Khalsa Bhaichara Shri Amrit (Methods of offering baptism to newly-born Sikh babies).

675 _____ : Ninda Nirodh. (P) Amritsar, Bhai Sucha Singh, 1910. 18 p.
Renounce slander, a reply to a tract by Bhai Narain Singh which contained remarks against the Bhasaur Singh Sabha.

676 _____ : Sade Dase Sat Guru Ik Rup Han. (P) Amritsar, Wazir Hind Press, 1906. 52 p. IOL
Our ten Gurus are the embodiment of the one True Guru.

677 _____ : Sahij Dhari Sikh. (P) Bhasaur, Teja Singh, 1907. 56 p. KC
Discussion of Sahajdhari Sikhs.

678 _____ : Samjhauta Prakash. (P) Amritsar, Sri Gurmat Press, 1919. 50 p.
A light on agreements, news and activities relating to the Panch Khalsa Diwan.

679 _____ : Singhan Da Panth Niyara. (P) Amritsar, Wazir Hind Press, 1900. 16 p.
The Sikh religion is separate from other religions.

680 _____ : Sri Guru Singh Sabha Bhasaur De Ikminbra De Bhajangi Singh Da

Chalana. (P) Amritsar, Wazir Hind Press, 1902. 2 p.

Reprint from the Khalsa Samachar (supplement) on the innovations in death ceremonies suggested by the Bhasaur Singh Sabha.

681 _____ : Sri Guru Singh Sabha Bhasaur Nun Khalsa Panth Sewaki Vich Zaruri Bhulenme. (P) Amritsar, Wazir Hind Press, 1904. 13 p.

Important omissions in the service of the Panth, as enunciated by the Bhasaur Singh Sabha. Discussion of gurdwara reform and elimination of accretions from Hinduism into the Sikh faith.

682 **TEJA SINGH, Principal :** The Growth of Responsibility in Sikhism. Lahore, Sikh Tract Society, 1919. 64 p. BM/IOL/KC/PPU

Interpretation of Sikh history.

683 _____ : Guru Nanak and His Mission. Lahore, Sikh Tract Society, 1918. 29 p. BM/BTSL/KC/PPU/IOL

684 _____ : Meditation on Divine Name. Lahore, Sikh Tract Society, 1918. 17 p. BM/KC/IOL

685 _____ : The Sword and Religion. Lahore, Sikh Tract Society, 1918.15 p.BM/KC/IOL

A vindication of fighting for a righteous cause.

686 **TEK SINGH, Bhai :** 'Aql Ki Pukar. (P) Amritsar, Chashma-i-Nur Press, 1895. 16 p.

The call of wisdom, an exhortation for Sikhs to abandon idol worship and return to the teachings of the Gurus.

687 **THAKAR DAS, Lala :** Sikh Hindu Hain. (PN) Hoshiarpur, Khatri Press, 1899. 84 p. PPU

The Sikhs are Hindus. (53)

688 **THAKAR SINGH, Bhai :** Sidq Jiwan. (P) Amritsar, Bhai Labh Singh, 1908. 124 p. BM

Life of faith, verses on the life of Baba Mani Singh who was killed by the Muslim Governor of Lahore.

689 _____ : Gurmat Hulas. (P) Amritsar, Wazir Hind Press, 1898. 28 p.

Discussion of Sikh marriage ceremonies and praise of a few Sikhs rejecting Hindu ritual.

690 _____ : Gursat Shahid Bilas. (P) Amritsar, Wazir Hind Press, 1902. 180 p. BTSL/IOL

Verses on the martyrdom of Guru Gobind Singh's sons.

691 _____ : Harpal Charitar. (P) Rangoon, Bhai Thakur Singh, 1912. 11 p. BTSL

The story of a Sikh who exchanged his wife, sister and daughter for a parrot, which he presented to Guru Hargobind, and of their ultimate restoration to him.

692 **THAKAR SINGH, Gyani :** Guru Panth Age Pukar. (P) Amritsar, Gyani Thakur Singh, 1911. 2 p. IOL

Appeal to the Sikh community, criticism of the activities of the Chief Khalsa Diwan.

693 _____ : Guru Singh Shahid Bilas. (P) Amritsar, Wazir Hind Press, 1903. 104 p.

Verses on the martyrdom of Baba Dip Singh.

694 _____ : Putri Nun Sikhya. (P) Amritsar, Gyani Thakur Singh, 1915. 16 p.

Guidance to a daughter, parental advice to a Sikh girl at the time of her marriage concerning her future behaviour in the husband's house.

695 _____ : Vadda Shahid Bilas. (H,P) 3/e., Amritsar, Chattar Singh, 1911. 191 p. BM/PPU/IOL

Verses on Sikh martyrs.

696 **THAKAR SINGH, Sardar :** Comparison of Guru Nanak with Jesus Christ. Amritsar, Wazir Hind Press, 1906. 22 p. BTSL/IOL

697 _____ : Life and Teachings of Guru Nanak. Amritsar, Wazir Hind Press, 1906. 102 p. BTSL/IOL

698 **TRALOCHAN SINGH, Sardar :** Panth Miloni. (P) Amritsar, Wazir Hind Press, 1902. 117 p.

Unity of the Panth, suggestions on how to unify the various Sikh sects into one nation.

699 _____ : Sri Guru Arjan Dev Ji Patshahi 5 Da Jiwan Britant. (P) Lahore, Anglo-Sanskrit Press, 1896. 76 p.

Life of Guru Arjan.

700 **TRILOK SINGH :** Do Vayakhayan. (P) Amritsar, Bhai Bahadur Singh, 12 p. BTSL

Two lectures on the life of Guru Gobind Singh.

701 **TRUMPP, Ernst:** The Adi Granth, Or Holy Scriptures of the Sikhs. Allen and Company, 1877. xii, cxxxviii, 715p. BM/IOL

Controversial translation of a portion of the Adi Granth by a German scholar. His choice of words and critical introduction to Sikhism created a stir in the Sikh community and helped generate a

TRUMPP, Ernst (contd)

reexamination of the scriptures by Sikh scholars.

702 _____ : Die Religion Der Sikhs. (German) Leipzig, Otto Schulze, 1881. 124p. BM/IOL

Statement of Trumpp's ideas on Sikhism and the Adi Granth.

703 **TULSI RAM SINGH, Gyani:** Dharmi Bir. (P) Gujranwala, Sundar Singh, 1917. 46p. BM

Verses on the martyrdom of Baba Mani Singh a famous contemporary of Guru Gobind Singh.

704 **UDHAM SINGH, Sant:** Vivah Padhti Pati Prakarma. (P) Amritsar, Sant Udham Singh, 1908. 32p. IOL

Criticism of Sikhs adopting Hindu customs in their marriage ceremonies.

705 **UMED HARI:** Amolak Sikhia Arthat Sir Munduan Ghate. (P) Lahore, Sri Gurmat Press, 1905. 24p.

An invaluable lesson, or the bad effects of cutting hair.

706 **UTTAM SINGH :** Janam Sakhi. (P) Amritsar, Uttam Singh, 1887. 116p. BM

Life of Baba Atal, son of Guru Hargobind.

707 _____ : Khalsa Sanskar Pustak. (HG) Lahore, Vidya Pustak Prakashak Press, 1884. 75p. BTSL

A book of Sikh rituals.

708 **UTTAM SINGH, Bhai:** Kesh Mahatam. (P) Lahore, Anglo-Sanskrit Press, 1892. 32p.

The importance of keeping hair, a commentary with quotations from Sikh scriptures.

709 **UTTAR SINGH, Bhai :** Khalsa Dharm Darpan Pahla Bab. (P) Lahore, Guru Gobind Singh Press, 1898. 48p.

The mirror of the Sikh religion, a theological discourse.

710 **VARIAM SINGH, Kavishar :** Naukar Di Nar. (P) Amritsar, Sri Gurmat Press, 1918. 16 p. BTSL

Wife of a servant, a didactic essay on the benefits of British rule in the form of a letter from a Sikh wife to her husband on the front.

711 **VIR SINGH, Bhai :** Atam Vidya Parthaye Lekh. (P) Amritsar, Wazir Hind Press, 1912. 36 p. PPU

Paper on religious education among Sikhs, read at the Fifth Educational Conference (1912).

721 _____ : Bijai Singh. (P) Amritsar, Wazir Hind Press, 1900. 112 p. BM/IOL/PPU

A novel on the themes of the moral superiority of the Sikhs and the power of the Sikh religion. The hero is a young Hindu who marries a devoted Sikh. Following various adventures and spiritual crises, the Hindu turns to Sikhism and changes his name from Ram Lal to Bijai Singh.

713 _____ : Rana Surat Singh. (P) 2/e., Amritsar, KTS, 1919. 456 p. PPU

Verses on Rani Raj Kaur, the widow of a Sikh prince Surat Singh, her great love for her husband, her devotion, spiritual progress, and ultimate enlightenment. The book tries to show the influence of Sikhism in moulding the character of human beings and in developing their latent spiritual powers.

714 _____ : Sikhan Di Parvirt Dasha De Parshan Ate Raja Lakhdata Singh Di Rahin Usda Sudhar. (P) Amritsar, Bhai Vir Singh, n/d. 80 p.

A dramatic production on the degraded condition of Sikhs and their reform through the efforts of Lakhdata Singh.

715 _____ : Srimati Sundriji De Dardnak Samachar. (P) Amritsar, Wazir Hind Press, 1898. 148 p. IOL/PPU

Story of Sundri, a Sikh heroine who suffered for her religion. Subtitle, a true picture of the heroism, fidelity and patience of the Khalsas of former times.

716 **WADHAWA SINGH, Sardar :** Granth Istri Updesh. (P) Amritsar, Sardar Wadhawa Singh, 1900. 16 p. PPU

A book of advice to women.

717 **WALJI, Pandit :** The Dawn of Nanak Saheb's Religion. (P) Bombay, Anglo-Vernacular Press, 1895. 12 p. PPU

Historical survey of Sikhism by a Christian. The author suggests links between Christianity and the intellectual milieu which produced the Sikh faith.

718 _____ : Hari Charitra Or Comparison between the Adi Granth and the Bible. Ludhiana, Mission Press, 1894. 215 p.

Attempt to show that Guru Nanak was influenced by Christianity.

719 **WARYAM SINGH, Bhai:** Bharti Nama (PN) Dhandari (Ludhiana), Bhai Waryam Singh, 1918. 8 p.

Verses on enlisting in the army.

720 _____ : Qarza Madad Jang. (PN) Amritsar, Sanatan Dharm Electric Press, 1918

12 p.

Loans to aid the war, an appeal for contributions to the British war effort.

721 **WASAKHA SINGH, Bhai :** Janam Sakhi. (P) Lahore, Punjab Economical Press, 1898. 16 p.

Life of Guru Gobind Singh.

722 **WAZIR SINGH, Bhai :** Sidqi Sikh. (P) Lahore, Gurmat Press, 1903. 8 p.

Verses on the devotion of a Sikh and his wife to their religion despite Muslim persecution.

723 _____ : Veda Dharm Partal Larai Nambar 2. (P) Amritsar, Wazir Hind Press, 1906. 130 p. IOL

Sikh criticism of the assumption that the Vedas are the storehouse of all spiritual and temporal knowledge.

724 **YATHARATH RAI :** Kapt Binash. (P) Peshawar, Sikh Book Agency, 1911. 199 p. PPU

Refutation of fraud, a comparison between the teachings of the Gurus and the Vedic faith. The work was a response to Hamare Gurus Sahib Vedon Ke Pairon The (Our Guru was a follower of the Vedas).

SECTION 2

ANONYMOUS SIKH PUBLICATIONS

SECTION 2

ANONYMOUS SIKH PUBLICATIONS

This section consists of anonymous Sikh publications arranged alphabetically by title. The entries follow the pattern introduced in the preceding section. The reader is referred to the general bibliographic discussion in the preface and introduction also.

Anonymous Sikh Publications

725 **ABCHALI JOT.** (P) Amritsar, KTS, n/d. 192p. PPU

Now the light has gone, tract on Sikh theology.

726 **ACHARAJ KAUTAK.** (P) Amritsar, Khalsa Youngmen Association, 1904. 32p. PPU/IOL

A miracle, reinterpretation of the foundation of the Khalsa and a review of Guru Gobind Singh's activities at Anandpur.

727 **ADHURI VIDYA JIND DA KHUN.** (P) Amritsar, KTS, 1909. 16p. BTSL

Incomplete education is the pit of life, a poem showing how an educated but irreligious girl lost her son, husband and all her possessions.

728 **AGYAKAR.** (P) Amritsar, KTS, 1911. 117p. PPU/IOL

Obedient, a treatise on women's household duties.

729 **AJAIN MARE GAI.** (P) Amritsar, KTS, 1902. 74p.

Now we are struck down, an essay on the strengthening of Sikhism by reform and reclamation of fallen Sikhs.

730 **AJ MANGAL WAR HAI.** (P) Amritsar, KTS, 1900. 32p. PPU

Today it is Tuesday, condemnation of fasts and superstitious rites.

731 **ANAND BIWAH PAR VICHAR.** (P) Amritsar, Punjab Commercial Press, 1906. 8p.

A discussion of Anand marriage, criticism of a statement allegedly issued by the Raja of Nabha against the Singh Sabhas and a simplified Sikh marriage ceremony. (3, 431)

732 **ANARTH.** (P) Amritsar, KTS, 1899. 6p.

Distorted meaning, criticism of incorrect interpretations of the Adi Granth.

733 **ANATH KANYA.** (P) Amritsar, KTS, 1916. 30p. PPU

Orphan girl, story of how an orphan became interested in Sikhism.

734 **ANDITHA PRITAM.** (P) Amritsar, KTS, 1913. 119p.

Unseen devotion, description of a Raja's love towards Guru Nanak whose teachings were explained to him by a Sikh. On hearing this Guru Nanak met the Raja and converted him.

735 **ANGREZI RAJ DIAN BARKATAN.** (P) Amritsar, Bhai Arjun Singh, 1916. 8p.

Blessings of British rule, description of the positive aspects of foreign rule published by a rais and secretary of the Ferozepur War Aid Committee.

736 **AN ISHWAR PARTHAE, GURUJI DE UPDESH.** (P) Amritsar, KTS, 1914. 19p. PPU

The preachings of the Guru on the tradition of irreligious worship.

737 **AN MULLI TAHLAN.** (P) Amritsar, KTS, 1900. 8p. PPU

Unpaid services, didactic tale on the necessity for women to learn new skills such as needle-work.

738 **ANOKHA BABU.** (P) Quetta, Guru Nanak Library, 1911. 32p. IOL

Strange Babu, a dialogue between a Hindu and a Sikh in which the Sikh tries to prove that the practice of keeping his hair uncut is based on philosophical grounds.

739 **ANOKHA BALAK.** (P) Amritsar, KTS, 1903. 32p.

A unique boy, an account of Guru Nanak's early life.

740 **ANYA MATI KANDA.** (P) Rawalpindi, Gulshan-i-Punjab Press, 1898. 4p.

A thorn for members of other religions, criticism of individuals who call themselves Sikhs but only stir up trouble for the Panth.

741 **APNE AUGUN.** (P) Lahore, Sikh Handbill Committee, 1910. 4 p. PPU

Our own perversions, a short essay on the realization of individual shortcomings among Sikhs.

742 **ARSHI NUR.** (P) Amritsar, KTS, 1917. 82 p. PPU

Heavenly light, a commentary on the Sikh Gurus and Sikh history.

743 **ASI TAN BHULLE HI RAHE.** (P) Amritsar, Khalsa Hamdard Agency, 1908. 8 p. IOL

We remain forgotten men, a religious discussion between two Sikhs on the Mazbhi Sikhs, a sweeper caste. The conclusion is that Mazbhis should be looked upon as real Sikhs as they abide by the religious rituals of the Sikh community.

744 **ATAM GHAT.** (P) Amritsar, KTS, 1900. 45 p.

Suicide, or the story of quarrels between mothers-in-law and daughters-in-law.

745 **AVTAR-I-ZAMANA.** (U) Amritsar, Roz Bazar Steam Press, 1914. 16 p.

Incarnation of time, a lecture delivered by a convert to Islam attempting to prove that reformers such as Guru Nanak were Muslims and prophets of their time.

746 **AZMAT-I-KHALSA.** (U) Amritsar, KTS, 1897. 16 p. BTSL

The glory of the Khalsa, survey of Sikh history.

747 **BABA NANAK AUR SWAMI DAYA-NAND.** (U) Lahore, Darshanand Tract Parcharak Mission, 1913. 16 p.

Attempt at re-establishing friendly relations between Sikhs and Arya Samajists.

748 **BABANIYAN KAHANIYAN.** (P) Amritsar, KTS, 1905. 32 p. IOL

Anecdotes connected with the life of Guru Nanak.

749 **BACHCHE PALAN DIAN MATTAN.** (P) Amritsar, KTS, 1911. 40 p.

Advice to Sikhs on the rearing of children.

750 **BALAK TE FAQIR.** (P) Amritsar, KTS, 1901. 16 p.

A child and a faqir, fictitious story about how a child's generosity changed adult attitudes.

751 **BALAN NUN GAHNE PAHNAWANE DE AUGAN.** (P) Amritsar, KTS, 1900. 28 p.

Essay on the evils of putting ornaments on children.

752 **BAL BIVAH DE DUKHRE.** (P) Amritsar, KTS, n/d. 32 p.

The woes of child marriage.

753 **BALIDAN.** (P) Amritsar, KTS, 1896, 40 p. PPU

Sacrifice, account of the martyrdom of Guru Gobind Singh's youngest son.

754 **BAL LILA.** (P) Amritsar, KTS, 1899. 32 p. BTSL

Childhood deeds of Guru Nanak.

755 **BAL SUDHAR.** (P) Lahore, Panjabi Prachar Book Agency, 1910. 16 p. BTSL

Reformation of children, discussion of family life and conduct of Sikh children.

756 **BARA MASA PAKHAND KHAN-DAN.** (P) Rupar, Swami Bishan Das, 1910. 12 p.

Refutation of imposters, a poem on the qualifications of Gurudom according to the Adi Granth.

757 **BHAGAT JAI DEV JI DA JIWAN CHARITTRA.** (P) Amritsar, KTS, 1904. 50 p. IOL

Biographical sketch of Bhagat Jai Dev, a Sanskrit poet whose hymns are in the Adi Granth.

758 **BHAGAT NAMDEV JI DA JIWAN CHARITTRA.** (HG) Amritsar, KTS, 1906. app.230 p. BTSL/IOL

Life of Bhagat Namdev.

759 **BHAI BIDHI CHANDJI DI ADUTI BAHADURI.** (P) Lahore, Sant Singh Musafiir, 1913. 32 p. BM

Poem of 184 verses describing the bravery of Bhai Bidhi Chand in recovering from Shah Jahan's stables two horses from Kabul which had been taken from the Sikhs who were bringing them to Guru Hargobind.

760 **BHAI JIWAN SINGH DA SIKHKHI JIWAN.** (P) Amritsar, KTS, 1905. 72 p.

The examplary Sikh life of Bhai Jiwan Singh.

761 **BHAI MAHNGA ATE MAI SUHAG BAI DI VITHIA.** (P) Amritsar, KTS, 1903. 106 p. BM/IOL/PPU

The story of a Hindu couple (Bhai Mahnga and Mai Suhag Bai) who after enduring many hardships and trials in search of a spiritual guide met Guru Amar Das and became true Sikhs. Subsequently republished in an English edition : Bhai Mahnga : Or the Search after Truth. Amritsar, CKD, 1911. 120 p. PPU

762 **BHAI PRABUDH SINGH JI DA JIWAN SUDHAR.** (P) 6 Pts. Amritsar, KTS, 1906-7. app.425 p. IOL

Bhai Prabudh Singh, how his life was reformed.

763 **BHAI SAIN DAS JI DA JIWAN.** (P) 7 Pts. Amritsar, KTS, 1909. app.315p. PPU/IOL

A brief account of Bhai Sain Das, a devoted disciple of Guru Arjan.

764 **BHAW PRAKASHNI TIKA JAITSARI DI WAR DI.** (P) Amritsar, KTS, 1898, 154 p.

Commentary on the Jaitsari Bani in the Granth Sahib, usually recited on the occasion of the death of a Sikh.

765 **BHUJANGIAN DA KHOLAK.** (P) Amritsar, KTS, 1901, 64 p.

Fictitious story on the value of Sikh union.

766 **BHULLER JAT ATHVA PANJABI MELE.** (P) Amritsar, Sardar Bal Singh, 1910. 66 p. IOL

Criticism of heavy drinking among Sikhs on the occasion of Holi.

767 **BHUYANGAN PUKAR.** (P) Kairon, Singh Sabha, 1908. 16 p. PPU

Verses addressed to Sikh women warning against unnecessary ornaments and advising them to wear only those articles permitted by the Gurus.

768 **BHUYANGAN VIRLAP.** (P) Amritsar, Khalsa Bhuyangan Diwan, 1908. 46 p. PPU/IOL

Call for Sikh women to give up customs borrowed from Hinduism.

769 **BIBI BHAIN.** (P) Amritsar, KTS, 1900. 88 p. BTSL

To my sister, verses on family quarrels. The author criticizes the desire for ornaments and showy dresses and suggests instead that Sikh women emphasize cleanliness and household duties.

770 **BIKHYA NIKHEDAN.** (P) Amritsar, KTS, 1904. 36 p.

Opposition to drugs.

771 **BINAI PATTAR.** (P) Amritsar, KTS, n/d. 63p. PPU

A letter of humble requests, a call for Sikhs to act upon the principles of their religion.

772 **CHACHA BHATIJA.** (P) Amritsar, KTS, 1900. 42 p.

Uncle and nephew, a dialogue on the Sikh faith. Topics discussed include the existence of God, the necessity of prayer and the attributes of divinity.

773 **CHIN DI AMIRZADI.** (P) Amritsar, KTS, 1899.

A Princess of China, a fictitious story on the theme of Sikh gallantry.

774 **DANGO DANGI.** (P) Amritsar, KTS, 1905. app.120 p. BTSL/IOL

A hot discussion, account of a debate on the principles of Sikh religion.

775 **DARHI DI DURGAT.** (P) Amritsar, KTS, 1897. 4 p.

The beard disgraced.

776 **DASAM GRANTH NIRNAYE.** (P) Bhasaur, Babu Teja Singh, 1919. 74 p.

Attempt to prove that the Dasam Granth is a mixture of the works of poets and the utterances of Guru Gobind Singh.

777 **DASAM GUR CHARITRA LAVINIAN.** (P) Amritsar, KTS, 1899. 88 p.

Verses on the life of Guru Gobind Singh.

778 **DASE GURU SAHIBANJI DA SAMPURAN JIWAN BRITANT.** (P) Amritsar, Sat Bivharak Agency, 1911. 392 p. IOL

Complete life sketches of the ten Gurus.

779 **DHARM HET BALI DAN.** (P) Amritsar, KTS, 1897. 40 p.

The sacrifice of life for religion, a story about two youthful martyrs.

780 **DHARM RAKHYA.** (P) Amritsar, KTS, 1896. 18 p. IOL

The protection of religion, a study o, the role of Guru Gobind Singh in defending Hindus. According to the author, the Guru helped Hindus in three ways: in dealing with Muslim oppression, in developing trade, and in performing good deeds for individuals.

781 **DHARMIK KHABRAN.** (P) Amritsar, 1909. 24 p.

Supplementary bulletin to Khalsa Samachar, December 1909. Information on Singh Sabha meetings and the second annual report of the Khalsa Pracharak Vidhyala, Tarn Taran.

782 **DHOKHE TON BACHO.** (P) Amritsar, KTS, 1899. 6p.

Beware of fraud, lecture to Sikhs on honesty and protection against thieves.

783 **DUMANA TE BHAMBIRI.** (P) Amritsar, KTS, 1910. 14p.

Discussion between the bee and the butterfly, in verse, illustrative of the dangers of leading an easy and idle life.

784 **EH TAN GARKI AI.** (P) Amritsar, KTS, 1899. 24p. PPU

This is destruction, a social tract examining the defects of wearing dresses that reveal too much, a fashion supposedly growing among a section of Hindu ladies.

785 **EH TANGAR KI AI?** (P) Amritsar, Khalsa Baradari, 1919. 4p.

EH TANGAR KI AI (contd)
What is this low caste ? A dialogue between Sikhs on the conversion of outcastes to Sikhism.

786 **FARZ.** (P) Amritsar, KTS, 1916. 197p.
Man's duty to himself and others.

787 **GARIB KAUR.** (SI) Amritsar, KTS, 1898. 3p.
Social essay on the necessity of ameliorating the condition of women in the lower ranks of life.

788 **GARIB NIWAZ.** (P) Rawalpindi, Sri Gurmat Pracharak Sabha, 1919. 16p. PPU
Lover of the poor, life sketch of Guru Gobind Singh.

789 **GHAR SUAR.** (P) 2 Pts. Amritsar, KTS, 1901. 160 p. PPU
Household duties, for Sikh women.

790 **GHARVICH SUARG.** (P) Amritsar, KTS, 1900. 29 p. BTSL/PPU
Heaven in the home, essay on religion and the Sikh household.

791 **GRAHI SIKHYA.** (P) Amritsar, Panjabi Prachar Book Agency, 1910. 47p. PPU
Homecraft, advice on Sikh family life and health.

792 **GURDUARA RAKAB GANJ.** (P) Amritsar, Wazir Hind Press, n/d. 2 p. KC
Statement of Sikh demands concerning proposed demolition of the Rakabganj Gurdwara in 1914.

793 **GURDUARA RAKAB GANJ SAHIB ATE 3 MAY DI COMMITTEE.** (P) Rawalpindi, Ramgarhia Sabha, 1914. 16 p. KC
Condemnation of the proposals made by the Chief Khalsa Diwan, Amritsar, in its meeting of May 3, 1914, regarding the Rakabganj Gurdwara.

794 **GURMAT PARKASH.** (P) Amritsar, CKD, 1915. 112 p. BM/PPU
Guide to Sikh customs, with an appeal for reforms in conduct and rituals.

795 **GUR SIKH WARI.** (P) Amritsar, KTS, 1913. 291 p. KC/PPU/IOL
Verses on Sikh contemporaries and successors of the Gurus.

796 **GURU DE TRAI DARSHAN.** (P) Amritsar, KTS, 1909. 32 p. BTSL/PPU
Three forms of God, a short story with the moral that Sikhs can meet God through emphasis on devotion, not entrapment in physical aspects of the world.

797 **GURU PRIKHYA.** (P) Amritsar, Gurumat Granth Pracharak Sabha, 1899. 48 p.
Test of a Guru.

798 **HAI HAI BACHCHI TUN KITHON ?** (P) Amritsar, KTS, 1897. 8 p.
Oh unfortunate daughter, from where have you come ? Story of a young Brahman widow who gave up her religion under the influence of a Christian missionary but finally was converted to Sikhism.

799 **HAI NI MERA NAK NAHIN RAHNDA.** (P) Amritsar, KTS, 1900. 40 p.
People will cease to respect me, attack on the prevalence of siapa (mourning rites) among Sikhs.

800 **HEROISM OF SIKH WOMEN; MARTYRDOM OF A SIKH YOUTH; BHAI HAR PAL; BHAI MADHO.** Amritsar, Khalsa Agency, 1906. 34 p. BM/PPU

801 **HIMMAT-I-KHALSA.** (P) Amritsar, KTS, 1897. 15p.
Energy of the Khalsa.

802 **HIND DA PURATAN ITIHAS.** (P) Amritsar, KTS, n/d. 30 p. PPU
Survey of Chinese accounts of Indian history.

803 **HINDUAN DA POL.** (P) Amritsar, Punjab Commercial Press, 1914. ii, 219p. BM
The hollowness of Hindus, a critical review of Hindu religious ideas and methods, prepared for distribution at the Seventh Sikh Educational Conference.

804 **HINDU MARTYRS.** Lahore, Arorbans Press, 1895. 81p. PPU
Description of the lives and deaths of Sikh martyrs.

805 **HIR WARE SHAH DE PHAL.** (P) Amritsar, KTS, 1898. 32 p.
The consequences of reading Waris Shah's Hir. The author argues that women should give up reading love tales and devote all their leisure to the study of religious books.

806 **HOLI HAI.** (P) Amritsar, KTS, 1902. 38 p. PPU
It is Holi, a request to Sikhs to curtail their licentiousness during the holi day.

807 **HUR MATI.** (P) Amritsar, KTS, 1904. 56 p.
Fictitious account of the evils of idleness and being stubborn.

808 **IK BABU NUN UPDESH.** (P) Amritsar, KTS, 1902. 16 p.

An admonition to a Babu, discussion of Sikh religion.

809 **IK DHATHE SIKH DA SUDHAR.** (P) Amritsar, KTS, 1917. 29 p. PPU
The reform of a fallen Sikh.

810 **IK KANNIYAN DE DUKHRE.** (P) Amritsar, KTS, 1899. 4 p.
A girl's misfortunes, a didactic story on the Sikh religion.

811 **IK PANJABI SINGH DI VILAYATI SAIR.** (P) Amritsar, KTS, 1898. 52p. IOL
A Punjabi Sikh's trip to Europe.

812 **IK PAVITTRA JIWAN.** (P) 13 Pts. Amritsar, KTS, 1902-3. app.500p. BTSL/PPU
A pious life, historical fiction on the theme of what it means to be a Sikh.

813 **ISTRI BHARTA.** (P) Amritsar, KTS, 1900. 55 p. PPU
Husband and wife, fiction on the responsibilities of a married couple.

814 **ISTRI SAMBODH.** (P) Amritsar, KTS, 1906. 16 p. PPU
Moral lessons for Sikh women.

815 **ISTRI VARAT DHARAM.** (P) Amritsar, KTS, 1904. 424 p. PPU
Religious discourse on a husband's duty towards his wife.

816 **ISTRIAN LIYE AMRIT DI LOR.** (P) Amritsar, KTS, 1898. 16 p.
The necessity of baptism for Sikh women.

817 **JADID SRI GUR BHAGAT MAL.** (P) Amritsar, Maghi Ram and Sons, 1914. 575 p. BM
A hagiology with commentary, comprising the stories of early Punjab saints, the life of Kabir, and the lives of other individuals judged influential in the emergence of Sikhism.

818 **JAGTI JOT.** (P) Amritsar, Bhai Kishan Singh, 1910. 16 p.
Glowing light, a brief account of the life of Guru Gobind Singh.

819 **JANG-I-CHAMKAUR.** (P) Amritsar, KTS, 1897. 60 p. PPU
Verses on the battle of Chamkaur.

820 **JANG NAMA GURU GOBIND SINGH JI.** (P) Lahore, Balmukand Press, 1900. 32 p.
Verses on the warfare of Guru Gobind Singh.

821 **JARWANIAN TON NIRMANIAN DA NISTARA.** (P) Amritsar, KTS, 1910. 36 p. PPU/IOL
Story of young girl and her grandfather, both of whom had great faith in Guru Gobind Singh. When the two were attacked by robbers, the Guru intervened and saved their lives.

822 **JEH EHI HAL RIHA TAN ASAN DUBBE.** (P) Amritsar, KTS, 1900. 20 p. PPU
We shall be undone if we remain in this state, commentary on the condition of the Sikh community.

823 **JHOK JAMIA PANJAB DA.** (P) Amritsar. Sikh Hand Bill Committee, 1912. 8 p. BTSL
Verses on the origin and development of Panjabi.

824 **JI MAINU WEHL NAHIN.** (P) Amritsar, Khalsa Young Men's Association, 1904. 50 p.
I have no time, didactic story on the necessity of education and utilizing personal resources.

825 **JINDRI DIAN JINDRI NAL GALLAN.** (P) Amritsar, KTS, 1905. 40 p. PPU
Tale of how Guru Nanak saved a sick person from an incurable disease.

826 **JIWAN DI KANI.** (P) Amritsar, KTS, 1912. 54 p. BTSL
Talk between a Sikh lady and her husband's brother on Sikhism and man's relation with God.

827 **JIWAN BHAI PARO JULKA.** (P) Amritsar, KTS, 1905. 32 p. IOL
Biography of Bhai Paro Julka.

828 **JIWAN BRITANT BHAI TARU SINGH JI SHAHID.** (P) Amritsar, KTS, 1912. 35 p. PPU
Life of Bhai Taru Singh.

829 **JIWAN BRITANT MAHARAJA RANJIT SINGH.** (P) Amritsar, 1918. xii,380 p. BM
Biography of Ranjit Singh.

830 **JIWAN BRITANT PAHLI PATSHAHI SIRI GURU NANAK SAHIBJI.** (P) Amritsar, Sat Biwharak Agency, 1910. 47 p.
Biography of Guru Nanak.

831 **JIWAN BRITANT SRI BABA ATAL RAI JI.** (P) Amritsar, KTS, 1898. 44 p.
Life of Baba Atal Rai, son of Guru Hargobind.

832 **JIWAN BRITANT SRI GURU ARJAN DEV JI.** (P) Amritsar, KTS, 1898. 86 p. IOL
Life of Guru Arjan.

833 **JIWAN SUDHAR.** (P) Amritsar, KTS, 1903. 24 p. PPU
Essay on how to reform life.

834 **JO PATTI SUADON PATTI.** (P) Amritsar, KTS, 1897. 48 p. PPU
Love of taste leads to destruction.

835 **JUA KINEN NA JITTIA SABH JUE JITTE.** (P) Lahore, Sikh Hand Bill Committee, 1910. 4 p. BTSL
No one won in gambling, gambling won all, leaflet directed against gambling. This is probably by Bhai Mohan Singh Vaid.

836 **JUE BAZI.** (P) Amritsar, KTS, n/d. 52 p. PPU
Gambling. The author utilizes scriptures and arguments from everyday life to convince Sikhs that they should not try to make money without working for it.

837 **KALGIAN WALE DE ADARSH SAMJHAN DA PRAYATAN.** (P) Amritsar, KTS, n/d. 98 p. PPU
Attempt to show that Guru Gobind Singh's mission was suppression of tyranny and the establishment of peace, not worldly aggrandizement.

838 **KALGIAN WALE DE KAMAL.** (P) Amritsar, Khalsa Samachar, 1918. 57 p. PPU
The achievements of Guru Gobind Singh.

839 **KALHINI DIURANI.** (P) Amritsar, KTS, n/d. 44 p. PPU
The troublesome family life of two stepwives.

840 **KARAM KAUR.** (P) 5 Pts. Amritsar, KTS, 1918. app.150 p. PPU
Story of a Sikh woman, Karam Kaur.

841 **KESIN NAHAWAN KI BICHAR.** (P) Amritsar, Amar Press, 1887. 2 p.
Rules for washing the hair.

842 **KHALSA BARADARI DI PUSHTI.** (P) Rangoon, Amrit Pracharak Jatha, 1908. 16 p.
Verses calling on Sikhs to form one united nation.

843 **KHALSA BARADARI UNATTI ASHRAM DIAN KUNJIAN.** (P) Amritsar, Wazir Hind Press, 1909. 16 p. BTSL
The keys to the advancement of the ashram of the Khalsa brotherhood, a proposal for the creation of a missionary force to carry Sikhism throughout the world.

844 **KHALSA DA GUR MANTAR.** (P) Amritsar, KTS, 1898. 2 p.
The religious formula of the Sikhs.

845 **KHALSA DHARM AUR VED.** (U) Rawalpindi, Dayanand Ved Pracharak Mission, n/d. 8 p.
The Sikh religion and the Vedas, quotations and commentary on the Granth Sahib by an Arya Samajist in an effort to prove that the Gurus believed in the Vedas. (614)

846 **KHALSA DIRECTORY, 1898.** (P) Amritsar, KTS, 1898. 102 p. PPU
Lists of Sikh aristocrats, officials, and members of Singh Sabhas.

847 _____ **1899.** (P) Amritsar, KTS, 1900. 206 p. BM/PPU
Lists of Sikh aristocrats, officials, priests and singers, professional men, and members of Singh Sabhas.

848 **KHALSA JANAM.** (P) Amritsar, KTS, 1907. 16 p.
Birth of the Khalsa.

849 **KHALSA KANNIYA WIWAH SANSKAR.** (P) Lahore, Khalsa Press, 1905, 36 p. PPU/IOL
Rules for marriage ceremonies performed according to Sikh rites.

850 **KHALSA DI NIND.** (P) Amritsar, KTS, 1899. 56 p.
Lethargy of the Sikhs.

851 **KHOT BURA.** (P) Amritsar, KTS, 1911. 39 p. PPU
Stories illustrating the results of evil deeds and hasty action.

852 **KHUAN PAR ZULM.** (P) Amritsar, KTS, 1899. 24 p.
Tyranny on the wells, tract on the dangers of impure wells and drinking dirty water.

853 **KHULQ-I-KHALSA.** (P) Amritsar, KTS, 1899. 16 p. PPU
The conduct of the Khalsa.

854 **KIRTAN SOHILA BHAW PRAKASHNI TIKA SAHIT.** (P) Amritsar, KTS, 1900. 32 p.
Sikh prayers, with commentary.

855 **KI VADDA HONA HAI?** (P) Amritsar, KTS, 1905. 16 p. PPU
What is greatness? Account of what qualities go into the making of a great man.

856 **KYA VED ISHVARI BANI HAI ?** (P) Lahore, Punjab Sewak Agency, 1912. 20 p.

Are the Vedas from God? A reply to Khalsa Mat Parkash, an Arya Samaj tract which criticized the Gurus and declared that the Adi Granth was a hypocritical pretension. The Sikh author counters with a denunciation of the Vedas, primarily relying upon evidence from Bengali and European scholars.

857 **LOHE RAKH.** (P) Amritsar, KTS, 1901. 22 p. BTSL.

The wearing of iron, criticism of Sikhs wearing iron as a charm to ward off evil spirits.

858 **MAHARAJA KHALSA.** (P) Amritsar, Khalsa College Student Association, 1918. 282 p. BM/IOL

Verses on the lives of Ranjit Singh and his generals, and a narrative of the period following his death until British annexation in 1849.

859 **MAHNDI.** (P) Amritsar, KTS, 1908. 16 p.

A moral poem which teaches that men should not make friends just to use others and then fling them away just as mehndi (Lawsonia Inermis) is thrown away when it has made the hands of women red.

860 **MAIN KI KITA TAIN KI KITA?** (P) Amritsar, KTS, 1899. 6 p. BTSL

What have I done, and what have you done? A dialogue between a staunch Sikh and a person who had left Sikhism and become a Sadhu. The latter is brought back to the religion of the Guru after a lengthy discourse.

861 **MAIN SIKH HAN.** (P) Amritsar, KTS, 1906. 24 p. PPU

I am a Sikh, fictitious account of a Muslim convert to Sikhism.

862 **MAKAN.** (P) Amritsar, KTS, 1906. 36 p. PPU

A condemnation of the system of paying condolatory visits on the death of friends.

863 **MAN MOKH SUDHAR.** (P) Ambala, Khalsa Bhujangi Sabha, 1903. 114 p. PPU

Reform of evil things, criticism of Hindu customs prevalent among Sikhs.

864 **MARG PARKASHINI.** (H) Adyar, Theosophist Office, 1906. 34 p. PPU

Light on Sikh theology.

865 **MARTYRDOM OF THE TWO INFANT SONS OF GURU GOBIND SINGH.** Lahore, Arorbans Press, 1895. 32 p. PPU

866 **MAHTAB SINGH DI BAHADURI.** (P) Amritsar, KTS, 1898. 24 p.

The bravery of Mahtab Singh.

867 **MERA ARSHI PRITAM.** (P) Amritsar, KTS, n/d. 96 p. PPU

My beloved in heaven, discussion of the Gurus and Sikh theology.

868 **MERA SATGUR PIYARA.** (P) Amritsar, Khalsa Dharam Pracharak Committee, 1912. 20 p.

My beloved Guru, a lecture on Guru Nanak written with the object of promoting mutual love and morality among Sikhs.

869 **MIRAN BHAI JI DA JIWAN.** (P) Amritsar, KTS, n/d. 45 p. PPU

Life of a Hindu who died in defiance of Muslim invaders.

870 **MURAKH GAND PAWE MUH MARI.** (P) Peshawar, Sikh Book Agency, 1910. 2 p. BTSL

The foolish man speaks whatever he likes, a handbill delineating the distinctions between Hindus and Sikhs.

871 **NASHANG KAUR KIKUR LAJ KAUR BAN GAI.** (P) Amritsar, KTS, 1901. 35 p.

Story of how a shameless woman was converted into a modest lady.

872 **NAVAN KISSA BAMBA DA.** (P) Lahore, Bhai Amar Singh, 1913. 15 p. BM

Poem denouncing the attempt to kill the Governor-General Lord Hardinge, by a bomb at Delhi in 1912. Appended is an affirmation of Sikh loyalty.

873 **NIMANIAN DA NISTARA.** (P) Amritsar, KTS, n/d. 36 p. PPU

Sketch of Guru Gobind Singh and his bravery.

874 **NIRMALA PRABHAKAR ATE SIKKHI PRABHAKAR.** (P) Lahore, Ramdas Narula, 1903. 338 p. BM

Verses on the religious rules of the Nirmalas and orthodox Sikhs.

875 **NISANG KAUR.** (P) Amritsar, KTS, 1906. 40 p. PPU

A tract containing instructions for Sikh women.

876 **NIYOG.** (U) Lahore, Khalsa Agency, 1905. 48 p. PPU/IOL

Criticism of ideas on Niyog supposedly preached by Arya Samajists.

877 **NUNH SAS DA SAMBAD.** (P) Amritsar, KTS, 1900. 24 p. PPU

Conversation between a mother-in-law and a daughter-in-law on the nature of Sikhism.

878 **ONE - FOURTH DASWANDH SCHEME, 1911.** Daska (Sialkot), Sardar Raghbir Singh, 1911. 18 p. IOL

Prospectus of a scheme for contribution of 1/40th of income of every Sikh family for the spread of religious, social and secular education among Sikhs.

879 **PALTAN NO. 14 SIKHS DI YADGARWALI BAHADURI.** (P) Amritsar, Recruiting Officer, 1915. 8 p.

Account of the heroic attack by the 14th Sikhs on the Turkish position in the Dardanelles.

880 **PANJABI PHULWARI.** (P) Amritsar, 1914. ix,216 p. BM

The garden of Panjabi, selections from Panjabi poets with biographical notices.

881 **PANTH HITKARI.** (P) Lahore, Panjab Steam Press, 1918. 8 p.

A supplementary bulletin of Panth Sevak Akhbar, Lahore, which describes a visit of the Maharajah of Nabha to the Vidhya Bahadur Panch Khand, Bhasaur.

882 **PANTH KHALSA JAG.** (P) Lahore, Sri Gurmat Press, 1910. 8 p. BTSL

Awakening of the Khalsa, an appeal to Sikhs to renounce current social and religious practices and return to the guidelines of life established by the Gurus.

883 **PANTH PRABODH.** (P) Lahore, Khalsa Press, 1901. 8 p.

Verses exhorting the Sikhs to rise from the lethargy and devote their energies to the religious and social uplift of the community.

884 **PANTH PUKAR ARTHAT PANTHIC RAVAN.** (P) Kaliana (Montgomery), Sardar Hukam Singh, 1918. 208 p.

Collection of opinions received from representative Sikhs in response to an appeal issued by Sardar Hukam Singh for the retention of Rag Mala in the Adi Granth. (919)

885 **PARSANG BABE ATAL SAHIB DE AVTAR DHARAN DA.** (P) Amritsar, Bhai Hakim Singh, 1910. 16 p.

Account of the deeds of Baba Atal, a son of Guru Hargobind.

886 **PARSANG BHAI MADHOJI.** (P) Amritsar, KTS, 1911. 31p. PPU

The story of a thief who killed the wife of Bhai Madhoji, a Sikh saint, but later repented and converted to Sikhism.

887 **PARSANG BHAI MANJH.** (P) Amritsar, KTS, 1912. 48 p. BTSL

The story of a village lambardar, Bhai Manjh, who became a follower of Guru Arjan.

888 **PARSANG SIRI NANAKANA SAHIB JI DA.** (P) Amritsar, Bhai Hakim Singh, 1910. 16 p.

Historical account of Nanakana Sahib, the birthplace of Guru Nanak.

889 **PASHCHA-TAP.** (P) Amritsar, KTS, 1903. 28 p.

Repentence.

890 **PATI BRIT DHARAM.** (P) Amritsar, KTS. 1897. 32 p. BTSL

The duty of a faithful wife.

891 **A PEEP INTO SIKHISM.** Amritsar, CKD, 1911. 32 p. BM/IOL

Select verses from the Adi Granth with English translations and explanations.

892 **PRARTHNA WISHE TE HIK MANOHAR.** (SI) Amritsar, KTS, 1906. 48 p. BTSL

A sermon on prayer.

893 **PRAVARON MURI MAI.** (P) Lahore, Sikh Sangat, 1910. 20 p.

Old woman who came back to the family, a tract illustrating the importance of publishing a correct text of the Adi Granth. The Lahore Sikh Sangat printed the work to encourage support for its publication programme.

894 **PREM KAHANI.** (P) Amritsar, KTS, 1912. 48 p. BTSL

A story of love, a novel depicting the life of a rich Sikh widower.

895 **PREM PATOLA.** (P) Amritsar, KTS, 1904. 16 p.

A collection of sacred songs for the moral and religious instruction of women.

896 **PREM PATOLA ARTHAT DO SACHCHE SIDKIAN DA BRITANT.** (P) Amritsar, KTS, 1905. 16 p.

Verses on two faithful Sikh soldiers.

897 **PREM SOMA.** (P) Gujranwala, Khalsa Updeshak College, 1910. 34 p.

Drink of love, story of Guru Arjan and his devoted disciples Musan and Samman.

898 **PRITAM JI.** (P) Amritsar, KTS, 1910. 144 p. IOL

A story illustrative of the idea that one cannot attain communion with God without an ardent love of Him.

899 **PUSHAP PATARI.** (P) 4 Pts. Amritsar, KTS, 1910. 60, 59, 63, 48 p. PPU

Basket of Flowers. Fictitious account of how a gardener, Gyan Singh, and his daughter, Lajvanti, remained true to Sikhism despite trials and hard moments.

900 **PYARE DA PYARA.** (P) Amritsar. KTS, 1910. 120 p. IOL

A story illustrating the love of Sikhs towards their Gurus.

901 **RAHIT NAMA.** (P) Lahore, Mufid-i-Am Press, 1893. 8 p.

Code of conduct for Sikhs.

902 **RAJA JI TE MISS.** (P) Amritsar, KTS, 1899. 106 p.

An imaginary story of an Indian Prince who neglected his duties, took to drinking and wanted to marry a European. Finally a patriotic and loyal Sikh servant brought him back to his senses.

903 **RAJ KUMAR.** (P) Amritsar, KTS, 1905. 22 p. PPU

The Prince, a fable.

904 **RANI RUP KAUR TE TIKKA MANNA SINGH JI DA SANGRAM, ARTHAT JANG MARAULI.** (P) Amritsar, KTS, 1903. 64 p. BM/PPU/IOL

A contest between Rani Rup Kaur and Tikka Manna Singh, or the battle of Marauli.

905 **RASBHINNRA GURPURAB.** (P) Amritsar, KTS, 1915. 93 p. PPU

Background on Sikh festivals.

906 **RIN HATTIA.** (P) Amritsar, KTS, 1904. 65 p.

Death to borrowing, didactic story on predicaments arising from borrowing for extravagant reasons.

907 **ROJDIAN RATAN TE VASAKHI DA GURPURAB.** (P) Amritsar, KTS, 1908. 28 p. IOL

Day to day instructions and the celebration of the Guru's birthday, verses on the difference between Sikhs in the past and present. The author suggests that the old custom of celebrating Sikh holidays should be reinstituted.

908 **SACHCHA GURU.** (P) Amritsar, KTS, 1900. 4 p. BTSL

A true Guru, discussion as to whether Christ or Guru Nanak was the most significant religious leader.

909 **SACHCHA RAH.** (P) Amritsar, KTS, 1900. 16 p.

The right path, essay on Sikh religion.

910 **SACHCHA RAHBAR.** (P) Gujranwala, Bhujanghi Club, Khalsa Updeshak College, 1910. 24 p. PPU

A true guide, commentary on Guru Nanak and Guru Gobind Singh. Appended is an attack on the caste system.

911 **SACHCHE SAJJAN ARTHAT IK WIGRE HUE SARDAR DA SUDHAR.** (P) Amritsar, KTS, 1901. 36 p.

A true gentleman, or reform of a Sikh Sardar who had fallen into evil.

912 **SACHCHI KHETI ARTHAT BHAJAN SIMRAN DA IK UTTAM UPDESH.** (P) Amritsar, KTS, 1899. 16 p.

The true sower or a piece of good advice on devotion to God.

913 **SACH KHAND YATRA.** (P) Amritsar, KTS, 1899. 64 p. BTSL/PPU

A journey to the land of the blessed.

914 **SADA GURPARAB.** (P) Amritsar, KTS, 1908. 16 p. PPU

A description of the celebration of Guru Nanak's birthday.

915 **SADA HAL.** (P) Amritsar, KTS, 1911. 32 p. PPU/IOL

Our condition, essay on the present state of Sikhs and how to reform them.

916 **SADE GHARANDI DASHA.** (P) Amritsar, KTS, 1911. 63 p. PPU/IOL

The condition of our homes, a call for reforms in Sikh family life.

917 **SADE GURAN DA GURPURAB AYA HAI.** (P) Amritsar, KTS, 1906. 40 p.

The birthday of our Guru has come, essay on days sacred to the memory of the Gurus and their celebration.

918 **SADI DARAVANI DASHA.** (P) Amritsar, KTS, 1900. 16 p.

Our terrible state, analysis of the critical condition of the Sikh community.

919 **SAMBODH PATTAR.** (P) Amritsar, Sri Gurmat Press, 1917. 27 p. PPU

Recommendation letters supporting the Panth Khalsa Diwan's publication of the Adi Granth. The tract attempts to refute the charges of the Khalsa Samachar that Teja Singh and his associates omitted several parts. (404, 884)

920 **SANJAM.** (P) 15 Pts. Amritsar, KTS, 1902. 312 p. PPU

Abstinence.

921 **SANSAR PAR HI NARK-SUARG.** (P) Amritsar, KTS, n/d. 76 p. PPU

There is heaven and hell in this world.

922 **SAPHAL GUR PARB.** (P) Amritsar, KTS, 1909. 66 p. IOL

A successful birthday, story of a Sikh

SAPHAL GUR PARB (contd)
lady who through her religious education brought back to Sikhism her brother, a notorious bandit.

923 **SAPTAMI DI BHETA.** (P) Amritsar, KTS, 1905. 32 p. BTSL/IOL
A present for the seventh day, the story of the conversion of a family to Sikhism.

924 **SARAB KALI SRI GURU NANAK DEV JI.** (P) Amritsar, Khalsa Samachar, 1918. 56 p. PPU
Life of Guru Nanak.

925 **SARA GARHI DA JUDH.** (P) Amritsar, KTS, 1899. 16 p. BM/BTSL
Account of the defence of Saragarhi, a fort on the frontier, by Sikh soldiers. Also reprinted in a Sindhi edition: Saragarhi A Jo Jang. Amritsar, KTS, 1905. 16 p. BTSL.

926 **SARDAR BAGH SINGH, FAUJADAR.** (P) Amritsar, KTS. 1910. 17 p.
Verses on Sikh soldiers, demonstrating Sikh loyalty, religious fervour and devotion to duty.

927 **SAT ASAT NIRNAY.** (P) 2/e. Lahore, Vaidraj Dharm Dev, 1915. 32 p.
Discussion of truth and untruth, an account of a debate between Arya Samajists and Sikhs which took place at Kami Pind in the Patiala State.

928 **SAT DHARAM DE RAKHYAK SRI GURU TEGH BAHADUR JI DA JIWAN BRITANT.** (P) Amritsar, KTS, 1914. 31 p.
Life of Guru Tegh Bahadur.

929 **SAT SIDHANT.** (P) Amritsar, Gurmat Granth Pracharak Sabha, 1899. 80 p.
True Principles, tract on Sikh theology.

930 **SAWAIYE SRI MUKH WAK.** (P) Amritsar, Akaljantra Press, 1882. 16 p.
Extracts from the Adi Granth, with an address by Bhai Gurmukh Singh on the necessity of learning Gurmukhi.

931 **SHAHIDGANJ.** (P) Lahore, Mufid-i-Am Press, 1898. 112 p. PPU
Verses on Hindu and Sikh martyrs.

932 **SHAHID NAMA.** (PN) Amritsar, KTS, 1900. 50 p. PPU/IOL
Verses on the martyrdom of Guru Gobind Singh's infant sons.

933 **SHER KHALSA.** (P) Amritsar, Dhyan Singh, 1917. vi,186 p. BM
Poetry on the struggles of Sikh heroes against the Muslims.

934 **SHRIMATI GOLAR KAUR.** (P) Amritsar, Sikh Agency, 1910. 105 p. IOL
Tragedy of early Sikh times in which the hero and heroine undergo great trials at the hands of Muslims.

935 **SHRIMATI RANJIT KAUR.** (P) Amritsar, Charan Singh, 1914. 208 p. BM/IOL
The story of Ranjit Kaur, a Sikh girl who was taken as a slave to Kabul and on escaping was murdered by Pathans.

936 **SHUDHI ARTHAT KHALSA PATAT PAWAN.** (P) Amritsar, Khalsa Baradari Karyasadak Dal, 1909. 178 p. PPU/IOL
Shuddhi or purification of fallen Sikhs, a dialogue between a Sikh in favour of converting men of other religious persuasions to Sikhism and another against it.

937 **SIAPE DA SIAPA.** (P) Amritsar, KTS, 1900. 48 p. BM/PPU
Criticism of siapa, a female custom in the Punjab of holding prolonged mourning meetings at the death of relatives, attended with great displays of grief.

938 **SIDAQ DE BERE PAR.** (P) Lahore, Sikh Hand Bill Committee, 1910. 4 p.
On the ship of truth, an essay on the advantages of total surrender to the will of God.

939 **SIDAQ KHALSA.** (P) Lahore, Laddha Singh, 1911. 252 p. BM
True Sikhs, a metrical narrative of the oppression of Sikhs by Muslim rulers.

940 **SIDAQ SAGAR, GUTKA.** (P) Amritsar, KTS, 1908. 48 p. BTSL/PPU
Commentary on devotional verses of Bhai Gur Das.

941 **SIDQI SHAHID BHAI MANI SINGH JI.** (P) Amritsar, KTS, 1899. 64 p. BTSL
Verses on a Sikh martyr, Bhai Mani Singh.

942 **SIKH HANDBILL.** (P) Lahore, Hand Bill Committee, 1908-1910. 80 p. PPU
Collection of handbills on Sikhism, both historical and contemporary problems.

943 **SIKHKHI TE PANTH UNNATI.** (P) Amritsar, KTS, 1906. 32 p.
Sikhism and its advancement.

944 **SIKH SACHCHI LEI.** (P) Amritsar, KTS, 1903. 26 p.
Story on the theme of Sikh commitment to truth.

945 **SIKH VIDYA DI PARTAL.** (P) Ferozepur, Bhai Takht Singh, 1915. 9 p. 18 charts.

A monumental study of Sikh education, 1913-14. Analysis and statistics arranged by individual institution are given on students, teachers and schools throughout India. Data is based on official reports, censuses, and first-hand research.

946 **SINGHANI PRABODH.** (P) Amritsar, KTS, 1906. 36 p. PPU

Knowledge for Sikh women.

947 **SRI AMRITSARJI PARTHAI BENATI.** (P) Amritsar, KTS, 1909. 20 p. PPU

Background on the Golden Temple and Darbar Sahib, Amritsar, with information on fairs and festivals.

948 **SRI DARBAR SAHIB JI DE SANKHEP HAL.** (P) Amritsar, KTS, 1919. 24 p,

History of the Golden Temple, Amritsar. This short account was followed quickly by a lengthy work, Sri Darbar Sahib. (P) 14 Pts. Amritsar, KTS, 1919. 229 p. PPU

949 **SRI GRANTH SAHIB KYON PARHNA LORIYE.** (P) Amritsar, KTS, 1900. 23 p. PPU

Why it is necessary to read the Granth Sahib.

950 **SRI GURU ANGAD SAHIB JI JIWAN BRITANT.** (P) Amritsar, KTS, 1906. 72 p. BTSL/IOL

Life of Guru Angad.

951 **SRI GURU GOBIND SINGH JI DE UPKAR.** (P) Amritsar, KTS, 1897. 16 p.

The message of Guru Gobind Singh.

952 **SRI GURU GOBIND SINGH JI MUKTI DATE.** (P) Peshawar, Sikh Book Agency, 1914. 34 p.

Story showing how a man can obtain salvation by reciting and acting upon the teachings of the Guru.

953 **SRI GURU GOBIND SINGH JI PATSHAHI 10 DA JIWAN BRITANT.** (P) Amritsar, KTS, 1895. 64 p. PPU

Biography of Guru Gobind Singh, the tenth Sikh Guru.

954 **SRI GURU GRANTH BANI BEURA.** (P) Amritsar, KTS, 1905. 116 p.

A glossary of words in the Adi Granth, with an explanation of musical tunes and tables showing the chronological arrangement of the teachings of the Gurus.

955 **SRI GURU GRANTH KOSH.** (P) Amritsar, KTS, 1900. 236 p.

A glossary of the Adi Granth.

956 **SRI GURU GRANTH SAHIB JI DE BHAGTAN DE JIWANAN PAR KUCHH CHANANEN DIYAN RISHMAN.** (P) Amritsar, KTS, 1904. 24 p.

Account of the lives of those holy men whose sayings are embodied in the Adi Granth.

957 **SRI GURU GRANTH SAHIB VICHCHON CHALANE DE SHABAD.** (P) Amritsar, KTS. 1898. 112 p.

Funeral verses from the Adi Granth with commentary.

958 **SRI GURU GRANTH SAHIB JI VICHCHON LANWAN.** (P) Amritsar, KTS, 1907. 70 p. PPU

The marriage ceramony prescribed by Sikh scriptures, with commentary.

959 **SRI GURU GRANTH SAHIB VICHCHON SHALOK BHAGAT KABIR BHAW PRAKASHNI TIKA SAHIB.** (P) Amritsar, KTS, 1902. 370 p. BTSL

The verses of Kabir extracted from the Adi Granth, with commentary.

960 **SRI GURU HAR RAI JI DA JIWAN BRITANT.** (P) Amritsar, KTS, 1897. 16 p. PPU

Life of Guru Har Rai.

961 **SRI GURU HAR RAI JI DA SANKHEP JIWAN CHARITRA.** (P) Amritsar, Khalsa National Agency, 1910. 32 p.

Verses on the life and work of Guru Har Rai.

962 **SRI GURU KIRPA KATAKHYA YA KHALSA MANODIK.** (P) Amritsar, Gurmat Granth Pracharak Sabha, 1899. 48 p.

Discourse on the grace of the Guru or appeal to the hearts of Sikhs. Essay on the true meaning of what Guru Gobind Singh had to say about giving religious gifts to Sikh priests in preference to Brahmans.

963 **SRI GURU NANAK AGAM.** (P) Amritsar, KTS, 1901. 16 p. BTSL

The advent of Guru Nanak.

964 **SRI GURU RAM DAS JI PATSHAHI CHAUTHI DA JIWAN BRITANT.** (P) Amritsar, KTS, 1897. 23 p. BTSL

Biography of Guru Ram Das, the fourth Sikh Guru.

965 **SRI GURU TEGH BAHADUR JI DA JIWAN BRITANT.** (P) Amritsar, KTS, 1895, 32 p. PPU

Biography of Guru Tegh Bahadur.

966 **SRI JAP JI SAHIB ARTHAN SAMET.** (P) Amritsar, KTS, 1899. 100 p.

Japji Sahib, with commentary.

967 **STORIES OF BABA NANAK.** Lahore, Sikh Tract Society, 1919. 18 p. KC

968 **SAUDAL SIKHIA.** (P) Amritsar, KTS, 1909. 47 p. PPU

Interesting advice, nine short stories with various morals and messages concerning conduct, translated into Panjabi from English sources.

969 **SUBHE DI SAIR.** (P) Amritsar, KTS, 1900. 64 p. BTSL

A walk in the morning, didactic verses exhorting Sikhs to study their sacred books and regulate their lives in accordance with the teachings of the Gurus.

970 **SUDESHI NUNH SARSARI NAZAR.** (P) Amritsar, KTS, 1911. 47 p. BM

A vivid description of the mistreatment of a daughter-in-law in her new home, and the evil consequences that arise.

971 **SUKHWATI KE CHINTAMATI ARTHAT BAL BIWAH DE DUKHRE.** (P) Amritsar, KTS, 1901. 30 p. PPU

A dialogue on the evils of early marriage between two Sikh women, Sukhwati and Chintamati.

972 **SUNDAR ISTRI TE SOHNA MAHAL.** (P) Amritsar, KTS, 1907. 18 p.

The beautiful woman and an attractive palace, an allegory describing how happiness and eternal life—the palace and the lady—can be obtained in three ways : devotion to God, charity, and service for the public good.

973 **SURBIRTA.** (P) Lahore, Khalsa Agency, 1902. 12 p.

Chivalry, account of the fight between Bhai Bachittra Singh and an elephant at the battle of Anandpur.

974 **TARIKH MUQADAMA KHALSA PANTH KI HAQIQAT.** (U) Lahore, Lala Ram Lal, 1914. 32 p. BTSL

Proceedings of a case against Bishambar Datt and Raunaq Ram for editing an anti-Sikh book, Khalsa Panth Ki Haqiqat. (554)

975 **THE TEACHINGS OF NANAK, RETURN GOOD FOR EVIL.** Rawalpindi, Royal Press, 1911. 18 p. PPU

Discussion of Sikh views on charity and retribution.

976 **TIN KUNJIAN ARTHAT SUKHI VASSAN DE SACHCHE DHANG.** (P) Amritsar, KTS, 1899. 16 p.

Three keys, or how to lead a happy life.

977 **UCHCH JIWAN.** (P) 2 Pts. Amritsar KTS, 1916. 82 p. PPU

Discourse for Sikhs on a virtuous life.

978 **UTTAM UPDESH.** (P) Amritsar, KTS 1903. 30 p.

A good piece of advice, comments on the history and present condition of Sikhism. The author compares Sikh educational efforts with those of the Japanese and challenges Sikhs to educate themselves, particularly Sikh women. Social evils such as drinking and reliance on moneylenders also are denounced, and the essay closes with an appeal for the use of Panjabi throughout the Punjab.

979 **UTH BABA, AJJA TERI WARHE GANDH HAI.** (P) Amritsar, KTS, 1909. 35 p. PPU/IOL

Oh Baba get up, this is your birthday, a story on the degradation and revival of the Sikh religion.

980 **UTTAM SIKHYAN.** (P) Amritsar, KTS, 1911. 47 p.

The best advice on how to lead a healthy life and acquire knowledge.

981 **VACHITRA SAPNE.** (P) Amritsar, KTS, 1910. 44 p. BTSL

Wonderful dreams, fictitious account on the attainment of morality from dreams.

982 **VIDYA DA PRACHAR HONA ZARURI HAI.** (P) Peshawar, Sikh Book Agency, 1912. 4 p. BTSL

Essay on the necessity of spreading education among Sikhs.

983 **WADHA GHALU GHARA.** (P) Amritsar, KTS, 1905. 24 p. BTSL/PPU

Description of Sikh opposition to Muslim invaders from Afghanistan.

984 **WAH, BHAIJI, WAH.** (P) Lahore, Bombay Press, 1910. 8 p. IOL

A dialogue between two Sikhs—one ignorant and the other well-versed in religious matters—showing that a nation can rise by paying due regard to its religion and by promoting a desire for social helpfulness.

985 **ZAINA DA VIRLAP.** (P) Amritsar, KTS, 1913. 64 p. PPU

The pleas of the wife of the Nawab of Sirhind for pity on the sons of Guru Gobind Singh, and her lamentations on their martyrdom.

SECTION 3

SIKH INSTITUTIONAL PUBLICATIONS

SECTION 3

SIKH INSTITUTIONAL PUBLICATIONS

This section consists of reports and publications pertaining to Sikh institutions. Items are arranged alphabetically by the name of organization, followed by its location. Additional information on location, such as district, has been placed in parentheses. Because Sikh organizations often were controversial and generated a secondary literature, extensive cross-references to items in other sections have been provided. Entries follow the pattern introduced in the first section. The reader also is referred to the bibliographic discussion in the preface and survey of the period in the introduction.

The presentation of institutional material involves several problems. The first, variation in spelling, has been met by standardizing the spelling of organizations and place names according to current usage in West Pakistan, Punjab State and Haryana. Titles are reproduced as they appear on title pages or in British catalogues except for shortened titles of annual reports. All reports are spelled "report" despite innumerable Panjabi variations. Another difficulty relating to Sikh organizations is that they changed over time, merged with each other, or adopted new names. The Bhasaur Singh Sabha, for example, sometimes maintained a separate identity and sometimes served as the nucleus for the Panch Khalsa Diwan. No attempt has been made to account for these institutional variations. Rather, the bibliographic entries follow the references in the title page or British catalogues. Finally, annotation in the section has been limited because many items do not require extensive commentary. For example, annual reports usually contain similar information—financial statements and a survey of activities during the period covered by the item. For further discussion of the material in the reports, see the survey of organizations and their literature in the introduction.

The following list contains terms common in titles and their English equivalents:

amdan	income, contribution
diwan	Sikh meeting, also used as the name of Sikh associations
kharch	expenditures
mahavidyala	high school, college
niyam, upniyam	rules, bylaws, regulations
mul sutra	principles, rules
pathshala	school
salana	annual
updeshak	preacher, missionary

Sikh Institutional Publications

986 **ABCHALNAGAR SAHIB, Nander (Deccan) :** Report (1911). (P) Amritsar, Wazir Hind Press, 1911. 15 p.

Financial statement of the Gurdwara where Guru Gobind Singh died in 1708.

987 **BABA BAKALA GURDWARA COMMITTEE, Amritsar :** Salana Report (1905-6). (P) Amritsar, Hukam Singh, 1907. 30 p. PPU

988 _____ : Dusre Varhe Report (1906-7). (P) Amritsar, Hukam Singh, 1909. 24 p. BTSL

989 _____ : Panjven Ate Chheven Sal Di Report (1909-10). (P) Amritsar, Hukam Singh, 1911. 38 p. BTSL/PPU

990 _____ : Salana Report (1917-18). (P) Amritsar, Wazir Hind Press, 1918. 72 p.

991 **BASAITH PRACHAR COMMITTEE, Gujranwala :** Basithan Nun Bachao. (P) Gujranwala, Basaith Prachar Committee, 1913. 16 p.

Appeal for missionary work among members of a depressed class in Kashmir, the Basith.

992 **BEDI YOUNG MEN'S ASSOCIATION Dera Baba Nanak (Gurdaspur) :** Report. (U) Gurdaspur, 1909. 22 p.

993 **BHUJANGAN ORIENTAL COLLEGE, Jaspalon (Ludhiana) :** Niyam. (P) Amritsar, Sri Gurmat Press, 1919. 8 p.

994 _____ : Report (1917-18). (P) Lahore, Managing Committee, 1919. 18 p. BTSL

995 _____ : Report (1919). (P) Lahore, Managing Commitee, 1920. 21 p. BTSL

996 _____ : Salana Diwan Da Samachar. (P) Lahore, Managing Committee, 1918. 8 p. BTSL

Information on the annual meeting of the College, 1918.

997 **CENTRAL KHALSA HOSPITAL, Tarn Taran :** Pahila Report (1915-16). (P) Tarn Taran, Dr. Harnam Singh, 1916. 18 p. PPU

998 _____ : Report (1917-18). (P) Tarn Taran, Dr. Harnam Singh, 1918. 18 p. BTSL

999 **CENTRAL KHALSA ORPHANAGE, Amritsar :** Anarth Pralap. (P) Amritsar, CKD, 1913. 4 p.

Useless crying, an appeal for funds in verse. (372)

1000 _____ : Central Khalsa Yatimkhana Amritsar Da Sakim. (P) Amritsar, CKD, 1909. 18 p. PPU

Scheme for improving the orphanage.

1001 _____ : Niyam. (P) Amritsar, CKD, 1906. 8 p. PPU

1002 _____ : Report (1906-7). (P) Amritsar, CKD, 1907. 43 p. BTSL

1003 _____ : Report (1912-13). (P) Amritsar, CKD, 1914. 94 p. PPU

1004 _____ : Report Aur Salana Imtihan Par Prikha Dian Ravan. (1908-9). (P) Amritsar, CKD, 1909. BTSL

Report and suggestions for the annual examination.

1005 **CHIEF KHALSA DIWAN, Amritsar:** Dharmsalan Te Gurdwarian Di Rahin Vidya Prachar Di Skim Te National Fund De Skulan Sanbandhi Niyam. (P) Amritsar, CKD, 1915. 36 p.

Scheme for imparting elementary education to the masses through Gurdwaras and dharmsalas, and rules for schools maintained from the National Fund of the Educational Committee, Chief Khalsa Diwan.

1006 _____ : Mul Sutra. (P) Amritsar, CKD, 1902. 18p: Mul Sutra. (P) Amritsar, CKD, 1906. 29 p. PPU: Mul Sutra. (P) Amritsar, CKD, 1918. 34 p. BTSL

The first item is a set of draft principles and regulations; the latter items are editions of the principles and regulations.

1007 _____ : Report (1902-3). (P) Amritsar, CKD, 1904. 39 p. PPU

1008 _____ : Report (1903-4). (P) Amritsar, CKD, 1904. 63 p. PPU

1009 _____ : Report (1904-5). (P) Amritsar, CKD, 1905. 37 p. PPU

1010 _____ : Report (1905-6). (P) Amritsar, CKD, n/d. 26 p. PPU

1011 _____ : Report (1909). (P) Amritsar, CKD, n/d. 70 p. PPU

1012 _____ : Report (1910-11). (P) Amritsar, CKD, 1911. 70 p.

1013 _____ : Report (1913). (P) Amritsar, CKD, 1915, 108 p. BTSL

1014 _____ : Report (1914). (P) Amritsar, CKD, n/d. 72 p. PPU

1015 _____ : Report (1915). (P) Amritsar, CKD, 1916. 85 p. PPU

1016 _____ : Report (1916). (P) Amritsar, CKD, 1917. 82 p. PPU

1017 _____ : Report (1917). (P) Amritsar, CKD, 1918. 141p. PPU

1018 _____ : Report (1917-18). (P) Amritsar, CKD, 1918. 82 p. PPU

1019 _____ : Report (1918-20). (P) Amritsar, CKD, 1922. 293 p.

1020 **CHIEF KHALSA DIWAN, Sind :** Balochastan Pracharak Jathe Di Report. (P) Amritsar, Wazir Hind Press, 1904. 12 p.

Report of the Diwan's preaching mission to Baluchistan.

1021 **DHARM PRACHARAK COMMITTEE (PREACHING COMMITTEE), Baddon (Hoshiarpur):** Niyam. (P) Baddon, Bhai Parduman Singh, 1919. 8 p.

1022 **DITT SINGH KANYA PATHSHALA, Rupar:** Benati. (P) Amritsar, Gurbakhsh Singh, 1907. 24 p.

Appeal for funds, with appended contribution lists and correspondence.

1023 _____ : General Te Parbandhak Kameti De Kaide. (P) Rupar, Managing Committee, n/d. 15 p, BTSL

Rules and regulations of the managing committee for the girls' school.

1024 _____ : Report. (P) Amritsar, Wazir Hind Press, 1909. 24 p. BTSL/PPU

Supplementary bulletin to the Khalsa Samachar, May 1909. Discusses history of the school, which was founded on the suggestion of Sikhs in Malaya in memory of Gyani Ditt Singh. Survey of operations and contributions, with letters proposing that a branch school be located near Ambala.

1025 _____ : Report (1907). (P) Rupar, Managing Committee, 1908. 24 p. BTSL

1026 **DOABA KHALSA HIGH SCHOOL, Jullundur City:** Niyam Te Upniyam. (P) Jullundur City, Manager, 1915. 24 p.

1027 _____ : Report (1915-16). (P) Jullundur City, Manager, 1917. 15 p.

1028 **DOAB SIKH DHARM PRACHARAK SABHA, Jullundur City:** Mul Sutra. (P) Amritsar, Wazir Hind Press, 1908. 12 p.

Rules and organizational background on the Sabha, founded in June 1908 to prepetuate the memory of the Gurus, to foster authentic Sikh rituals and to spread Sikh brotherhood. Sahjdhari Sikhs were included in its membership, politics was excluded. Officers for 1908 were Parduman Singh, President, and Amar Singh, Secretary.

1029 **EDUCATIONAL COMMITTEE, Burma:** Tisri Report (1913-15). (P) Amritsar, Bhai Vir Singh, 1916. 15 p.

1030 **EDUCATIONAL COMMITTEE, CHIEF KHALSA DIWAN, Amritsar:** Aijukeshanal Kameti Chief Khalsa Diwan De Sanbandhat Ashram Lai Dharmik Vidya. (P) Amritsar, EC, 1914. 12 p.

Scheme for spreading religious education to the ashrams affiliated with the Educational Committee.

1031 _____ : Report (1909-10). (P) Amritsar, EC, 1910. 42 p. BTSL/PPU

1032 _____ : Report (1910). (P) Amritsar, EC, n/d. 71 p. PPU

1033 _____ : Report (1911). (P) Amritsar. EC, n/d. 48 p. PPU

1034 _____ : Report (1912). (P) Amritsar, EC, n/d. 74 p. PPU

1035 _____ : Report (1913). (P) Amritsar, EC, 1914. 95 p. PPU

1036 _____ : Report (1914-15). (P) Amritsar, EC, 1915. 70 p. PPU

1037 _____ : Report (1915-16). (P) Amritsar, EC, n/d. 76 p. PPU

1038 _____ : Report (1916-17). (P) Amritsar, EC, n/d. 85 p. PPU

1039 _____ : Report (1917-18). (P) Amritsar, EC, n/d. 67 p. PPU

1040 _____ : Report (1918-19). (P) Amritsar, EC, n/d. 101 p. PPU

1041 _____ : Report (1919). (P) Amritsar, EC, 1920. 81 p. BTSL/PPU

1042 **EDUCATIONAL CONFERENCE :** Aitki Zarur Chalange. (P) Ferozepur, Reception Committee, 1915. 4 p. BTSL

Surely we shall go this time, an appeal for large Sikh attendance at the Eighth Educational Conference (1915).

1043 _____ : Ideals of the Sikh Educational Conference. Amritsar, EC, 1914. 16 p.

Short history and summary of the Conference's programme, compiled by Bhai Inder Singh.

1044 _____ : Kanfrans. Ton Shaiharan Te Pindan Nun Labh. (P) Amritsar, EC, 1916. 8 p. BTSL

Benefits to the cities and villages from the Conference.

1045 _____ : Mul Sutra. (P) Amritsar, EC, 1914. 24 p.

1046 _____ : The Proceedings of the First Sikh Educational Conference. (P) Amritsar, EC, 1908. 175 p. PPU

1047 _____ : Report (Second, 1909). (P) Amritsar, EC, 1909. 186 p. PPU

1048 _____ : Report (Third, 1910). (P) Amritsar, EC, n/d. 132 p. BTSL/PPU

1049 _____ : Report (Fourth, 1911). (P) Amritsar, EC, n/d. 184 p. PPU

1050 _____ : Report (Seventh, 1914). (P) Amritsar, EC, n/d. 19 p. PPU

1051 _____ : Report (Eighth, 1915). (P) Amritsar. EC, 1915. 23 p. PPU

1052 _____ : Report (Ninth, 1916). (P) Amritsar, EC, n/d. 23 p. PPU

1053 _____ : Report (Tenth, 1917). (P) Amritsar, EC, n/d. 28 p. PPU

1054 _____ : Report (Eleventh, 1918). (P) Amritsar, EC, n/d. 24 p. PPU

1055 _____ : Rules of the Constitution of the Sikh Educational Conference. Amritsar, EC, 1914. 4 p. BTSL

1056 **GOLDEN TEMPLE, Amritsar :** Dastur-ul-Amal Gurdwara-i-Sri Amritsarji. (U) Amritsar, Manager, Golden Temple, 1899. 20 p.

Rules of management compiled by Bhai Suchet Singh.

1057 _____ : Report Jaman Kharch (1906). (P) Amritsar, Gurbakhsh Singh, 1907. 14 p. BTSL

Report of income and expenditure of construction at the Golden Temple.

1058 _____ : Report Jaman Kharch (1907-8). (P) Amritsar, Gurbakhsh Singh, 1908. 12 p. BTSL

1059 _____ : Report Verva Amdan Ate Kharch (1910-11). (P) Amritsar, Manager, Golden Temple, n/d. 7 p. PPU

1060 _____ : Report Verva Amdan Te Kharch (1918-19). (P) Amritsar, Manager, Golden Temple, 1919. 7 p. BTSL

1061 _____ : Statements of Accounts, 1912-1913. Amritsar, Manager, Golden Temple, 1914. 6 p.

1062 **GURDWARA BARI SANGAT, Calcutta :** Dastur-ul-Amal Gurdwara Sangat. (P) Calcutta, Gurdwara Committee. 1915. 16 p.

Rules for the upkeep and management of the Gurdwara.

1063 **GURMUKHI KANYA PATHSHALA, Lahore :** Pahili Report (1906-13). (P) Lahore, Singh Sabha, 1914. 29 p. BTSL

1064 **GURU ARJAN CLUB, KHALSA BOARDING HOUSE, Lyallpur :** Niyam Upniyam. (P) Lyallpur, Guru Arjan Club, 1914. 7 p.

1065 **GURU NANAK CLUB, Amritsar :** Rules and Regulations of Sri Guru Nanak Club, Khalsa College, Amritsar (1907). Amritsar, Guru Nanak Club, 1908. 8 p.

The constitution was enacted in a general meeting on May 12, 1907. The aims of the club included religious instruction, mutual help, and study of the lives of the Gurus.

1066 _____ : **GURU NANAK DHARMSALA, Gujranwala :** Report (1913-14). (P) Gujranwala, Singh Sabha, 1914. 4 p.

1067 **GURU NANAK KANYA PATHSHALA, Amritsar :** Niyam Upniyam. (P) Amritsar, School Committee, 1917. 12 p.

1068 _____ : Report (1918). (P) Amritsar, School Committee, 1919. 8 p.

1069 **GURU NANAK KANYA PATHSHALA, Quetta :** Prabandh De Qaide. (P) Quetta, Managing Committee, 1908. 8 p.

Rules and constitution of the school.

1070 _____ : Report (1906-7). (P) Quetta, Managing Committee, 1908. 32 p.

1071 **GURU NANAK KHALSA COLLEGE, Gujranwala :** Report (1916-19). (P) Gujranwala, Khalsa Committee, 1919. 66 p. BTSL/PPU

1072 **KANYA MAHA VIDYALA, Ferozepur :** Niyam Upniyam Aur Sankhep Itihas. (P) Ferozepur, Manager, 1912. 8, 8, 35 p. BTSL

Rules and history of the school, with appended information on courses and required texts.

1073 _____ : Pyare Viran Te Bhainan Agge Bhain Dei Fariyad. (P) Ferozepur, Bhai Takht Singh, 1910. 20 p. BTSL

Verses on the importance of female education.

1074 _____ : Report (1906-7). (P) Ferozepur, Bhai Takht Singh, 1907. 8 p. BTSL

1075 _____ : Report (1913). (P) Ferozepur, Manager, 1914. 28 p. BTSL/PPU

KANYA MAHA VIDYALA, Ferozepur (contd)

1076 _____ : Report (1914). (P) Ferozepur, Bhai Takht Singh, 1915. 41 p. BTSL/PPU

1077 _____ : Sikh Kanya Maha Vidyala Firozpur Sanbandhi Parsanasa Pattar, Panthak Ashram. (P) Ferozepur, Bhai Takht Singh, 1911. 74 p. BTSL/PPU

Recommendation letters on the school and a short history, with comments on female education among Punjabi Sikhs.

1078 _____ : Truth and Bare Truth about the Sikh Kanya Maha Vidyala, Ferozepore. Ferozepur, Manager, 1915. 12 p.

Information on the school and a plea for support, compiled by Bhai Sohan Singh.

1079 **KANYA MAHA VIDYALA, Rawalpindi :** Report (1908). (P) Amritsar, Wazir Hind Press, 1908. 4 p. BTSL

1080 **KANYA PATHSHALA, Chunian (Ambala) :** Pahli Report (1907-8). (P) Chunian, Managing Committee, 1909. 40 p.

1081 _____ : Sikh Kanniyan Pathshala Chuniana De Mukhtasar Britant. (P) Chunian, Managing Committee, 1908. 4 p.

Brief account of the Sikh girls school, compiled by the Secretary of the Managing Committee, Bhai Gurbakhsh Singh.

1082 **KHALSA BIRADRI, Amritsar :** Niyam Upniyam. (P) Amritsar, Khalsa Biradri, 1908. 16 p. BTSL

1083 **KHALSA COLLEGE, Amritsar :** Report (1902-3). (P) Amritsar, Sunder Singh Majithia, 1903. 24 p.

1084 _____ : Report (1903-4). (P) Amritsar, Sunder Singh Majithia, 1904. 24 p.

1085 **KHALSA DIWAN, Amritsar :** Niyam Arthat Qanun Khalsa Diwan. (P) Amritsar, Gobind Press, 1887. 20 p.

1086 _____ : Report (1890). (P) Amritsar, Khalsa College Committee, 1890. 16 p.

Report includes discussion on the founding of Khalsa College, Amritsar.

1087 **KHALSA DASWAND COMMITTEE, Patiala :** Report (1906-7). (P) Patiala, Sardar Bachitra Singh, 1907. 20 p. BTSL

Report of a committee established to encourage tithing among Sikhs. The funds were to be spent on religious and educational projects. Rules and constitution of the committee are appended.

1088 **KHALSA DIWAN, Bhasaur :** Gurmat Ate Phaisle. (P) Bhasaur, Teja Singh, 1901. 16 p. IOL

Religious discussion and resolutions at the annual conference, February 23-25, 1901.

1089 _____ : Salana Diwan Samachar. (P) Bhasaur, Teja Singh, 1917. 24 p.

Announcements and draft resolutions for the 1917 annual conference.

1090 **KHALSA DIWAN, Bunga Ramgarhia (Amritsar) :** Karvai Khalsaji De Diwan Di Jo Panth Khalsa Valon Bunga Ramgarhian Vich 10 November 1901 Nu Hoia. (P) Amritsar, Wazir Hind Press, 1901. 22 p. BTSL

Report of the conference, with lists of members of sub-committees and delegates selected for the meeting by different Singh Sabhas.

1091 **KHALSA DIWAN, Dhan Pothohar (Rawalpindi) :** Report (1913). (P) Amritsar, Wazir Hind Press, 1905. 26 p. BTSL

1092 **KHALSA DIWAN, Ferozepur:** Gurmate Ate Faisale. (P) Ferozepur, Bhai Takht Singh, 1901. 8 p. BTSL

Religious discussion and resolutions at a conference on July 14-15, 1901.

1093 _____ : Gurmate Ate Faisale. (P) Bhasaur, Singh Sabha, 1901. 8 p. BTSL

Review of the proceedings of the 1901 meeting, with suggestions for amending and implementing the resolutions.

1094 _____ : Report. (P) Ferozepur, Bhai Takht Singh, 1904. 12 p.

Proceedings and resolutions at a conference on September 24-25th, 1904.

1095 **KHALSA DIWAN, Gujranwala :** Report (1908-10). (P) Gujranwala, Khalsa Diwan, 1910. 35 p. PPU

1096 **KHALSA DIWAN, Jullundur:** Gurmate. (E,P) Peshawar, Gurmukhi Press, 1911. 8 p.

Message of Sikhism, the proceedings of a religious meeting at Jullundur on July 31st and August 1st, 1909.

1097 **KHALSA DIWAN, Lahore :** Masawwada Qanuni Nem Khalsa Diwan. (P) Lahore, Bhai Gurmukh Singh. 1884. 37 p.

Draft rules and regulations of the Diwan.

1098 **KHALSA DIWAN, Lyallpur Colony :** Tije Report (1907-8). (P) Lyallpur, Khalsa Diwan, 1908. 26 p.

1099 **KHALSA DIWAN, Machi Singh (Montgomery) :** Report (1905). (P) Amritsar, Wazir Hind Press, 1905. 8 p.

1100 **KHALSA DIWAN, Manjha :** Niyam Upniyam. (P) Kairon, Singh Sabha, 1904. 15 p.

1101 _____ : Report (1904-6). (P) Kairon, Sham Singh, 1906. 16 p. PPU

1102 _____ : Report (1906-8). (P) Amritsar, CKD, 1908. 38 p. PPU

1103 _____ : Tisri Report Aur Pahili Report, Sub-Committee, Chief Khalsa Diwan. (P) Amritsar, CKD, 1909. 18 p.

Third report on the Diwan and the first report of the Chief Khalsa Diwan's Manjha Sub-Committee (1908-9).

1104 **KHALSA DIWAN, Malerkotla:** Amdan Kharch Te Report, Salana Diwan. (P) Ludhiana, Army News Press, 1907. 8 p.

Report on proceedings and finances of an annual meeting at the Malerkotla Gurdwara, January 1907.

1105 **KHALSA DIWAN, Mastuane :** Report Khalsa Ji De Diwan Di Jo Mastuane Vich 14, 15, 16 March 1907 Nu Hoia. (P) Mastuana, Sant Teja Singh, 1911. 36 p. BTSL/PPU

Report of a conference on Sikhism and the condition of gurdwaras.

1106 **KHALSA DIWAN, Nabha :** Niyam. (P) Nabha, Durga Press, 1906. 18 p. PPU

1107 **KHALSA DIWAN, Vancouver :** Report (1906-9). (P) Amritsar, Wazir Hind Press, n/d. 14 p. BTSL

1108 **KHALSA GURMUKHI PRIMARY SCHOOL, Valtoha (Amritsar) :** Report (1914-15). (P) Valtoha, Sardar Khushal Singh, n/d. 12 p.

1109 **KHALSA HIGH SCHOOL, Ambala City :** Niyam. (P) Amritsar, Punjab Commercial Press, 1917. 16 p.

1110 **KHALSA HIGH SCHOOL, Damdama Sahib (Patiala State) :** Niyaman Da Kharara. (P) Damdama, Manager, 1916. 18 p.

Draft rules for administration of the School.

1111 **KHALSA HIGH SCHOOL, Gujranwala :** Khalsa High School, Gujranwala, Te Sri Hazur Lat Sahib Bahadur. (P) Gujranwala, Khalsa Committee, 1912. 32 p.

Account of the laying of the foundation stone performed by the Punjab Lieutenant Governor.

1112 **KHALSA HIGH SCHOOL, Lahore :** Report (1914). (P) Lahore, Mufid-i-Am Press, n/d. 24 p.

1113 **KHALSA HIGH SCHOOL, Lyallpur :** Report (1914-15). (P) Lyallpur, Managing Committee, 1915. 32 p.

1114 _____ : Report (1915-16). (P) Lyallpur, Managing Committee, 1917. 28 p.

1115 **KHALSA PRACHARAK VIDYALA, Tarn Taran :** Dusri Report (1907-8). (P) Amritsar, Santokh Singh, 1908. 24 p. PPU

1116 _____ : Pahili Che Masak Report (1906-7). (P) Amritsar, Managing Committee, 1907. 16 p. PPU

1117 **KHALSA PRESS, Lahore:** Report (1895-1900). (P) Lahore, Khalsa Press, 1901. 8 p.

Financial statement, with information on publications.

1118 **KHALSA SABHA, Nabha:** Niyam. (P) Lahore, Khalsa Press, 1897. 16 p. PPU

1119 **KHALSA SCHOOL, Gujranwala :** Qaw'id. (P) Gujranwala, Qaumi Press, 1895. 8 p.

1120 **KHALSA TRACT SOCIETY, Amritsar:** Report (1897). (P) Amritsar, KTS, 1898. 80 p. BTSL

This, and subsequent reports, contain information on the constitution and operation of the society, its finances, distribution system, and contributors. Brief comments on tracts published during the year often are included.

1121 _____ : Report (1899). (P) Amritsar, KTS, 1900. 78 p. PPU

1122 _____ : Report (1901). (P) Amritsar, KTS, 1902. 48 p.

1123 _____ : Report (1902). (P) Amritsar, KTS, 1903. 54 p. PPU

1124 **NAM DEV SHRIMONI DIWAN, Lahore:** Report Langar. (P) Lahore, Langar Committee, 1919. 14. p.

Finances of a Sikh free kitchen in Lahore 1917-19.

1125 **PANCH KHALSA DIWAN, Bhasaur:** Dashera Bhav Panth Jagawa. (P) Bhasaur, Panch Khalsa Diwan, 1916. 39 p. PPU

Expression of disappointment at the closing of the Diwan's girls school, and an appeal for funds to reopen it. Teja Singh probably wrote the tract.

1126 _____ : Dharmak Kanfrans De Tisre Varshak Samagam Di Report. (P) Bhasaur, Teja Singh, 1918. 30 p. PPU

Report of the third annual religious conference (twenty-fourth diwan of the Panch Khalsa Diwan), held at Bhasaur in 1918.

PANCH KHALSA DIWAN, Bhasaur: (contd)

1127 _____ : Diwan De Salana Samachar. (P) Bhasaur, Teja Singh, 1903. 31 p. PPU

Survey of activities, 1903.

1128 _____ : Khalsa Rahit Parkash. (P) Bhasaur, Panch Khalsa Diwan, 1908. 132 p. BM/PPU

A statement on the essence of Sikh religion and style of life by a militant reform organization.

1129 _____ : Panth Hitkari Maharaja Ripduman Singh Ji Sahib Bahadur Nabha Pati Ji Vidya Bhandar—Panch Khand Vikhe Upkarta Sahit Darshan. (P) Lahore, Punjab Steam Press, 1918. 8 p.

Review of the visit of the Maharaja of Nabha to the Diwan's school.

1130 _____ : Salana Diwan Sanbandhi Samachar. (P) 2 Pts. Bhasaur, Teja Singh, 1916. 30, 31 p. BTSL/PPU

Resolutions and proceedings, 1916.

1131 _____ : Samachar Ate Apil (1910). (P) Bhasaur, Teja Singh, 1910. 47 p. BTSL

Rules and regulations, with a brief account of the Diwan and its girls school.

1132 _____ : Vidiya Bhandar Sanbandhi Skim Ate Niyamavali. (P) Bhasaur, Teja Singh, n/d. (c 1908). 16 p. PPU

Educational projects of the Diwan, with revised draft rules for the girls school.

1133 **PARVAR SAHAIK DEG, Gujranwala:** Anand Vivah Sahaik Fund De Sankhep Ate Sadharan Samachar. (P) Ferozepur, Bhai Takht Singh, 1910. 10 p.

Prospectus of a special fund begun for the exclusive use of Sikhs.

1134 _____ : Sikh Parvar Sahaik Deg, Samachar. (P) Gujranwala, Teja Singh, 1909. 12 p. PPU

News about the Sikh Family Relief Fund.

1135 **PURANA KHALSA DIWAN, Gujranwala:** Chauthe Sal Di Karravai Report. (P) Lahore, Bombay Machine Press, 1911. 16 p. BTSL

Report on the finances and operation of the Sikh association, fourth year (1910-11).

1136 **RAMGARHIA SABHA, Punjab :** Appeal. Amritsar, Ramgarhia Sabha, 1918. 4 p.

A call for members of the Ramgarhia community to attend the annual conference and to uplift themselves.

1137 _____ : Ramgarhia Sabha Panjab De 7th Session Di Karvai Report. (P) Amritsar, Sundar Singh, 1911. 15 p. PPU

Report of the annual conference held at Amritsar, on April 13, 1911.

1138 **SINGH SABHA, Abbottabad :** Panth Wich Halchali Paunwali Afwah Wichar. (P) Amritsar, Singh Sabha, 1915. 4 p.

Rumours and thoughts creating confusion in the Panth, a refutation of the charge that the Sabha had altered portions of the Granth Sahib.

1139 **SINGH SABHA, Agra :** Athven Salana Diwan Report. (P) Amritsar, Wazir Hind Press, 1905. 8 p. BTSL

Report of the eighth conference, January 27-29, 1905.

1140 **SINGH SABHA, Ambala Cantoment:** Updeshak Report. (P) Lahore, Khalsa Press, 1901. 4 p.

Report of the Sabha's missionary programme, 1900-1

1141 **SINGH SABHA, Amritsar :** Niyam. (P) Amritsar, Chashma-i-Nur Press, 1890. 16 p,

1142 **SINGH SABHA, Bhasaur :** Gurmate Ate Faisale. (P) Bhasaur, Teja Singh, 1904. 16 p.

Religious discussions and decisions of the Sabha.

1143 _____ : Khalsa Panth Sevki Vich Zaruri Bentian. (P) Bhasaur, Teja Singh, 1904. 13 p. BTSL

An urgent appeal to the helpers of the Panth, request for financial assistance.

1144 _____ : Salana Report (1897-8). (P) Bhasaur, Teja Singh, 1898. 8 p.

1145 _____ : Sanbodh Pattar. (P) Bhasaur, Singh Sabha, 1917. 24 p. PPU

Reply to editorials in the Khalsa Samachar which supposedly criticized the Sabha and Sikh activities in general.

1146 _____ : Vir Sudhar Pattar. (P) Bhasaur, Teja Singh, 1904. 73 p. PPU/IOL

The proceedings of the eighth and ninth annual conferences of Sabha, 1903-4.

1147 **SINGH SABHA, Bhatinda :** Do Salana Jor Mel. (P) Amritsar, Wazir Hind Press, 1905. 4 p.

Report on a bi-annual conference, March 14, 1905.

1148 **SINGH SABHA, Ferozepur :** Khalsa Fund Report (1900-2). (P) Ferozepur, Bhai Takht Singh, 1902. 21 p. BTSL

Financial statement of fund which was

utilized for education and preaching by members of the Sabha.

1149 _____ : Khalsa Fund Report (1902-3). (P) Ferozepur, Bhai Takht Singh, 1903. 22 p. BTSL

1150 _____ : Khalsa Fund Report (1903-4). (P) Ferozepur, Bhai Takht Singh, 1904. 38 p. BTSL

1151 _____ : Khalsa Fund Report (1904-5). (P) Ferozepur. Bhai Takht Singh, 1905. 46 p. BTSL/KC

1152 _____ : Khalsa Fund Report (1905-6). (P) Amritsar, Wazir Hind Press, 1906. 72 p. BTSL

1153 _____ : Khalsa Fund Report (1906-7). (P) Amritsar, Wazir Hind Press, 1907. 88 p. BTSL

1154 **SINGH SABHA, Gharjakh (Gujranwala) :** Report (1904). (P) Gujranwala, Dr. Mahan Singh, 1904. 16 p. PPU

Report on the activities of the Sabha, with information on its updeshak school and orphange.

1155 _____ : Report (1904-5). (P) Gujranwala, Dr. Mahan Singh, 1905. 39 p. PPU

1156 _____ : Report (1908). (P) Amritsar, Wazir Hind Press, 1909. 16p. BTSL

1157 **SINGH SABHA, Hong Kong :** Report (1906-7). Hong Kong, Singh Sabha, 1907. 24p. BTSL/KC/PPU

1158 _____ : Report (1907-8). (P) Hong Kong, Singh Sabha, 1908. 12p. BTSL/PPU

1159 _____ : Report (1909-10). (P) Amritsar, Singh Sabha, 1910. 16p. PPU

1160 **SINGH SABHA, Hoshiarpur :** Salana Diwan Di Report. (P) Hoshiarpur, Singh Sabha, 1906. 8p.

Report of the annual conference, June 2-4, 1906.

1161 **SINGH SABHA, Kanjla (Patiala) :** Salana Report Karravai Singh Sabha Kanjla Riasat Patiala Babat Dursa Salana Jormel. (P) Lahore, Khalsa Press, 1899. 8p. PPU

Report of the second annual conference, February 25-26, 1899. A supplement to the Khalsa Akhbar, March 17, 1899.

1162 **SINGH SABHA, Lahore :** Chetavni Jo Sri Guru Singh Sabha Lahaur De Salana Diwan Di Khushi Vikhe. (P) Lahore, Sri Gurmat Press, 1907. 8p. PPU

Warning to the Sikhs gathered for the annual conference, a treatise on true sacrifice and the principles of Sikhism.

1163 _____ : Dharm Ate Vidya Pracharak Sri Guru Singh Sabha Lahaur Di Report. (P) Lahore, Singh Sabha, 1880. 35p. PPU

Survey of the Sabha's educational and religious activities.

1164 _____: Niyam Ate Upniyam. (P) Lahore, Khalsa Press, 1897. 16p.

1165 _____: Report (1884). (P) Lahore, Gulzar-i-Muhammadi Press, 1884. 16p.

1166 _____ : Report Sodhak Kamaiti. (P) Amritsar, New Anglo-Gurmukhi Press, 1897. 23p.

Report of the reformation committee appointed to evaluate current editions of the Granth Sahib and to suggest an authentic version.

1167 _____ : Report Sri Guru Singh Sabha Lahaur De Jalse Di Jo 21 Magh Sammat Nanak 422 Nun Hoia. (P) Lahore, Vidya Prakashak Press, 1892. 30p.

Report of the conference on the founding of Khalsa College, Amritsar.

1168 _____ : Salana Diwan Sri Guru Singh Sabha Lahaur Da Britant. (P) Lahore, Singh Sabha. 1905. 21p. PPU

Account of the annual conference at Lahore, April 8-10, 1905.

1169 **SINGH SABHA, Patiala :** Khalsa Dasvandh Kameti Report. (P) Patiala, Patiala Printing Press, 1906. 20p.

1170 **SINGH SABHA, Phusang (Malay States) :** Report. (P) Amritsar, Wazir Hind Press, 1908. 8p.

1171 **SINGH SABHA, Samanstaun (South Africa) :** Report (1905-6). (P) Amritsar, Wazir Hind Press, n/d. 8 p. BTSL

1172 **SINGH SABHA, Sangla Hill (Gujranwala) :** Memorandum of Association and Rules of Sri Guru Singh Sabha, Sangla Hill. Sangla Hill, Singh Sabha, 1914. 18 p.

1173 **SINGH SABHA, Shanghai :** Sri Guru Singh Sabha Shanghai De Gurduare Di Ninh Da Pathar Rakhan Vale Di Karvai Di Report. (P) Amritsar, Wazir Hind Press, 1907. 8 p. PPU

Report of the foundation stone ceremony of a gurdwara in Shanghai.

1174 **SINGH SABHA, Sialkot :** Kam Di Sankhep Report Te Khalsa Hai Skul Di Amdan Te Kharch Da Chittha. (P) Sialkot, George Printing Works, 1913. 8 p.

Report of the Sabha and its Khalsa High School, 1912-13.

1175 **SINGH SABHA, Simla :** Niyam Ate Upniyam. (P) Simla, Singh Sabha, 1919. 56 p.

1176 _____ : Report (1898-9). (P) Amritsar, Wazir Hind Press, 1899. 8 p. BTSL

1177 **UDASIN SAT SABHA, Gujranwala :** Pratham Samagam Ki Report. (P) Lahore, Bombay Machine Press, 1912. 15 p.

Report on the first Udasi Sat Sabha conference held at Sialkot, March 22-24, 1912. Included are rules of the organization, lists of donors and resolutions.

1178 **VIDVA ASHRAM, Amritsar :** Report (1910-1915). (P) Amritsar, Bhai Murari Singh, n/d. 78 p.

Report on the Sikh widow's home which the Chief Khalsa Diwan began on June 8, 1908.

1179 **YOUNG MAN'S SIKH ASSOCIATION, Amritsar :** Niyam Upniyam. (P) Amritsar, Young Man's Sikh Association 1917. 14 p.

1180 **YOUNG MEN'S SIKH ASSOCIATION, Lahore :** Rules and Regulations. Lahore, Young Men's Sikh Association, 1917. 7 p.

SECTION 4

SIKH PERIODICALS

SECTION 4

SIKH PERIODICALS

This list of Sikh periodicals is based primarily on two British series, the catalogue of books published in the Punjab and the annual reports on the Punjab press compiled by the Special Branch of the Punjab Police Department and preserved in the National Archives of India, New Delhi (reports for 1880, 81, 82, 83, 85, 87, 89, 91, 92, 93, 99, 1901, 02, 03, 05, 10, 11, 23). Supplementary information has been drawn from secondary works and research by the author in the newspaper collection of the Sikh Kanya Mahavidyala, Ferozepur. For locations of the papers, consult "Depositories of Sikh Printed Documents" (Appendix A).

Background on each periodical, when available, has been arranged according to the following format :

a. Name, language, place of publication, press, source, and dates. Abbreviations : B (Began), CL (Closed), E (English), H (Hindi), P (Panjabi), R (Report on the Punjab Press), U (Urdu). Background from newspaper reports is indicated by "R" followed by the years of the report in which the publication appeared. For example, R:81-87 signifies that reports from 1881 to 1887 included the periodical. If "R" does not appear, secondary works or the periodical itself served as a source. In cases where beginning and closing dates are uncertain, the approximate date of publication has been noted.

b. Circulation statistics (c). Frequency of publication is indicated by d(daily), tri-w(thrice a week), bi-w(twice a week), w(weekly) and m(monthly). Information is not repeated each year but changes only when the frequency of publication alters. For example, the *Aftab-i-Panjab* (1181) was bi-weekly in 1880, converted to a tri-weekly in 1883, and resumed bi-weekly publication in 1891. Annual circulation figures are supplied when available.

c. Background on proprietor (prop.), printer(pr.), editor (ed.), publisher (pub.) and general information (info.). The date of the report from which the data has been taken follows it in parentheses (e.g., (83) indicates that the preceding came from the 1883 press report).[1]

Reliance upon British documents as a major source for this section naturally places limitations on the reliability and use of the material. Occasional gaps in the reports, for example, mean that some journals and papers have been omitted. More importantly, circulation figures sometimes are incongruent, as are facts on newspapermen and their antecedents. Assessment of individuals' position in society, ideology, and the drift of editorial policy also tends to vary with the reporter and the general British outlook. Despite these limitations, if evaluated in the light of research and other sources, the following information should be helpful—not as a final statement but as an initial attempt to assemble data relevant to the evolution of Sikh journalism.

1. The disjointed-nature and variety of sources on the periodicals made impossible a narrative on each item or even more detailed background. The format employed in handling the data is derived from a model in a more comprehensive treatment of Punjab journalism : N.G. Barrier and Paul Wallace, *The Punjab Press, 1880-1905 : A Data Paper.* (East Lansing, MSU South Asia Occasional Papers Series, forthcoming winter of 1969-70).

Sikh Periodicals

1181. AFTAB-I-PANJAB. (U) Lahore, Aftab-i-Hind Press. R:80-01. B: 66.

C : bi-w(80), tri-w(83), bi-w(91), w(99); 660(80), 550(81), 550(82), 550(83), 500(85), 350(87), 300(89), 300(91), 300(92), 600(93), 140(99), 150(01).

Prop : Diwan Buta Singh, Kalal, Kuka Singh, once a servant of Rani Jindan, from whom he acquired the title of Diwan. Shortly before the Multan rebellion, Buta Singh attempted to create a disturbance in favour of the Rani and was kept a state prisoner in Allahabad for seven months. In 1866 he started the *Aftab-i-Panjab.* A branch of the press at Ajmer printed the Rajputana Government Gazette. The British considered Buta Singh very religious and before the arrest of Ram Singh in 1872, a zealous Kuka. Since then he did not associate openly with the sect although he supposedly believed in their tenets. Buta Singh was wealthy and a member of the Lahore Singh Sabha (80). In 1882 Buta Singh became Vice-President of the Lahore Singh Sabha (83). Diwan Aya Singh (90). Diwan Atar Singh, Khatri, age 24(01).

Ed : Faqir Muhammad, Sheikh, aged 37, never in government service. He once taught in mosques, then served an apprenticeship at the Koh-i-Nur Press and became editor in 1872. "Good character" (80). Nabi Bakhsh (85). Hafiz Umar Daraz (91). Jai Gopal (93). Diwan Aya Singh (99). Diwan Atar Singh (01).

Info : Not in pay of princely states. Discussed local news, Sikh developments and education. Although not very critical of the British, the paper noted misbehaviour of government servants. Published translations from English papers and cuttings from the vernacular press. The press also printed Gurmukhi books on religious subjects (80). Supported abolition of cow slaughter, became hostile to British and played up cases in which Europeans were defendants. Supported placing Punjabis in important posts (83). General and political essays, some religious news (93).

1182. AZAD KHALSA. (P) Amritsar, Azad Khalsa Press. R:03. CL:03.

C : m(03); 500(03).

Prop : Bhai Sundar Singh, son of Bhai Teja Singh, Lambardar of Akal Bunga (Khatri, Pujari of Akal Bunga), 22. Also ed.(03).

Info : A Sikh paper representing a faction critical of the work of the Chief Khalsa Diwan, Amritsar. Also advertised Ayurvedic medicine. Supposedly little influence (03).

1183. BAR. (P) Lyallpur. B,CL:07.

C : w(07); 45(07).

Ed : Kirpal Singh.

Info : Agrarian news and essays on farming techniques. Published essays on Sikh religion and requests for patronage (jobs and education) reserved for the rural Sikh community.

1184. BIR. (P) Amritsar, Sri Gurmat Press. R:10-11.

C : m(10); 500(10), 500(11).

Prop : Mahtab Singh, son of Lakhbir Singh (tailor), 36, bookseller. Judged a man of ordinary position. Also ed., pub.(10).

Info : "Tat Khalsa paper," advocating Sikh unity and reform. Ordinary influence, no security required under the 1910 Press Act (11).

1185. DITT SINGH MAGAZINE. (P) Rupar (Ambala), Wazir Hind Press, Amritsar. B,CL:11.

C : m(11); 500(11).

Prop : Gurmukh Singh, son of Dhian Singh (Jat), Rupar. Also ed., pub.(11).

Info : A short-lived magazine on Sikh education, religion and social reform, founded as a memorial to Bhai Ditt Singh of Lahore who died in 1901.

1186. DODHARA KHANDA. (U) Amritsar, Faryad Press. R:11.

C : m(11); 1,150(11).

Prop : Suchet Singh, son of Ganga Singh (Jat), 36. Supposedly of ordinary position. Also ed., pub., and pr. (11).

Info : A Sikh paper critical of the manager and pujaris of the Golden Temple; no interest in politics but the British felt its influence was bad because the paper stirred up dissension. The editor supposedly had a grudge against the manager because his father was dismissed for misconduct, and he himself had been turned out from Patiala at the suggestion of several pujaris. He used the paper to try to force the government and the management to give him his father's old position. "A man of straw" (11).

1187. DUKH NIWARAN. (P) Amritsar, Wazir Hind Press. R:11. B: 06, CL:20.

C : m(11); 1,500 (11).

Prop : Bhai Mohan Singh Vaid, Arora, 36, resident of Tarn Taran. Also ed., pub. (11).

Info : A Sikh paper advocating the teaching of Gurmukhi and printing medical advice. The paper ran continually at a loss, but Mohan Singh published it for fifteen years because he felt that the Sikh community needed as many spokesmen as possible. The British considered the *Dukh Niwaran* and its editor of little significance. For a more sympathetic appraisal, see the diary excerpts and narrative in Munsha Singh Dukhi, *Jiwan Bhai Sahib Bhai Mohan Singhji Vaid* (2/e., n/d., n.p.)

1188. DURBAR. (E) Amritsar, George Press. R:23.

C : m(23); 775 (23).

Prop : Khalsa College Council, Amritsar.

Ed : Principal of the college.

Info : A college magazine consisting of articles by students and news on Sikh education. Warned in 1916 under section 3 of the 1897 Press Registration Act because of material borderingon "sedition" (23).

1189. FAUJI AKHBAR. (H,P,U,) Lahore, Mufid-i-Am Press. R:10,11.

C : w(10); 2,000(10), 6,000(11).

Prop : R.S. Munshi Gulab Singh and Sons, Lahore (11).

Ed : Bhai Nikka Singh, 61, a clerk in the Civil and Military Gazette Press, Lahore (10); Major Kay (11).

Info : The paper was begun with the objects of inculcating ideas of loyalty among troops, particularly the Sikhs. The Punjab government subsidized the paper by purchasing at least 1,000 copies each week for free distribution in the army. The Paper included editorials on martial bravery and the virtues of the British government, and articles on current military subjects.

1190. GURMUKHI AKHBAR. (P) Lahore, Delhi Punjab Press (80), Amritsar, Aftab-i-Panjab Press (86). R:80-93. B: Nov. 10, 80, CL:95.

C ; w(80), tri-m (93); 300 (81), 250(84), 275(86), 265(87), 325(93).

Prop : Bhai Gurmukh Singh, son of Khan Singh, Jullundur City, 30. Educated in English and Hindi, a prominent member of the Anjuman-i-Panjab, employed as a Professor of Mathematics and Panjabi in the oriental branch of the Panjab University College. Other proprietors included Harsha Singh, son of Natha Singh

(Arora, Granthi of the Tarn Taran gurdwara), teacher of Gurmukhi in the Panjab University College; Dharm Singh, son of Dyal Singh (Lahore druggist), employed in the Civil and Military Gazette Press (80). Gurmukh Singh and Lahna Singh (86). Antar Singh, previously employed by the Raja of Faridkot as a house agent in Simla. A member of the Amritsar Singh Sabha (90).

Ed : Gurmukh Singh and Harsha Singh (80). Antar Singh (93).

Info : The Paper received financial support from the Maharaja of Nabha but did not concern itself with news of princely states. Published editorials, articles, and letters on Sikh religion and society, considered an organ of the Lahore Singh Sabha (80). Printed political and religious essays, moderate, leaned toward the Congress, and supported the spread of Singh Sabhas. The British felt that its editor, Antar Singh, had no status or influence (93).

1191. HAMDARD-I-KHALSA. (U) Amritsar, Chashma-i-Nur Press. R:99-03. B:99, CL:04.

C : m(99), tri-m(01); 350(99), 300(01), 300(03).

Prop : Suchet Singh, son of Ganga Singh (Pujari, Golden Temple, Jat Sikh), 22 (99). Judged of no influence (01). Also pub., ed. (03).

Info : General news, Sikh religion, critical of Nirmalas and other sections of the Sikh community (99). Strong tone, advocated separatism of Sikhs from Hindus. Irregular in its issues (01).

1192. ISTRI SATSANG. (P) Amritsar. c.04-08.

C : w(04-08).

Info : Published material on female education and Sikh social reform.

1193. JAT GAZETTE. (U) Rohtak, Hariana Press. R:23.

C : w(17); 590(23).

Prop : The Jat Association, Rohtak (Rai Sahib Chaudhri Chhottu Ram, pleader; Chaudhri Lal Chand, Rai Bahadur, pleader; Chaudhri Kanhaiya Lal, Jat zamindar, village Matunhail, Rohtak; Dr. Ramji Lal, medical doctor, Hissar).

Ed : Molar Singh, Sikh convert from Hinduism, Jat, Kiloi village, Rohtak, 39. Also pr., pub. Policy editor : Chhottu Ram, Jat of village Garhi (23).

Info : Represented the Jat zamindars. The British considered the paper to be serving a "useful purpose" in developing rural interests and recruiting. The editors were warned four times in 1917 and 1918 for printing "objectionable matter" (23).

1194. JAT VIDDYA PRACHAR. (P) Lahore, Gulzar-i-Muhammadi Press. c. 88-89.

C : m(88).

Ed : Uttam Singh.

Info : Social and religious essays directed toward Jat Sikhs, with emphasis on frugality, investment of money, and education.

1195. KHALSA. (E) Lahore, Guru Gobind Singh Press. R: 99-02. B: Jan. 99, CL: April 01.

C : w(99); 450(99), 350(01).

Prop : Khalsa Press Committee, including Bhagat Lakshman Singh, Chanda Singh, and Mahtab Singh (01).

Ed : Bhagat Lakshman Singh, Khatri, schoolmaster, 36. Also, Bhai Maya Singh, Manager of the Khalsa Press (99).

Info : The first Sikh newspaper in English, partially financed by a grant from Colonel Diwan Jiwan Singh, Finance Minister of Patiala. The paper supported "Ham Hindu Nahin" and was critical of the Arya Samaj. For a summary of its policies and chief articles, see *Bhagat Lakshman Singh Autobiography* (Calcutta, 1966), pp. 133-169.

1196. KHALSA ADVOCATE. (E) Lahore, Tribune Press; Wazir Hind Press, Amritsar. R:03-11,23. B:03, continued until merging with the *Khalsa* in 1923 to become the *Khalsa Te Khalsa Advocate (P)*.

C : m(03), w(11); 1,000(03), 900(05), 846(11), 500(23).

Prop : Khalsa Advocate Committee (03). Khalsa Press Syndicate, Amritsar, with Bhai Jodh Singh as Secretary.

Ed : Bhai Hukam Singh (03). Dewa Singh, Arora, 35 (05). Bahadur Singh, Arora, 40 (11). Subsequent editors included Gian Singh and Jodh Singh.

Info : Devoted to Sikh interests, with discussion of politics, social problems, and local events. "Moderate" (05). The British felt the tone of the paper had become more favourable to the government by 1911 (11). Between 1911 and 1922, the *Khalsa Advocate* tended to be a spokesman for the Chief Khalsa Diwan, Amritsar. During that period it was warned three times for printing "objectionable matter" and once for a registration violation. In 1922 the Diwan made over the paper to the newly–formed Khalsa Press Syndicate (23).

1197. KHALSA AKHBAR. (P) Lahore, Gulzar-i-Muhammadi Press; Khalsa Press. R:89-05. B: June 83, CL: 05.

C : w(89); 275(89), 400(93), 632(99), 1172(01), 1132(02), 1100(03),

1100(05).

Prop : Lahore Singh Sabha (89). Lahore Khalsa Diwan, with Bhai Gurmukh Singh as General Secretary (93).

Ed : Bhai Jhanda Singh, Faridkot, followed by Bhai Gurmukh Singh and Bhai Ditt Singh (89). Bhai Maya Singh, age 43 (05).

Info : The premier Sikh newspaper in the nineteenth century. Carried social and religious news, critical of Sikh and Hindu opponents. Pro-Panjabi (93). The newspaper suspended operation during drawn-out libel trials against Bhai Ditt Singh, but it began again in 1893 with the financial assistance of the Maharaja of Nabha, Hira Singh. For further background on the paper, see Giani Amar Singh, *Singh Sabha Lahir De Ughe Sanchalak Giani Ditt Singhji* (Amritsar, 1962).

1198. KHALSA AKHBAR. (U) Lahore, c.11-21.

C : w(12).

Ed : Sardar Singh, 1919.

Info : Strong supporter of Sikh reform and the Chief Khalsa Diwan. Also critical of British policy toward the Sikhs and Indian nationalism.

1199 KHALSA BAHADUR. (U) Lahore, Guru Gobind Singh Press. R:99-05. B:97, CL:05.

C : w(99), bi-m(01); 500(99), 500(01), 500(02), 500(03), 800(05).

Prop : Rajindar Singh, carpenter, resident of Sialkot, 38. His father was once Inspector of Police in the United Provinces. Rajindar Singh had served as Station-Master at Miani on the North-Western Railway but received a sentence of two years and suspension when convicted of breach of trust in 1899. He wrote *"Are the Muhammadans Our True Friends?"*, for which he was prosecuted in 1894 for stirring religious tension. In that case, however, he escaped punishment because witnesses withdrew their original statements. Rajindar Singh travelled frequently for the Lahore Singh Sabha and gave speeches at religious gatherings. In 1897 the Maharaja of Patiala gave him Rs. 5,000 to support the newspaper. He was appointed a member of the Press Deputation at the time of the Diamond Jubilee (1897) but the Punjab government removed his name from the list. Also ed.(01).

Info : Political, social and religious news (99). Published regularly, provided a Sikh interpretation of events (03).

1200. KHALSA DHARM DEPAK. (P) Batala, Gurmat Press, Amritsar. R:10. c.05-10.

C : w(06), bi-m(10); 500(10).

Prop : Harnam Singh, son of Chatar Singh (Granthi of Dera Nanak), 48. Harnam Singh also was a preacher, a former convert first to Christianity, then to the Arya Samaj. Following several preaching tours with Arya Samaj groups, he returned to Sikhism. Also pub., ed. (10).

Info : News on the Sikh religion, non-political but loyal to the government. Circulation limited to the Sikh community (10).

1201. KHALSA DHARM PARCHARAK. (P) Amritsar, Chashma-i-Nur Press. R:01. B,CL:01.

C : m(01); 300(01).

Prop : Lahora Singh, Arora, 36, formerly a copyist, druggist, and schoolmaster at the Khalsa Jubilee School. Also ed.(01).

Info : Irregular in issue, published excerpts from Sikh scriptures and religious news (01).

1202. KHALSA GAZETTE. (P) Lahore. c. 1885-1900.

C : w(96).

Info : The paper originally was published in Urdu under the editorship of Bhai Maya Singh. In 1894, Dyal Singh became editor. The paper contained religious articles and news on Sikh affairs.

1203. KHALSA MAGAZINE. (U) Lahore, Guru Gobind Singh Press. R:01 B,CL:01.

C : m(01); 100(01).

Prop : Hazur Singh, also ed. (01).

Info : Dealt primarily with Sikhism, little local news (01).

1204. KHALSA PARKASH. (P) Lahore, Aftab-i-Panjab Press. R:91-99. CL:99.

C : w(91); 200(91), 200(92), 300(93), 250(99).

Prop : Diwan Buta Singh, also owner of the Aftab-i-Panjab (91).

Ed : Bur Singh, son of Faqir Attar Singh, Amritsar. Received Rs. 12 a month (91). Daya Singh (93).

Info : Sikh religion, general and political news (91).

1205. KHALSA SAMACHAR. (P) Amritsar, Wazir Hind Press. R:99-11. B:99, still in existence.

C : w(99); 500(99), 1,000(01), 1400(03), 3,000(05), 3,000(11), 3234(19).

Prop : Wazir Singh and Bhai Vir Singh, Arora, owners of Wazir Hind Press. Judged by the British to have "no social status." Also ed., pub. (99). Bahadur Singh Arora, 40, ed., pub., printer (11.)

Vir Singh, 1919.

Info : General and political news, supported the religious ideas and reforms of the Chief Khalsa Diwan (03).

1206. KHALSA SEWAK. (P) Amritsar, Amar Press (03); Chashma-i-Nur Press (05); Khalsa Sewak Press (11). R:03-11. B:03.

C : m(03); 1,000(03), 200(05), 1,000(11).

Prop : Jiwan Singh, shopkeeper, son of Bhai Arjan Singh, 45. Also pub., ed. (03).

Info : Begun by several Sikhs to propagate their religion. Reprinted articles and proceedings of various Singh Sabhas and the Chief Khalsa Diwan (03). Promoted female education. Tone reportedly bitter against non-Sikhs, particularly Arya Samajists (05).

1207. LOYAL GAZETTE. (U) Lahore, Loyal Press. R:11.

C : w(11); 1,307(11), 2,500 in 1919.

Prop : Lal Singh, son of Harnam Das, Arora Sikh, age 40, "Status good," an "orthodox Sikh of the old fashion" according to the British (11).

Ed : Amar Singh, son of Gulab Singh, Pindigheb, Attock, Khatri Sikh, 30. Passed entrance examination from Kashmir State School (11).

Info : Began as a loyal, pro-British paper, but by 1911 its strong political articles led to a demand for security. A principal aim of the paper supposedly was to unite Hindus and Sikhs by discrediting the Arya Samaj, which the proprietor held responsible for all tension between the two communities (11).

1208. LYALL GAZETTE. (U). B: June 11.

Info : Begun by Sardar Amar Singh (b. 1889), subsequently a leader of the Khalsa National Party. The newspaper later became the *Sher Panjab*. Amar Singh discussed politics, religion and social issues, taking a position akin to that of the Chief Khalsa Diwan.

1209. LYALL KHALSA GAZETTE. (U,P) Sialkot, Guru Gobind Singh Press. R:91-93.

C : w(91); 150(91), 150(92), 150(93).

Prop : Archandar Singh, carpenter. His brother, Rajinder Singh, became proprietor in 1892 (92).

Ed : Gurdit Singh, Halkari, Sialkot. Employed on fixed salary (91). Rajinder Singh (93).

Info : Political and religious news. Chief aim to promote Sikh social and moral advancement (91).

1210. MASIK PATTAR. (P) Amritsar, Wazir Hind Press. R:11.

C : m(11); 500(11).

Prop : Chief Khalsa Diwan, Amritsar.

Info : Contained monthly financial statements and information on the work of the Diwan, including preaching tours, meetings, resolutions, and correspondence.

1211. NANAK PARKASH, KAPURTHALA. (U) Lahore, Ravi Ben Nazir Press. R:87-93. B:Nov. 87.

C : m(89); 300(87), 300(89), 300(91), 300(92), 350(93).

Prop : Bawa Arjan Singh, Khatri, Kapurthala. His father, Hukam Singh and grandfather, Nihal Singh, held positions with the Kapurthala State. Arjan Singh supposedly left Kapurthala and resided in Lahore because his criticism of administration created enemies. Also ed. (91).

Info : The paper discussed caste, religion, the affairs of Kashmir and Kapurthala, and Singh Sabha activities. Kapurthala subscribed to a hundred copies (91).

1212. NAU RATTAN. (P) Amritsar, Sri Gurmat Press. R:11. c.08-14.

C ; bi-m(11); 600(11).

Prop : Lahora Singh, son of Tara Singh, Arora. Physician of Amritsar, 43. Also pub. (11).

Ed : Teja Singh, brother of Lahora Singh, 35 (11).

Info : Dealt with Sikh religious affairs, with news and notes on medical subjects.

1213. NIRGUNYARA. (P) Amritsar, Wazir Hind Press. R:02-11. With occasional gaps, still in existence.

C : bi-m(02); 1,300(02), 1,600(03), 2,000(05), 1,800(11).

Prop : Owned by the Khalsa Tract Society and supervised by one of its sub-committees (02).

Ed : Kanhya Singh, Arora, head clerk, Khalsa Tract Society, 29 (02).

Info : Religious news, primarily selections from Sikh scriptures with commentary (02).

1214. PANCH. (P) Lahore, Model Press. c.19.

C : w(19); 1,000(19).

Ed : Ram Singh.

1215. PANJAB DARPAN. (P) Amritsar, Khalsa Mitra Press. R:85. B,CL:85.

C : w(85); 350(85).

Prop : Lahora Singh, subsequent prop. and ed. of Nau Rattan and other Sikh newspapers. He and his father, Tara Singh, were well-known Gurmukhi copyists and had been employed in that capacity in several Lahore presses (85).

Info : The paper closed because it did not pay. Although the *Panjab Darpan* discussed religious and secular matters, the proprietor had no journalistic experience and generally extracted news from Urdu papers. On October 19, 1885 he printed a portrait of Maharaja Dhulip Singh (85).

1216. PANJAB DARPAN. (P) Amritsar, Coronation Printing Press. R:23.

C : w(19); 800(23).

Prop : Sucha Singh, son of Bhai Hans Raj, Arora, 44. Good status (23).

Ed : Ratan Singh Azad, son of Kanshi Ram. Also pub. and pr. (23).

Info : The British considered it a "moderate paper of the Sikhs" but with occasional "strong tone." Warned for objectionable matter in 1919 and required to contradict a false statement in 1922. The editor was prosecuted under 124-A, IPC, in 1923, but discharged (23).

1217. PANJABI. (P) Ludhiana, Khalsa Press. R:11.

C : w(11); 400(11).

Prop : Natha Singh, Jat Sikh, retired Surgeon, First Grade, 57 (11).

Ed : Chaudhuri Parduman Singh, Jat Sikh, Lambardar and Honorary Jamadar, Transport Corps, 29 (11).

Info : Social, religious and general news on the Sikhs.

1218. PANJABI BHAIN. (P) Ferozepur City, Bombay Steam Press, Lahore. R:11. c.08-30.

C : m(11); 2,000(11), 1,050(19).

Prop : Although the Ferozepur Singh Sabha owned and published the periodical, Bhai Takht Singh, manager of the Sikh Kanya Mahavidyala, took responsibility for its administration (11).

Ed : Vir Singh, Jat Sikh, former schoolmaster in the 14th Sikhs but employed at the Mahavidyala since 1908, 42 (11). Takht Singh, 1919.

Info : Articles on religion, the family, and household duties. Non-political and devoted to female education (11).

1219. PANTH. (P) Gujranwala, Sri Gurmat Press, Amritsar. R:11, c.06-12.

C : bi-m(11); 300(11).

Prop : Lal Singh, son of Jawala Sahai, Arora, former updeshak of the Chief Khalsa Diwan, 31. Also ed. Lal Singh quit the Diwan and began his own paper. The British judged him a "scheming person" who "needs watching" (11).

Pr : Budh Singh, son of Amar Singh, Brahman, prop. of Sri Gurmat

Press, 36. A pujari in the Golden Temple and author of *Tawārikh Khalsa* (11).

Info : A Sikh religious paper, "with little influence" (11).

1220. PANTH MITRA. (P) Amritsar. c.04-05.

C : w(04).

Info : Sikh religious and general news.

1221. PANTH SEWAK. (P) Lahore, Universal Printing Press; Sardar Press, Amritsar (23). R:23. c.13-CL:23.

C : w(19); 2,000(19), 1,000(23).

Prop : Chanda Singh, formerly a school teacher. Also ed. (23).

Pub : Gurbachan Singh, also pr. (23).

Info : Political organ of the "Young Sikh Party" opposed to the Chief Khalsa Diwan. Blacklisted by the British in 1919, it was restarted in Amritsar in 1920. Warnings for objectionable matter in 1914, 1919.

1222. PATIALA AKHBAR. (U) Patiala, Patiala Akhbar Press (80); Newal Kishore Press (83); Rajinder Press (01). R:80-05.

C : w(80); 300(80), 300(81), 300(82), 290(83), 360(84), 360(84), 670(86), 365(87), 200(89), 304(91), 304(92), 215(99), 300(03), 300(05).

Prop : Munshi Newal Kishore, Kair, also prop. *Oudh Akhbar,* Lucknow (80). Riki Kesh (81). Abdul Rahman (86). Din Muhammad (87) Syed Raja Ali Shah (93).

Ed : Registered as Riki Kesh, Brahman, but the real editor was Jaswant Rai, an employee of the Patiala Council and partisan of the President, Sir Dev Singh. Jaswant Rai, according to the British, had spent several years in jail on counts of bribery and was a "sharp, intelligent, but unprincipled man"(80). Maulvi Din Muhammad, Hasangarh village, Rohtak. He was employed first as a teacher, then in 1879 became associated with the paper. A Wahabi, Maulvi Din Muhammad frequently attacked Shias and other religious opponents (83). Pandit Raj Narain Arman. (99).

Info : The President of the Council controlled the paper and checked proofs before copies were struck off. The Council gave the paper Rs. 200 a month in return for 30 copies of each edition (80). Known for its support of the Council of Regency, with historical and literary information pertaining to Sikhism and Sikh Phulkian States.

1223. RAH NUMA KHALSA. (U) Gujranwala, Narindra Press. R:02-06.

C : bi-m(02), m(03); 350(02), 450(03), 400(05).

Prop : Gyani Mihan Singh, son of Attar Singh, Arora, 25. Also ed. (02).

Info : Articles on social and political affairs of the Sikhs. "Little influence" (05).

1224. RAMGARHIA PATRIKA. (P) Lahore, Sri Gurmat Press; Amritsar, Bharat Printing Press (23). R:03-05, 23.

C : m(03), bi-m(23); 500(03), 450(05), 500(23).

Prop : Ramgarhia Sabha, Lahore (03). Ramgarhia Sabha, Punjab (23).

Ed : Bhai Baisakha Singh, Ramgarhia, Lahore (03). Sowaran Singh, son of Ladha Singh. Also pub. (23).

Info : Organ of the Ramgarhia community, with general news on social reform and Sikhism (03). Ramgarhia paper, an admirer of the Akali movement (23).

1225. RISALA-I-SRI GURU PARTAP SURAJ UDAI. (U,P) Lahore, Nanak Parkash Press. c.82.

C : m(82).

Ed : Bedi Udaya Singh.

1226. SACH KHAND. (P) Lahore. c.16-17.

C : m(16).

Prop : Giani Sucha Singh.

Info : Religious and social news; emphasis on spread of Panjabi.

1227. SACHA DHANDORA. (P) Lyallpur. c.09.

C : w(09).

Info : Dealt primarily with politics. The British considered it seditious and tried to prevent widespread distribution among troops. Background in Nahar Singh (ed), "Developments in Sikh Politics," English Section, *Gurduara Gazette* (P), April 1969, 7-62.

1228. SEWAK SINGH PATRIKA. (P) Lahore, Sri Gurmat Press. R:05. B:05.

C : m(05); 300(05).

Prop : Budh Singh, 30(05).

Ed : Mian Singh, 30. Also pub., pr. (05).

Info : Articles on Sikh religion (05).

1229. SHER-I-BABAR. (U) Lahore. c.08-09.

C : w(08); 500(08).

Prop : Bishan Singh.

Info : Reform paper that defended Sikh symbols and *Jhatka*, a method of slaughtering animals favoured by the Sikhs. Anti-Hindu.

1230. SHUDDHI PATTAR KHALSA DHARM PARKASHAK. (P) Lahore, Anglo-Sanskrit Press. R:99. B:May 96, CL:99.

Prop : Lahore Shuddhi Sabha (96-98). Harnam Singh (99).

Ed : Bhai Sundar Singh, July-December 1896. Bhai Attar Singh, January-March, 1897. Bhai Mihan Singh, April-September 1897. Bhai Bur Singh, October 1897-December 1898. Ram Chand, 1899.

Info : A Sikh reform paper which championed purification of "defiled" Sikhs and converts from other religions, and acceptance of those individuals by the Sikh community. A controversial journal, continually challenged on the grounds that the Shuddhi Sabha was a tool of the Arya Samaj. Each issue contained details on the shuddhis or purification carried out during the month.

1231. THE SIKHS AND SIKHISM. (E) Gujranwala, Mercantile Press, Lahore. R:05. B:03, CL:05.

C : w(05); 500(05).

Prop : Bhai Sohan Singh, son of Bhai Mul Singh (an appeal-writer in the Gujranwala district court), Second Master, Khalsa High School, Gujranwala, 25. Also ed. (25).

Info : Articles on Sikh religion and politics. Opposed to the Arya Samaj and Sikhs who claimed that Sikhism was a Hindu sect.

1232. SIKH SEPOY. (P) Ferozepur City. B:Sept.17, CL:20.

C : m(17); 350(19).

Prop : Sikh Recruiting Committee, Ferozepur.

Ed : Tek Singh.

Info : A journal dedicated to "Crown, Country and Community." Contained recruiting news, poems on loyalty, and essays about Sikh heroes and martial bravery.

1233. SINGH SABHA GAZETTE. (P) Amritsar, Chashma-i-Nur Press. R:93. B:92,CL:95.

C : w(93); 500(93).

Prop : Lahora Singh, Natha Singh, Nar Singh Das, and Darbara Singh. Earlier a copy writer, Lahora Singh, edited the paper. Natha Singh owned Farma Press, Amritsar, and Nar Singh Das was proprietor of the Chashma-i-Nur Press. Darbara Singh was a student and son of Gyani Sardul Singh, Inspector of Municipal Board Schools, Amritsar (93).

Info : Politics and religious emphasis. Supported Singh Sabha reforms and leaned toward the Congress, occasionally reprinting political extracts from other papers (93).

1234. SINGH SAHAI. (U) Amritsar, Qanun-i-Hind Press (93); Singh Sahai

Press (99). R:91-03. Merged with the *Punjab Gazette* in 1904, with both papers closing by the end of the year.

C : w(91), m(99), w(02); 300(91), 300(92), 300(93), 200(99), 250(01), 150(02), 150(03).

Prop : Bawa Narain Singh, pleader of Vairowal, Amritsar (91). Bawa Arjan Singh, Khatri Sikh, Kapurthala, 51(99).

Ed : Daulat Ram, married to a sister of Bawa Narain Singh. While Daulat Ram was in jail for gambling in 1891, Narain Singh became editor (91). Arjan Singh (93).

Info : Religious and political news, strong advocate of Sikhism. The proprietor supposedly was hostile to the British (91). "Tone abusive," irregularly issued (01). "Requires watching" (02).

1235. SIRI GURUMAT PARCHAR. (P) B:92.

C : m(92).

Info : Devoted to Sikh missionary efforts and news about reform.

1236. SRI GURMAT PARKASHAK. (P) Lahore. c.86-89.

Ed : Bhai Autar Singh.

1237. SRI GURU NANAK DARSHAN. (P) Lahore, Model Electric Press. c.19.

C : w(19); 1,000(19).

Prop : Sant Sumer Singh.

1238. TEACHER. (E) Lahore, Gujrat Mercantile Press. R:10.

C : m(10); 200(10).

Prop : Kanhya Singh, son of Hakim Singh of Dinga, Khatri. Also ed. and pub. (10).

Info : Dealt primarily with education and the spread of Sikh religion. The British claimed it had no influence outside Dinga (10).

1239. VIDYARK PANJAB. (P) Lahore. R:81. B,CL:81.

C : m(81); 200(81).

Prop : Gurmukh Singh (81).

Info : Published by the Lahore Singh Sabha (81).

1240. VISKARMA. (P) Amritsar, Gurmat Press. R:10. c.09-21.

C : m(10); 600(10).

Prop : Viskarma Committee of the Ramgarhia Sabha, Amritsar, headed by Budh Singh, son of Amar Singh, 46. Also ed., and prop. (10).

Info : Urged technical education among young Sikhs and further training of females. Also published religious scripture and commentary (10).

APPENDIX A

DEPOSITORIES OF SIKH PRINTED DOCUMENTS

APPENDIX A

DEPOSITORIES OF SIKH PRINTED DOCUMENTS

This note surveys the background and contents of several representative depositories of Sikh literature.[1] Special attention has been paid to how and why material was collected because that process determined the character of each holding. The sketches are based on the compiler's research, supplemented with information supplied by librarians.

The Evolution of Sikh Collections

Both Sikh and British libraries contain collections of printed documents on Sikhism. Among the Sikhs the historical awareness that fostered research and writing also resulted in the preservation of their literature. Sikh organizations, most notably, schools, maintained libraries which still contain old records.[2] The most substantial holdings nevertheless remain those collected through the effort of individual scholars. One early example was the personal library of Sardar Attar Singh of Bhadaur, an author and active member of the Lahore Singh Sabha. After gathering books and manuscripts for thirty years Attar Singh contributed them to the Punjab Public Library, Lahore.[3] Other collections grew up in Ferozepur and Tarn Taran. The manager of the Sikh Kanya Mahavidyala, Bhai Takht Singh, devoted his life to training Sikh girls and preserving documents on the history of Sikhism. Every spare rupee went into research books, which were catalogued, placed in protective cupboards, and cleaned regularly. The Library, renamed the Bhai Ditt Singh Library after the death of the Lahore leader in 1901, soon became a chief depository for Sikh publications. Scholars contributed their holdings to the institution, and many visited Ferozepur to study in the library.[4] In Tarn Taran Bhai Mohan

1. The note does not include references to all existing institutions or private libraries. The collections under discussion were selected because of their comprehensiveness and availability to scholars.
2. *Khalsa Pracharak Vidyala Dusri Salana Report, 1907-8* (Amritsar, 1908), pp. 19-22. There is unfortunately no survey of these libraries available.
3. Shamsher Singh Ashok, *Bhai Kahan Singh Nabha* (Gurar, 1966), p.33.
4. Munsha Singh Dukhi, *Jivan Bhai Sahib Bhai Mohan Singh Ji Vaid* (Amritsar, n/d.), pp. 63, 252.

Singh Vaid amassed 'the most phenomenal assortment of documents collected by a single Sikh. Bhai Mohan Singh was a scholar who appreciated the value of books as records of current events. Realizing that future students would require sources on Sikh institutions, he preserved works including handbills, tracts, broadsides, reports and theological tomes. His daily diary records how Bhai Mohan Singh pursued individual items and proudly placed them in his library. The result was a collection totalling over 12,000 volumes.[1]

India Office and British Museum officials were equally concerned with preserving a record of Sikh history, and through their perserverance, there are now well-developed Sikh collections in London.

Until 1867 neither the India Office Library nor the British Museum had adequate channels for securing India works. Their reliance on individuals and private dealers ended, however, with the passage of Act XXV of 1867 (Registration of Books) which required publishers to submit copies of items printed in India. After 1867 India Office librarians marked quarterly lists of publications supplied by local governments, and desired items were then forwarded from India. In 1889 the British Museum also began to secure books through the official channels.[2]

Librarians frequently requested Sikh items from the Punjab government, which secured copies and shipped them to the London depositories. The Punjab government also purchased books from the Sikh princely states. As the states did not publish regular catalogues, the supply of items fromou tside British India rested on the initiative of Punjab officers associated with the Director of Public Instruction.[3]

Controversial Sikh items banned after 1907 remained outside these channels. London librarians were unaware that they had not received the proscribed literature until the Bombay government raised the issue in 1914. At that time the Government of India decided not to send the material on the grounds that its transmission through the mail would be troublesome and even dangerous. The British Museum refused to accept the ruling and claimed copies of all proscribed works under Imperial copyright. When the Government of India backed down and agreed to send the books to the two London libraries, librarians agreed to lock up the proscribed matter until its use by the public became "unobjectionable."[4] For the next three decades, arrange-

1. For Mohan Singh's attitude toward history and sources, see Munsha Singh, pp. 14, 54, 244-45. He also paid the expenses of a historian, Bhai Karam Singh, and assisted in his research.
2. Based on correspondence in two sets of IO records, Books and Publications and Records Library, and the Punjab correspondence books in the BM Archives.
3. Based on Punjab correspondence in the BM Archives.
4. Note by M. Seton, Nov. 13, 1914, and Records Despatch 1, Jan. 22, 1915, Register and Records, 3336 of 1914 (IOL).

ments for shipping this special category of publications to England kept breaking down, but a stream of Punjab banned items, including Sikh material, reached England until 1947.

The British Museum and India Office Library

Although the exact size of the Sikh collections in the two libraries cannot be gauged, the chart below denotes the number of items in languages in which Sikh literature is represented :

Vernacular Publications, BM and IOL[1]

	Regular Collections		Proscribed	
	BM	IOL	BM	IOL
Hindi, Hindi-Hindustani	10,600	23,000	536	622
Panjabi	1,650	6,000	51	44
Urdu	14,000	16,000	168	196

Many of the Panjabi and Urdu tracts pertain to Sikhism, as do a few Hindi works. Moreover, each collection contains over 500 English-language items on or by the Sikhs. The publications include the range of subjects discussed in the introduction and the first two sections.[2] In the proscribed sections are Ghadr tracts, Akali and revolutionary material, biographies, and anti-Sikh pamphlets by Hindus and Muslims.[3] The India Office Library has newspapers (e.g. the *Tribune, Pioneer,* and *Civil and Military Gazette)* with articles on Sikhs, but both libraries lack Sikh serial holdings. They also do not have much Sikh organizational material, probably explained by its infrequent inclusion in the quarterly book lists. The librarians did not have a chance to order annual reports and proceedings.

Scholars are reliant on catalogues for ordering specific works because both libraries have closed stacks. The fundamental guides to the pre-1900 vernacular Sikh material in the India Office Library are the Blumhardt catalogues, arranged by subject with author-title indexes.[4] The printed guides to English-language works begin to run out after 1910, and then the reader is

1. British Museum statistics supplied by Mr. J.H. Eisenegger and Mr. Peter Stocks; IOL statistics from Stanley C. Sutton, *A Guide to the India Office Library* (London, 1967), p. 17. Proscribed totals based on personal tabulation, July of 1968.
2. The following exemplify the range : *Akhiri Paighambar* (Sialkot, 1894); Sardar Gurmukh Singh, *Guru Nanak Prakash*(Lahore, 1891); Thakar Singh, *Sidk Jivan* (Amritsar, 1908); Avatar Singh, *Hornan Dharma Nalon Khalsa Dharm Vich Ki Vadha Hai* (Amritsar, 1895).
3. For example, a reprint of the first Ghadr newspaper, Nov. 1913, *Ghadr Parti Ki Sangrah* (San Francisco, 1922); *Ghadr Di Gunj* (San Francisco, 1914). For excerpts from some of the pre-1920 material, see Appendix B.
4. J.F. Blumhardt : *Catalogue of the Library of the India Office, Vol. II : Hindustani Books*(London, 1900); *Hindi, Panjabi, Pushtu and Sindhi Books* (London, 1902). Printed guides to the Hindi and Panjabi collection should be ready by the mid-70's.

dependent on acquisition lists, a card system, and entries pasted in loose-leaf volumes. The duplicate copy of the Punjab book catalogue kept by the India Office provides a cross-check for specific titles. If an item has been marked in the catalogue, it is probably somewhere in the collection.

The British Museum has printed catalogues for Hindi and Panjabi volumes. The Urdu catalogue ends at 1908, but later works can be easily traced in a well-maintained author-title card index.[1] English-language entries are arranged in large books ringing the main reading room.

The libraries have made their proscribed publications available to scholars since the summer of 1968. The India Office collection is divided by language and stored in boxes. Although not indexed, the boxes or individual items can be examined in a special reading room. The British Museum holding consists of approximately two hundred bundles wrapped in the original covers as received from India. The staff has prepared a handlist of titles, and tracts can be requisitioned for use in the Student's Room.[2]

Library, National Archives of India

The library of the National Archives of India has a similar collection of proscribed pamphlets. These items currently are being "deproscribed" by individual state governments, and until this has been completed, material cannot be filmed or quoted at length. In addition to Sikh tracts resembling those in London, the library has bundles of old Sikh newspapers (e.g., *Kirti, 1929-30, Ghadr,* and over a hundred issues from other papers).[3] A set of the Punjab Gazette containing most of the Punjab book catalogues also can be found in the library.

Punjab Public Library, Lahore

The Sikh collection in the Punjab Public Library primarily consists of the holdings contributed by Sardar Attar Singh of Bhadaur and books supplied by the Punjab government after the library became a despository of publications acquired under the 1890 Press Regulation Act. There is a six-volume printed catalogue on English items, and for Urdu, an up-to-date card index. Most of the Hindi and Panjabi works, however, have not been catalogued or even

1. J.F. Blumhardt: *Catalogue of Hindustani Books* (London, 1889); *Supplementary Catalogue of Hindustani Books,* 1889-1908 (London, 1909); *Catalogue of Hindi, Panjabi, Sindhi and Pushtu Books* (London, 1893); *Supplementary Hindi Catalogue*, 1893-1912 (London, 1913); and L.D. Barnett, *Second Supplementary Catalogue* (London, 1957); L.D. Barnett, *Panjabi Printed Books in the British Museum, A Supplementary Catalogue* (London, 1961).
2. The author currently is compiling a guide to proscribed literature, to be completed by the summer of 1972, which will union-list the IOL and BM collections.
3. The proscribed section contains 100 Urdu, 110 English, 550 Hindi, and 30 Panjabi tracts. Many Urdu and Panjabi items, and approximately 125 Hindi works, pertain to the Sikhs.

moved since 1947. Although statistics on the Sikh volumes are unavailable, the number undoubtedly exceeds five thousand, concentrated in the nineteenth century.[1]

Khalsa College, Amritsar

Despite being small and recent in comparison with several other depositories, the collection of the Khalsa College Library and the Sikh History Research Department includes approximately 500 rare English and vernacular works on Sikhism. Periodicals are numerous, as are theological studies. The library also has a sampling of organizational material such as annual reports and proceedings of the Sikh Educational Conference.

Bhai Takht Singh Library, Ferozepur

The research library at the Sikh Kanya Mahavidyala, Ferozepur, was the central depository for Sikh printed documents prior to the death of Bhai Takht Singh in 1937. Administrative problems after partition, coupled with flooding, have led to the partial destruction of the collection, but it remains a significant library of theological works, tracts, organizational reports, and newspapers. A recently prepared card index contains entries on the 3,000 individual items in the collection. A set of sixty bound volumes of miscellaneous tracts pertaining to Sikh institutions and religious debates before 1920 is particularly notable. As indicated by the list below, the Sikh newspaper holding is one of the most valuable in existence:

Bir, 1910-15
Civil and Military Akhbar, 1906-10
Dukh Niwaran, 1908-12
Hak, 1919-20
Istri Satsang, 1904-08
Jat Gazette, 1916-21
Khalsa, 1899-1902
Khalsa Advocate, 1903-20[2]
Khalsa Akhbar, 1894-1904, 1912-19
Khalsa Dharm Depak, 1906-9
Khalsa Gazette, 1890-1900
Khalsa Samachar, 1900-20[3]
Lyall Gazette, 1913-18

1. Based on a rapid shelf-reading in 1968. This suggests that the collection could well be the most important on the nineteenth-century Punjab. No other depository, for example, has depth prior to the 1890's.
2. On microfilm, Nehru Memorial Museum and Library, New Delhi.
3. On microfilm, Nehru Memorial Museum and Library; University of Missouri Library, Columbia.

Namdev Pattar, 1913-14
Nau Rattan, 1908-14
Panjab Darpan, 1917-24
Panjabi Bhain, 1909-15
Panth Mitra, 1904-05
Panth Sewak, 1914-22
Prem, 1909
Sacha Dhandora, 1909
Shuddhi Pattar, 1896-98

Bhai Mohan Singh Vaid Library

The family of Bhai Mohan Singh Vaid transferred his library to Punjabi University, Patiala, in 1966. The collection has now been accessioned, rebound and shelved in a special room. A card index should be completed by the end of 1970, with a printed catalogue projected for 1971 or 1972.

The collection consists of 2,645 English, 8,624 Panjabi, 4,752 Hindi and 2,594 Urdu titles. With the exception of the *Khalsa Akhbar* (1886-88), the library has few newspapers because Mohan Singh's periodicals were distributed between the Bhai Takht Singh Library and the Khalsa College Library. The heart of the collection lies rather in tracts and institutional material. Among the former are the voluminous literary products of Mohan Singh Vaid, Khalsa Tract Society issues, "Tat Khalsa" pamphlets, and an assortment of religious publications. Organizational works include sets of Sikh Educational Conference and Chief Khalsa Diwan proceedings, and reports from schools, hospitals, Singh Sabhas, and other institutions.

APPENDIX B

A NOTE ON SIKH PROSCRIBED MATERIAL

APPENDIX B

A NOTE ON SIKH PROSCRIBED MATERIAL

The publication of tracts and newspapers by Sikhs aligned with revolutionaries in Europe and North America created a significant political crisis for the British government in India. This note surveys the literature and the response of the Government of India. Appended are excerpts from works typlifying the concerns of Sikh politicians in exile. Besides illustrating themes discussed in the note and the introduction to the guide, these selections present a sample of vernacular and banned material hitherto unavailable to scholars. They also give another side of Sikh politics, a counter to the posture of loyalty among Punjabi Sikhs residing in India.

Organizations and public meetings in London stimulated some of the earliest Sikh nationalist publications. The revolutionary India House often conducted meetings in which Sikh students were prominent. At a 1908 birthday celebration honouring Guru Gobind Singh, for example, proceedings emphasized the martial attributes of the "Sikh brotherhood" and called on Punjabis to lead in throwing the British from India. Such meetings produced pamphlets for distribution among Sikh troops and agriculturists.[1] Nationalist networks in France and Germany generated similar works during the First World War.

Racism and working conditions fostered an even more pronounced political effort among Sikh immigrants in North America. Over ten thousand Punjabis, primarily Sikh, set up residence in California, Washington, and British Columbia between 1899 and 1910. Travelling to a foreign country because of agricultural problems in the Punjab and visions of new employment, these immigrants confronted exploitation and a blatant variety of white superiority exemplified in the "drive the coloureds out" movement in California.[2] It

1. See the last two items in the appendix. For background, Indulal Yajnik, *Shyamaji Krishnavarma* (Bombay, 1955), Khushwant Singh, *Ghadar 1915* (New Delhi, 1966) and the Isemonger report cited in the bibliography.
2. Conditions discussed in Rajani Kanta Das, *Hindustani Workers on the Pacific Coast* (Berlin, 1923). Also, the "back-lash" literature in the reels of U.S. Justice and Immigration Department files, National Archives of India, New Delhi.

is not surprising that Punjabis withdrew into the affairs of their own community or organized cultural organizations which served as nuclei for nationalist activities. In Canada the daily life of Sikhs revolved around gurdwaras and branches of Singh sabhas. Sikh leaders also established newspapers and fought a rear guard action against Canadian legislators who were determined to stem the "yellow tide."[1] Although strained at all times, Canadian-Indian relations suffered a particularly serious blow with the Komagata Maru incident in 1914. Following two months of lawsuits and fights between Sikhs and police, a Japanese ship loaded with several hundred Punjabi would-be immigrants, the Komagata Maru, had to return to India. That event, and subsequent police firing at Budge Budge harbour in October of 1914, furnished popular themes for Sikh publications.[2]

California became another centre of Sikh associations and literary activity. In Stockton, for example, Punjabis organized the "Hindustani Workers of the Pacific Coast" in the summer of 1913. Soon afterward they acquired a printing press and a building in San Francisco, renamed the "Yugantar Ashram." The movement produced revolutionary cells throughout East Asia and India. It also led to the publication of a controversial newspaper, the *Ghadr* (initially in Urdu, later Panjabi and Hindi). The paper's name, "Mutiny" or "Rebellion," reflected the matter found in its columns. The first issue of November, 1913, contained articles on British rule, American sympathy for Indian freedom fighters, notes on Russia and Ireland, Sikh immigration, and Canadian *zulum* (mistreatment or atrocities). Ram Singh, the head of the militant Kuka sect, was converted into a nationalist hero :

> "The Kukas looked upon service under the British as a sin and preached to all to raise the standard of rebellion. At last they openly fought in 1872. But how can a waking brother in a household of sleeping men successfully fight a band of thieves ? The heroic Kukas, men and children, were blown from the cannon's mouth, and all brave Indians kept silent and looked on."

The *Ghadr* preached a message of revolution. The "Ghadr party" associated with the paper outlined a programme for undercutting British power and then publicized that plan in literature smuggled into India :

> A band from the revolution has arrived in America.

1. Khushwant Singh, *Ghadar*, pp. 14-18.
2. See appended selection from *Shamsher Khalsa*.

> It has, after fleeing the Punjab of slavery, founded a second free Punjab in California, where brother can talk to brother, where men can deliver lectures, publish newspapers, and form associations. In short, they can do in America all those things which have been prohibited in the Punjab. Now they will make war on their enemies in India. Although they are far from their homeland, they can be there in spirit. To keep up the fight it is now necessary that a newspaper be begun and books published. These can be circulated among the Indians in the U.S. and secretly sent to India. We should also learn the arts of war and secure help from other countries. For this work we have set up a Sabha, the Pacific Coast Hindustan Sabha. This is not an Ashram but a fort from which we will shoot cannons at the British *raj*. This is not a newspaper, but a cannon which will spare no tyrant. This paper is printed in ink but it has been prepared with blood.[1]

The works emanating from Sikh centres shared several features. First, they emphasized the economic and social conditions of Indians. Frequent comparison was made between *zulum* in India and treatment of Indians residing in America and Canada. The poems in "Echo of the Mutiny" (*Ghadr Di Guni*, appended), for example, consistently described Indians as being labelled "coolies" or "black people treated like dogs." The authors tended to link situations in India and North America, reacting sharply to attitudes and policies from which there seemed no respite. Underlying this theme was the assumption that respect for Indians abroad would come only when India was either free or had risen again to an exalted position in the world. Such orientations toward internal developments in India nurtured a sense of national spirit among immigrants, a phenomenon similar to the ideological themes and activities of overseas Chinese also living on the west coast.

Besides noting threats to Indians, tracts attempted to deal with a problem facing Congress leaders in India, the increasing divisions within the Indian population on the basis of religion and social structure. Communalism posed embarrassing questions for exiled politicians. Between 1907 and 1913 Hindu-Muslim revivalism and political struggles within widened legislative arenas had

1. Selections from GI Home Political files, Jan. 1914, 42-43A, National Archives of India.

contributed to rioting and a fresh surge of religious hate literature. The editors of *Ghadr* and other publications frequently accepted a monolithic interpretation of the challenges these events presented to an image of united India—they blamed most trouble on a British policy of divide and rule.[1] Hindus, Muslims, and Sikhs were exhorted to forestall British tactics and to join hands despite "minor" conflict of interest. After all, the writers claimed, didn't Indians share a heritage of heroes, sacrifice, and world greatness ?

Although theoretically addressed to the Indian nation, much of the literature pertained to the Punjab and Sikhs. Punjab land revenue supposedly was collected cruelly, colonists in newly irrigated areas were being mistreated, and the provincial government showed disrespect for the "legitimate political aspirations" of the educated classes. In addition to discussing specific problems affecting Sikhs such as politics in Khalsa College and army conditions, articles attempted to stir Sikh spirits by repeatedly emphasizing their symbols and self-image. Use of terms such as "Khalsa", *Kirpan*, "Panth", the interchanging of "lion" and "Singh" for dramatic purposes, references to martial bravery, and finally, the accusation that Sikhs had been British lackeys during the 1857 Mutiny and therefore betrayed their Gurus—these were designed to arouse a dormant community. The authors frequently did not differentiate clearly between the "Sikh nation" and the "Indian nation," nor did they see the inconsistency of stressing Sikh nationhood at the potential cost of affecting Sikh cooperation with other Indians. The nationalist abroad, whether Hindu, Muslim, or Sikh, usually did not appreciate the implications of appeals to the tradition or particularistic aspects of individual communities. The spread of communal identity was judged less important than efforts to combat British imperialism.[2]

The British adopted a variety of tactics to meet threats from hostile writers. The most common manoeuvre was wholesale proscription of offensive works. Between 1908 and 1911 the Government of India passed ordinances and legislation to halt the flow of revolutionary propaganda. Act VII of 1909 "for the prevention of incitements to murder and other offences in newspapers" gave magistrates a right to forfeit material and the press upon which it had been printed. A stronger bill in 1910, "for better control of the press," extended forfeiture to virtually every piece of controversial printed matter. Customs and postal officials could search unsealed packages and confiscate

1. For example, "Echo of the Mutiny," poems one, seventeen; Gurmukhi pamphlet, both items appended.
2. This general problem surveyed by Lajpat Rai in V.C. Joshi (ed) *Lala Lajpat Rai Writings and Speeches* (New Delhi, 1966), v. II.

papers, books, and posters judged "seditious," interference extended subsequently to sealed mail. Moreover, magistrates could require presses to deposit substantial bonds which were forfeit if their products were declared illegal. War legislation, such as the Defence of India Act, 1915, extended ever greater power to the executive.[1]

The British paid particular interest to Sikh publications because of the Sikhs' central role within the Indian army. Despatches in 1908 and 1909, for example, warned the Secretary of State for India that London pamphlets were directed at Sikh troops.[2] These tracts were proscribed and seized upon entry at Bombay, followed by banning of all the products of the Ghadr party in California, the *Shamsher-i-Khalsa* of Stockton, and the *Swadeshi Sewak* of Vancouver.[3] Seizure of works published in the Punjab tended to be limited to items occasioned by specific events rather than the publications of a particular group. For example, in 1914 Michael O'Dwyer made a tour of the canal colonies and attempted to placate Sikh feelings on the partial destruction of the Rakabganj gurdwara in Delhi. When the *Khalsa Akhbar* published a sharp attack on the Lieutenant Governor for his comments, the edition in question and the press on which it was printed were confiscated.[4]

The tactic of conciliating Sikh opinion and winning allies among moderates tempered the policy of repression. On one occasion, for example, the British attempted to gain Sikh support by seizing an Ahmadiya paper which attacked the Gurus.[5] In the face of propaganda aimed at troops, the government also ran a newspaper, *Fauji Akhbar,* for circulation among North Indian soldiers. The publicity campaign intensified during the First World War when semi-official publicity committees in each province supplied information to "friendly" newspapers and extended patronage to editors adopting a pro-British policy. Once again cultivation of Sikh support received high priority.[6]

A final assessment of events between 1914 and 1920 would be premature, but the Indian government apparently sought to avoid alienating local Sikh groups while vigorously intercepting external propaganda aimed at the Punjab. Leaving aside North American publications, only a handful of Sikh works were

1. An accessible summary of the legislation, with background, is in G.K. Roy, *Law Relating to Press and Sedition* (Simla, 1915).
2. Minutes and documents in GI Home Political files, March 1909, 148-50A; July 1908, 137-39A.
3. Minutes and documents in GI Home Political files, Jan. 1914, 42-43A; June 1914, 110-11A; Oct. 1914; 333-35A.
4. Summarized in GI Home Political files, Aug. 1914, 65-66A.
5. Discussion, GI Home Political files, Aug. 1914, 12A.
6. For the *Fauji Akhbar,* GI Home Political files, May 1919, 689-92A; publicity committees, Nov. 1919, 281-87A.

banned prior to 1919. Conditions in the Punjab were not conducive to circulation of revolutionary literature. The times had changed by 1921, and with the acceleration of Sikh political writing, the government shifted attention from external threats to immediate dangers at home. Just as Sikhs joined other political prisoners in jail, so their literature was added to the list of works notified as banned in the gazettes. The lengthening list of Sikh proscribed tracts serves as a gauge to the widening gulf between the rulers and their once "most-loyal" subjects.

Banned Literature Relating to Sikh Politics

The initial selection consists of translated poems from the Punjabi "Ghadr Echo" (San Francisco, 1914), one in a series of pamphlets published by the Hindustan Ghadr Association for distribution in North America and India. The remaining selections are extracts from Government of India Home Political files. Comparison of the official translations with copies of original works indicates that the British versions accurately convey the ideas of the authors. The first extract is poetry on the Komagata Maru incident taken from the Panjabi *Shamsher Khalsa* ("Sword of the Khalsa") published in Stockton, California, July 1914. The second, a Gurmukhi tract, was published in London and proscribed after being discovered among Sikh troops. The final piece contains selections from an English-language "Khalsa Pamphlet" distributed at a meeting in Caxton Hall, London, 1908.[1]

Echo of the Ghadr

Poem One

Humanity throughout the world is now awake. Oh sleeping India, why don't you arise ?

Your clothes are torn and your body emaciated. Why is there no zeal in your body or strength in your heart ?

The world calls us "black thieves." Where is our old prosperity and happiness ?

Neither your colour nor your looks resemble that of old. Where did you lose your pomp and self-respect ?

You have no education or goodness or wealth. Where even is your sense of politics and your self-respect ?

Why are there no persons such as the great poet Kalidas, the philanthropic ruler Bhoj, or strong men like Arjuna ?

Why are there no strong Hindus of India nor strong Muslims, the sons of crusaders.

1. The author thanks Sri Ganpat Rai, Ambala, for assistance in editing and translating the first piece. The *Shamsher Khalsa* number is taken from GI Home Poll, Oct. 1914, 333-35A; the remaining two items, GI Home Poll, March 1909, 148-50A.

After dividing them, the oppressor has finished them both. Why don't you turn into poison to kill him ?
Repression is at its height and hell is loose. Why don't the Sikhs rise and attack ?
The world calls us "coolie." Why doesn't our flag fly anywhere ?
We are faced with innumerable miseries. Why aren't our hearts upset ?
It seems that we are good for nothing. Why aren't we honoured anywhere ?
From the beginning we have been yoked to thralldom. Why don't we even dream of freedom ?
How shall we survive, are we slaves forever ? Why aren't we involved in politics ?
Wherever we go, we are treated like dogs. Why is no person kind to us ?
The goal is far away and our pace is slow. Why are we inert ?
The blood has dried and only the skeleton remains. Why don't we burn it at the cremation ground ?
In the conflagration our house is ablaze. Why don't we put out the fire ?
Only a handful of oppressors have taken our fields. Why has no Indian cultivator risen and protected his land ?
Our children cry for want of education. Why don't we open science colleges ?
Have we ever been brave heroes ? Are there no battlefields on which we can play ?
We have many tricksters among us who are killing the nation. Why shouldn't these dishonest men die ?
Are there no valiant heroes, sons of India like Tilak ? Why doesn't our jewel, Sri Aurobindo, shine like a light of humanity ?
Har Dyal has been kind to India. Why doesn't our friend Ajit Singh offer sacrifices ? [1]
The time will come, and our eyes will bear witness. Why doesn't God avenge those who spend their lives in misery ?
Our weapons have been hidden. Why doesn't the *kirpan* (sword) shine like thunder ?
Oh brave Singhs, the time is not for sleeping. Why don't you look at the world around you ?
The oppressor is acting like a monkey. Why don't you take his life ?
He has devoured Turkey, Iran, and China. Why doesn't Japan awake and lead ?
Oh Ye, the blood of our revered fathers. If you unite, Satan must die.

1. Har Dyal and Ajit Singh were revolutionary leaders. Har Dyal was influential in the Ghadr movement in California, while Ajit Singh headed a gang of revolutionists in the Punjab before fleeing to Persia in 1910.

If you Singhs show courage, you can achieve success. Having lived a long life, why can't you sacrifice yourselves ?

Poem Three

Arise, ye sons of dear India, why have you slept so long ?
In the moonlight you have slept, but see, now the sun has risen.
You are in the clutches of bad sleep. It will not leave you without taking your life.
The red serpent is all around you. Where are your war flags ?
How have we become short-statured and cowards. Where are our youths who are eight feet tall ?
We cowards survive today without self-respect. Where are the heroes of the country ?
Today we are called the dirty black people *(kala log)*. Where is India's glory ?
When they confiscated our India, where have they left our religion ?
One who cannot swim the river cannot live in a seastorm, prepare to fight.
You are sluggish and keep sitting drugged. O idiots, where is your intellect ?
Had brave Hari Singh been alive, he would have taken up the sword. [1]
He would have sacrificed his life for self-respect, the same as the lion-hearted Shivaji.
You cowards are afraid of death. How can you think of becoming lions in battle ?
One hero should stand against one hundred and twenty-five thousand. That is the order of the Guru.
You sons of the Guru are Singhs, and there is much oppression. Where are your lion-like traits ?
Oh ye brave Singhs, join together to gather up the dropped pearls. Why must all be lost ?
We will fight for India, we will kill and be killed. Cry loudly, where is your tongue and heart ?

Poem Six

In what conditions do you sit idle, Oh brothers of India ?
Just look at Japan, see the heights of its achievement.
You are concerned with religion. You are anxious to protect your faith and way of worship.
You are quarreling, and Hindu-Muslim conflict is prevalent.

1. Hari Singh Nalva was the leading general of Ranjit Singh.

The jewel of India is rotting in the earth because you are fighting over the Vedas and the Koran.

If beef, pork and *jhatka* (meat prepared according to Sikh custom) troubles you, just see how the whites eat all varieties of flesh.

Why don't you stop these horrible men ? They are the real enemy of your religions.

It is written in political books that he who plays tricks is not a friend.

In famines our children die of starvation, but the English live off our income.

We are in a sad situation, what to do ? We are left only with kicks.

We grow wheat to eat, but receive only barley in exchange. The revenue collectors do not leave behind a single pice.

The British have taxed us heavily. Poor shopkeepers are starving to death.

Why do you sit silent in your own country, you who make so much noise in foreign lands ?

Noise outside India is of little avail. Pay attention to activities within India.

Go and speak with the soldiers. Ask them why they are asleep, men who once held swords.

Muslims, Pathans, Dogras and Sikh heroes should join together.

The power of the oppressor is not big if we unitedly attack him.

Indians have been victors in the battlefields of Burma, Egypt, China, and the Sudan.

It is shameful that we help enemies. We are acting like slaves.

"Damn the service of others," thus spoke the Guru full of wisdom.

The honour of our old heroes and saints will last forever, those who sacrificed for their nation.

Poem Eight

Let the earth give way so that we may drown. For what else were these 30 crore people born ?

Hurry up and unite, O Hindus and Muslims. Why do you sit in disunity ?

Hurry up and prepare for mutiny. O Singhs, have you turned away your face ?

The Gurus founded this Panth for the welfare of others, otherwise, what was the need ?

Open your eyes and look at the world. Why have your brothers left your boat to drown ?

The British have plundered our country. Why have you turned your backs and fallen asleep ?

Why do you disgrace the name of Singh ? What have you given away, your birthright of being lions ?

Where once there was a spring garden in full-bloom, what must there now be autumn ?

People say that the Singhs are cruel and insensitive. Why did they turn the tides during the Delhi Mutiny ?

The country would have enjoyed freedom. How and why did they commit this blunder ?

Oh ye lion-hearted, we are the children of lions. Why do you sit in cages with broken courage ?

Cry loudly, "let us kill the whites." Why do you sit shamelessly ?

Poem Eleven

Thought from the Sikh scriptures :

> *A hero can be recognized only if he fights for his religion. He shall not leave the battlefield even if he is cut to pieces.*

The Guru laid the foundation of the Panth for the welfare of others.

Oh Singhs, the Guru himself did wonders on the battlefield.

The Guru finished tyranny in India after waging war, Oh Singhs.

For the sake of protecting India, he sacrificed his own sons.

Those who tasted battle have taught us how to fight, Oh Singhs.

In the battlefield they advieved martyrdom for which God had sent them.

The sons of the Guru were bricked alive to put an end to tyranny, Oh Singhs.

When the Guru was kind, Oh Singhs, he taught us how to wage war.

When the Guru was ready to leave for Puri, he sent Banda to keep guard over the Punjab, Oh Singhs.

When Banda gave protection, the Panth was happy and prosperous.

When Banda died, the Panth took the reins of command in its own hands, Oh Singhs.

There were many brave heroes in the Punjab who stood as guards.

Afterwards Ranjit Singh became strong and loosened hell on opponents, Oh Singhs.

There were brave generals like Hari Singh who were pure-hearted and independent.

Phula Singh Akali was a great hero who always had God's protection, Oh Singhs.

He put to death the sinners while crying "Akal, Akal," Oh Singhs.

When he died, we gave up our valiant traits, Oh Singhs.

We abandoned the path and followed the wrong way. That is why we are in such trouble.

When Dhuleep Singh was imprisoned, there was an earthquake in India, Oh Singhs.

Following his arrest, he was taken to England. The Panth then slept again, Oh Singhs.[1]

The Panth was disunited and fell into the net of slavery, Oh Singhs.

The tyrant entered the Punjab and impoverished the country.

Had Nabha and Patiala not sided with them, Oh Singhs, the oppressors would never have dared to come here.

With their help the Punjab was conquered, those leaders who were disloyal to their salt, Oh Singhs.

Oh friends, they behaved worse than the lowest Sikhs *(chandal)*.

Today they are companions of the whites ; they are filling their own bellies, Oh Singhs.

When we went into deep slumber, we did not think of the country, Oh Singhs.

When the mutiny occurred in 1857, the Panth had fallen greatly.

Although the ruler of Nabha showed his loyalty, even he lost more land.

Had we loved the mutiny, Oh Singhs, the country would have been free by now.

Had we protected the mutiny, the children of mother India would not have been sold, Oh Singhs.

Pick them up and put them in your lap, Oh Singhs. There is nothing wrong with berries that have dropped on the ground.

The Guru laid the foundation of the Panth and you should have taken up His work, Oh Singhs.

How can we blame others, Oh Singhs, when our leaders are in a very sad plight.

Rai Bahadurs (title-holders) have ruined the country, Oh Singhs. They love the monkeys.

They have become courageless like cowards; they are damaging the roots of the country, Oh Singhs.

They have sold us to the English, Oh Singhs, they have become collaborators.

We wander in vain in foreign lands, Oh Singhs. It is hell to live there.

The whole world treats us like dogs, there is no one to protect us.

1. The son of Ranjit Singh, Dhuleep Singh, attempted to return to the Punjab but was intercepted at Aden and forced to give up claims for his father's kingdom.

The sinful tyrants have injured us even in Canada, Oh Singhs.
When we met Bhai Bhagwan Singh, where then were the songs of the Gurus.[1]
The foreign sinners took him in a ship, Oh Singhs, and he was put in a cage.
Keep your promises, Oh Singhs, to avenge Bhagwan Singh.
Deputations are of no avail. Take in your hands the sword and shield.
God gives victories to those who dare, Oh Singhs, the God named Akal Parukh.
Where had the son of the Tenth Guru gone who prevented the recovery of revenue in Lyallpur colony.[2]
Today he is rotting in foreign lands, he has not a pice.
He has maintained the honour of his name, Ajit (undefeated), but he roams in a sad plight, Oh Singhs.
He left behind his brothers, father, dear ones, and sons, Oh Singhs.
Bright sons of India like Tilak are rotting in jails; drown those whites who put him in prison.
Barkatullah is sitting in Japan, Oh Singhs; he has complete faith in God alone; Krishna Varma has settled in France. Just think of Madame Cama.[3]
Gandhi, the devotee, is rotting in jail. There was untold repression in Africa where fearless children were killed, Oh Singhs.
Oh Singhs, in Africa sisters and brothers, mothers and fathers have been separated.
The oppression has exceeded all limits. Oh Singhs, you must teach these tyrants a lesson.
We dare be called Singhs in name only, our life is worth less than that of the jackel.
Maintain the honour of the name Singh, O Singhs, throw the red colour of revolution throughout India.
The Khalsa College has been taken over by white monkeys, Oh Singhs.
Sundar Singh Majithia has played havoc, Oh Singhs. He has adopted ways worse than the *chandals*.[4]
The Golden Temple was built by the great Guru, Oh Singhs, but our leaders are now its commission agents.
You honour the Gurdwaras, but in Delhi the wall of Rakabganj Gurdwara has been destroyed, Oh Singhs.
Had the Sikhs been active and wise, they would have taught the British a lesson.

1. Bhagwan Singh was a Sikh leader in Canada.
2. An allusion to Ajit Singh, who led an agitation in the Lyallpur canal colony in 1907.
3. All revolutionaries.
4. Sundar Singh Majithia was a Sikh leader who cooperated with the British in reforming the constitution of Khalsa College in 1908. Allegedly the reforms shifted control of the College to the government.

Oh Singhs, had there been brave Dip Singh, he would have taken up the sword and shield.

Oh Singhs, had there been Mahtab Singh of Mirankot, he would have demonstrated his valour to the whites.[1]

We are their sons and grandsons, but we are not ashamed in the least, Oh Singhs.

When the mosque at Cawnpur was demolished, the Muslim crusaders showed their strength, Oh Singhs.

The biggest dacoit immediately made peace on seeing their zeal.

Oh Singhs, the second mutiny must now come. We must consider it our child and nurture it.

The Punjabis are in a deep sleep, Oh Singhs, but the lion of Bengal is awake.

Oh Ye Hindus, Muslims, Mughals and Pathans, you must unite and drown the fleet of the British.

Oh Singhs, we are all sons of mother India, there is no distinction among us.

Unburden yourself of the load of Bharat Varsha, Oh Singhs. You are the sons of mother India.

Make immediate preparations for carrying out the mutiny, Oh Singhs. God will give you victory.

Song Seventeen

Oh Ye born of the blood of aged fathers, let us sit and pass resolutions.

You have India's glory on your mind. After considering the situation, let us make good decisions.

We have tired of just observing; let us work out a programme for doing something.

Oh Ye sons of the Guru, why are you full of zeal ? Do something to satisfy your hearts.

We should make cowards lions before acting, convert men who have said "sir, sir" for ages.

We should be cautious lest on a rapid ascent we fall down.

We should first memorize the alphabet, then learn mathematics.

We should first handle fire and pistols, then we will not be afraid of guns and rifles.

We should throw away our sleepiness so that the enemy may not kill us while we doze.

1. Sikh hero noted for his bravery. Mahtab Singh rescued the Golden Temple in Amritsar and killed its desecrators.

We should forget petty thoughts so that at the proper time, we will not be led astray.

We should develop brotherly love so that we cannot be divided.

We should not close our eyes like pigeons, and seeing the cat, we should fly away.

Seeing the enemy, we should strike at his nose, we should not give a light blow to the neck as when we kill hens.

We should harden our soft hearts so that they do not weaken at the wrong time.

Leaving aside the clothes of beggars, we should become lions; we should also acquire a sense of politics.

Let me tell you some things along the way, you who are valiant Sikhs.

First, strike continually at the head of the enemy. Do not strike at one spot on the head but at many places.

Secondly, by beating him with shoes, run the enemy out of his home and even out of town.

To prevent his returning to trouble you, dig out his very roots.

This enemy initially is the traitor within; we shall deal with the whites after we teach the unfaithful a lesson.

If they are willing to be treated like gentlemen, we shall plead with them.

If they desire honour, we will meet them as meekly as possible (lit., with grass in our mouth and a cloth around our neck).

If they do not come to terms through dialogue, then we must consider other ways to make them understand.

It will be difficult to achieve success unless the number of traitors decreases.

We cannot permit one person to bear the burden. We should all share the load of tribulation.

You must meet the traitors in the way they deserve, with full force.

In this way you should unite and form a branch of the Ghadr party.

Then we shall send some brave persons to India. We first must test our might in the islands.

After the testing, we should select those who are ready to die. They will organize secret societies.

Some branches should be left in foreign lands, branches with deep roots.

We can then commit dacoities on the government, and in this way awaken the Punjab and the whole country.

At some places we should use guerilla warfare and adopt the methods that best suit us.

Oh friends, shine like Bengalis, take an oath, and let us seize the gauntlet.

We can have bliss by sacrificing our lives for India.
We should die fighting like brave persons and not like dogs.
Either we should kill ourselves or kill the opponent. We should not turn our backs like cowards.
If we live at all, we should live bravely. Only then can we achieve heaven.
We should prove our salt by dying for the country and making our name known throughout the world.
If we face tribulations we should do so with a smiling face, and preserve the name of India.
Let us, Oh friends, see our country free—help to save future generations from extinction.
If you fight with England and defeat the rulers, the jewel of India will shine brightly.
Holding in our hands the beautiful tri-colour flag, we shall raise the cry of "Bande Mataram."

Shamsher Khalsa

Introduction

The Shamsher will appear continually, it will invigorate broken hearts.
It will point out the duties of man, it will banish the sleep of the idle.
Think of the present conditions and gird your loins, shake off your sleep and rise.
Unite all the communities as you think necessary after reading this paper.
The *Sher Shamsher* has come roaring into the field.
It will devote itself to the service of the nation.
Our nation and brethren have been waiting for this a long time.
It will fulfill all desires, it will be full of good articles.
Its perusal will cause the faces of brothers to bloom.
When it takes up the service of the Khalsa, who will not be pleased with the Shamsher ?

True Cry

Indian brothers, listen to the cry.
Time is passing, be ready, and love the sayings of the Guru.
I will tell you of some troubles.
You sleep soundly, but I will shake you into wakefulness.
I implore you humbly (with grass in mouth).
Why are you disgracing yourselves with disunity ?
Indian brothers, listen to the cry.
Others have *pakhha* houses, you have not even a hut.
Others have blankets of silk, you have not even a dirty and torn quilt.

Our honour is rolled in the dust, people deride and hate us.
Indian brothers, listen to the cry.
We left the jewel India, for the sake of money we cut off relations with our family.
We have earned money after bearing a lakh of troubles.
You should consider that this is not really our money.
Indian brothers, listen to the cry.
People have electric lamps, we have not even oil lamps.
Brothers, you drink and sleep in intoxication.
Our clothes are torn, who will mend them now ?
Our clothes are not just torn, they are ripped to pieces.
Thieves are breaking the house, but you lie asleep.
Oh brothers, we have been looted while sleeping.
Oh brothers, wake a little.

Cry of Pain

Oppression has passed all bounds.
Oh brothers, we have been afflicted, of this an account is necessary.
You know a ship containing Indians came to Canada.
Our brothers reached Canada after a lakh of troubles.
No one cared for them.
Indians in Canada cared and helped them as they could.
Canadians were astonished with Indian unity.
All spent their money to share the pain of the voyagers.
They filed cases in court and became poor having spent their funds.
A painful piece of news arrived yesterday, that the voyagers have been ordered to return.
One's hair stands on end to hear of their troubles.
They could not get food or water for several days.
They remained in hunger and suffered.
At last a fight occurred and the Indians triumphed.
The police fought with five weapons (fully armed), the Indians had neither sword nor shield.
At last they attacked the whites with lumps of coal and reduced them to whimpering cowards.
Policemen became wounded and then excited, being enraged they killed three Indians.
Our brothers attained martyrdom, they taught us a lesson.
We Indians are simple-minded, and others play tricks on us.

Now the last moment has come.
Our hearts are aflame at other news.
Indians who have aroused the nation have been arrested.
Harnam Singh, Balwant Singh, and Bhag Singh, these brothers are in jail today in Canada.
Oh brothers, let us remove this difficulty.
Let us devote our precious lives to do good for others.
This body of ours is fated to be eaten up by death in the end.

A Lover's Cry

Let us relate a story of a hero, a hidden gem of the community.
We will tell you true things.
Get up, brothers, have you lost your courage ?
His name is Gurditt Singh.
He has taken up the task of rousing the nation.
He has worn the garland of troubles.
He has sacrificed body and mind for the nation.
People call it national love.
The ship sailed directly to Canada.
The leader brushed aside all Canadian laws.
And revealed as false the false complaints.
The ship sailed on the 15th April 1914.
He met trouble at the start, with a false snare spread at Hongkong.
It makes one's hair stand on end to read the account.
After undergoing much trouble the Sikhs sailed.
They were stopped as soon as they landed in Canada.
Had the ship belonged to another country, no one would have dared look at it.
It was notified it could not land.
Inhabitants of all countries go to India, but we are not welcome in Canada.
Have you not considered this ? We have been betrayed.
We cannot bear such troubles.
All people bitterly oppose us, they call us dogs.
When the ship reached Canada, the whites made a row.
Now our brothers must be sent back.
We are puppets in the hands of whites (lit., the *gora log* make us dance on their fingers).
They tell lies and loot us.
Rise up, Oh Indians, why do you delay ?
A daughter of India has brought a ship.

Brothers, you are asleep, open your eyes.
Why don't you demand your rights ?
If you are men, where is your courage ?
The Canadians have already sent back Gurditt Singh.
All men call us mad.
Famine and plague always break out in India.
We are now mistreated in other countries, here our lives are even in danger.
When you read this account, prepare for action.
Sacrifice for the nation.
You will not be born a human being again unless all brothers join together and do good.
The Guru has urged such a union.
A whip is required for a fool, a hint suffices for a sensible person.
We salute the motherland.

Gurmukhi Pamphlet

Dear Khalsa Ji,

If we compare our present state with our past, which of us is so stone-hearted that he will not shed tears ? The *Khalsa Advocate* is correct in saying that the brave Sikhs, whom the Muslims could not subdue, have today become spiritless. Now at a mere hint they will inordinately flatter the authorities. Whatever a *faringhee* may say is regarded as infallible (lit., a line engraved on stone) by our *jo-hukm* brothers; none dares so much as offer a remonstrance. Dear Khalsa. Where is your lion's roar which none could hush ? What has become of that sword which was ever ready to destroy the rule of the wicked ? Awake, O Nation. If you value your life, awake. Dear brethren. Mother Bharat has been ruined, and if you do not awake she will be swept from the earth. Many of our brothers say "we eat the salt of government, why should we be untrue to that salt ?" Oh simpletons, whose is the salt and by whom is it eaten ? The real fact is that the *faringhee* are eating your salt. Nor is that all. They sweep everything from here and are filling their houses by robbing us. Never labour under the delusion that you eat the salt of the British. We eat the salt of her that gave us being, who brought us up, and who still feeds us, namely, dear Mother Bharat. There is no sin like the betrayal of one's country, and you should never commit that even by mistake.

You are told by the government that "Hindus and Muslims are both your enemies and we alone wish you well." All this is untrue. Can we hope for good at the hands of those who differ from us in country, language, religion, colour, customs, usages, and race, and who hate us, calling us *kala log ?* No, never. Hindus and Muslims, who are old inhabitants of this country, are our brothers, and they and we are the children of the same Motherland. We have a common country, a common language, common habits, and common interests. Dear Khalsa, a nation always involves itself in trouble because of internal dissension. You should all unite to make India's name glorious once more so that you may be respected at home as well as abroad. You should first drive the foreigners from the country. The wrongs which the English have done and still are doing to us and to our brethren, are known to us all. We Sikhs could boast of one country of our own. They have taken even that from our hands. They took us to foreign countries and involved us in troubles there while they disgrace us in our own territory. They have even introduced mismanagement into the Golden Temple, the centre of our religion. They appointed a mere child to the post of Head Granthi. The poor Sikhs convened meetings and submitted numerous petitions, but did anything come of them ? Absolutely nothing. These foreign tyrants are amenable only to the bludgeon, which alone brings the crooked and recalcitrant to their senses. If any of our regiments had said "appoint us this or that man or we will leave your service and return to our homes," we should have seen the government quivering.

Dear friends. One can get along with another person only by treating him as he should be treated. We cannot refrain from praising and thanking those soldiers who refused point-blank to fire on their fellow countrymen on the occasion of the Rawalpindi riots, and who even threatened to blow up their white comrades.[1] Well done, good men. You still have left in you a spark of the fire which Guru Kalgidhar Maharaj kindled in the Sikhs. Such incidents encourage us and indicate that we possess the spirit requisite for making progress. Indeed, why shouldn't this be so ? Can the nation which produced warriors like Rama, Arjan, Bhim, Guru Gobind Singh, and Banda, and the land which gave birth to Mahatmas like Guru Nanak and Martyr Mani Singh,and the soil which bore heroes like Bikramaditya, Asoka and Ranjit Singh be ever swept from the earth's surface ? Never. It is bound to rise and acquire glory. Hopeful signs are visible even now. See Prafulla Chaki, Khudiram Bose and Kanai Lal have given their lives for the country. Patriots like Tilak Maharaj, Aurobindo Ghose, and Ajit Singh are making sacrifices which greatly encourage us to destroy our enemies and to bring vengeance, and which purge our hearts of selfishness. Sikhs. You constitute the sword of

1. The reference is to riots in Rawalpindi in early May of 1907. There is no indication in official proceedings that troops refused to obey orders, nor was there any order to fire on Punjabis.

the country, and your enemies are practicing oppression on you with the aid of that sword. They pay you only Rs. 10 but receive hundreds in salaries themselves. Guru Gobind Singh forged this sword to slay the enemy, and it is a shame to you if you do not now wield it to destroy the *faringhee*. The Guru who gave you the sceptre is weeping at the sight of your degraded condition. If you therefore help Bengal, Maharashtra, and Madras with troops, today the enemy will be destroyed, and tomorrow our country will be restored again. Take a vow before the Guru this day with a true heart to use no foreign-made goods, especially British; to deposit no money in English banks; to buy no promisory notes; to look on all Indians as brothers; to sacrifice yourself for your country; to seize the sceptre; to establish secret societies everywhere; to devise means and to prepare to subvert foreign rule. To unite to destroy the *faringhee* with one stroke at the right time. Sat Sri Akal.

Khalsa Pamphlet

It was in the year 1698 A.D. that one of those historical moments which make or unmake an epoch dawned its eventful light on the scenes of Anandpur. There were called the innumerable disciples of the great Guru, and from far and near Punjab had sent her hundreds and thousands of stalwart hearts and fiery souls to wait on the pleasure of their youthful leader. At last the auspicious day dawned, and the sea of human mass began to move and converge at the appointed place. Thousands of the faithful disciples, painting different pictures of the probabilities of the coming event before their mind's eye, stood on the tiptoe of expectation. Suddenly a figure—young, stalwart, and commanding—rushed forth from the central tent, and jumped upon the platform with lightning-like rapidity. From his eyes beamed a noble blast, round his face shone a resplendent halo, and in his hand bristled a sharp, naked, dazzling sword.

At this sudden emergence of the commander the infinite multitude in spell-bound awe stood hanging on the lips of the young conjurer. The well-known figure raised aloft the dazzling sword, and pointing to its burning flame, in tones irresistible and deep, began to let his disciples know his will and pleasure. His lips moved, and like the rumblings of the volcano, came out the deep, distinct swords : "I want to soak this sword in the blood of man. The insatiable Goddess of Duty demands a bloody sacrifice."

Those alone who not only believe in the truth of principle, but are ready, nay, greedy, to catch at the first opportunity of offering their breasts to be thrusted by a pointed steel so that uncompromising Goddess of Duty might be propitiated—they alone are the Khalsa—the liberated—the chosen. To test and to choose such martyr spirits from amongst his disciples this fiery ordeal was gone through and those who passed triumphantly through it were taken by the Guru in the tent one by one, each time killing a goat instead, without letting the rest know of this substitution, and when the fifth martyr was chosen the Guru asked all of them to come out, and declared these as the first Khalsa—the liberated. These five proved that the Bharat race was not dead, that the inherent powers of the Mother were only slumbering, and that there were in the nation's heart potentialities, which, if but a master voice can evoke them out, would flame forth to avenge the national injuries, to redeem the national honour. The five were the five elements out of which the great Guru wanted to evoke a nation. ....

Now, over the whole forest the jackals of famine and tyranny and treachery are stalking victorious—where is the Singh, the lion who at his thundering will assert the lordship of his native soil ? This Khalsa the Guru created as a sword in the hand of Mother Bharat—for Punjab alone the Great Guru and his sons and followers poured forth their blood in unmeasured quantities—and now the whole body of the motherland from Himalyas to Cape Comorin is dying, her life blood sucked off. Punjab, where every stone has a tale of some Sikh martyrdom to tell; Bengal, where Guru Tegh Bahadur and Nanak lived and preached; the Deccan, where the ashes of the mighty dead are treasured in by the Godavari, are groaning under the death disease. Patna, the very birthplace of the Khalsa is a weeping slave, and Anandpur—the city of joy is buried under the heap of treachery and shame. The Guru told the Brahmins that to repeat the prayers is no Dharma, but to act the prayers is the real Dharma. Will he not hurl the same lance at us when he sees us repeating his prayers like parrots—unconcerned amidst the wailings and weeping of three hundred millions—as if there was a music keeping tune with our Japjis and Shabads. The sword which he gave to protect Dharma and Desh—has not that very sword traded on treachery.

A Sikh was hailed as a patriot by the motherland at home and as a hero by the world abroad. But, Oh shame. Now Sikh has become a nickname for treachery at home; a synonym for a labourer or a coolie on the coasts of both the Pacific and the Atlantic.

But this cannot last long. The Guru will not leave us. Even as he said the sparrows shall kill the hawks. The trumpet call of duty is sounded and it is never too late to mend.

Therefore awake, Oh Khalsa, arise, Oh Khalsa, and never again shall we be fallen. Sat Sri Akal.

APPENDIX C

SELECT BIBLIOGRAPHY ON SIKH HISTORY AND LITERATURE

SELECT BIBLIOGRAPY ON SIKH HISTORY AND LITERATURE

Aduti Jivan Britant Panth Ratan Babu Teja Singh Ji Sahib. (P) Amritsar, Guru Khalsa Press, n/d., 139 p.

Life of Teja Singh Overseer, Bhasaur, controversial leader of the Bhasaur Singh Sabha and the Panch Khalsa Diwan.

Amar Singh, Gyani : *Giani Ditt Singhji.* (P) Amritsar, Kirpal Singh and Sons, 1962, 159 p.

Life of Giani Ditt Singh (1853-1901).

Balbir Singh Dil : *Panjabi Kahani Da Vikas.* (P) Ludhiana, Lahore Book Shop, 1952. 257 p.

Survey of Panjabi fiction, with background on authors.

Barque, A.M. (ed) : *Eminent Sikhs of To-day.* Lahore, 1942, 162 p.

Biographical sketches of Sikh leaders such as Gurbaksh Singh Kapur, Dr.Mohan Singh Uberoi, and Sardar Gurmukh Nihal Singh who were active in social and literary movements.

Charan Singh and Darbara Singh : *The Work of the Sikh Educational Conference.* Amritsar, Charan Singh, 1944, 39 p.

Survey of the history of the Conference, with sketches of each session.

Das Visakha Singh : *Malva Itihas.* (P) 3 Pts. Vihara, Gurmat Parcharak Singh Sabha, n/d., 566, 600, 776 p.

The second volume provides information on Sikh institutions in the British period and biographical sketches of Sikh leaders. A large section also deals with the Ghadr movement and the Lahore conspiracy cases.

Educational Committee, Chief Khalsa Diwan : *Golden Jubilee Book.* (P) Amritsar, Educational Committee, 1958, 300 p. *Silver Jubilee Book.* (P) Amritsar, Educational Committee, 1935, 161 p.

Resolutions and information on each session of the Sikh Educational Conference, with biographical sketches.

Fauja Singh : *Kuka Movement.* Delhi, Motilal Banarsidass, 1965, 235 p.
Survey based on British documents.

Gadar Parti Da Itihas. (P) Jullundur, Desh Bhagat Yadgar Committee, 1961, 289 p.
The first part of a history of the Ghadr party and related overseas revolutionary activities of the Sikhs (1912-1917). The second part has not been published.

Ganda Singh (ed) : "The Akali Dal and Shiromani Gurdwara Parbandak Committee, 1921-2," *Punjab Past and Present,* I, Pt. 2 (October 1967), pp.252-310.
Reports by the C.I.D. on Sikh religious and political developments.

____(ed) : *Dr. Bhai Jodh Singh.* (P) Patiala, Khalsa College, 1962, 202 p.
Collection of essays on the life and work of Bhai Jodh Singh, a Sikh theologian and educationalist.

____: *A History of the Khalsa College Amritsar.* Amritsar, Khalsa College, 1949, 145 p.
The most thorough study on the College and connected activities of the Sikh community.

____: *Kukian Di Vithia.* (P) Amritsar, Guru Ram Das Printing Press, 1946, 264p.
History of the Kukas, or Namdhari sect.

____ (ed) : *Panjab, 1849-1960.* (P) Ludhiana, Panjabi Sahit Academy, 1962,
Contains useful essays on the Kukas, Arya Samaj, Singh Sabhas and politics in the pre-1920 period.

Gurbakhsh Singh : *Meri Jivan Kahani.* (P) 2 Vols. Prit Nagar, 1969.
Autobiography of a Sikh journalist and poet. The first volume covers the period 1895-1924.

Gurcharan Singh and Surinder Singh : *Mohan Singh Te Usdi Kavita.* (P) Amritsar, Hind Publishers, 1953, 192 p.
Life and work of a famous Punjab poet.

Gurdial Singh Phul : *Ik Jivan Prakash.* (P) Jullundur, Hazuria and Sons, 1962, 143 p.
Biography of Bhai Jodh Singh.

Gurditt Singh, Baba : *The Voyage of the Komagatamaru.* Calcutta, n/d., 202 p.
Autobiography of a Ghadr leader, translated from Gurmukhi.

Gurditt Singh Premi : *Panjabi Sahit Di Bhumika.* (P) 2/e., Phagwara, Amar Publishers, 1965, 206 p.
An introduction to Panjabi literature.

Hira Singh Dard : *Jivan Charittra Baba Gurditt Singhji.* (P) Lahore, Akal Agency, n/d., 156 p.

A proscribed life of Gurditt Singh, Ghadr leader. Available in the library of the National Archives of India, New Delhi.

Isemonger, F.C. and J. Slattery : *An Account of the Ghadr Conspiracy, 1913-1915.* Lahore, 1919.

C.I.D. version of the revolutionary activities of Sikhs in North America and the Punjab, with biographical data and political analysis. Available in the National Archives of India and the India Office Library.

Jagjit Singh : *Ghadr Parti Lahir.* (P) Amritsar, Sudarshan Press, 1955, 728 p

History of the Ghadr party.

____: *Singh Sabha Lahir.* (P) Tarn Taran, 1941.

History of Singh Sabhas in the Punjab.

Jaswant Singh Jas : *Baba Gurdit Singh : Kamagatamaru.* (P) Jullundur, New Books Company, 1965, 244 p.

Study of Ghadr activities and the voyage of the Komagata Maru culminating in the shooting incident at Budge Budge Harbour, October 1914.

Kahan Singh, Bhai : *Gurushabad Ratnakar Mahan Kosh.* (P) 2/e., Patiala, Language Department, 1960, 835, 99 p.

An unrivalled encyclopedia of Sikh history and literature, first published in 1930 in four volumes and reprinted with appendices by Teja Singh. Includes background on books, authors, and specialized vocabulary.

Ker, James Campbell : *Political Trouble in India, 1907-1917.* Calcutta, 1917.

Confidential C.I.D. publication that surveys Punjab politics and provides sketches of local leaders including Sikhs.

Khushwant Singh : *A History of the Sikhs.* (Volume 2). Princeton, 1966.

A standard assessment of Sikh developments in the British period. Of particular importance are chapters on the Singh Sabhas and the Ghadr movement and concluding notes on authors and Panjabi literature.

Kirpal Singh Kasel and Parminder Singh : *Panjabi Sahit Di Utpati Te Vikas.* (P) 3 Vols. Ludhiana, Lahore Book Shop, 1952.

History of Panjabi literature.

Kulbir Singh : *Sardar.* (P) Jullundur, Punjab Kitab Ghar, 1967, 439 p.

Short lives of Sikh leaders such as Kahan Singh of Nabha, Sundar Singh Majithia, Sardar Trilochan Singh, Bhai Vir Singh, and Sardar Thakur Singh. Based primarily on interviews.

Lakshman Singh, Bhagat : *Bhagat Lakshman Singh Autobiography* (ed. by Dr. Ganda Singh, Patiala). Calcutta, 1966, 323 p.

Life and times of a Sikh educational and social leader.

Lal Singh (ed) : *Kalani Taswir.* (P) Panch Khand, Khalsa Parliament. 1935, 138 p.

Letters on Sikh affairs by Teja Singh Overseer, with notes on his life.

Mihar Singh Ravel : *Sir Sundar Singh Majithia.* (P) Amritsar, 1942.

Eulogies and biographical sketches on one of the foremost leaders of the Chief Khalsa Diwan. Sundar Singh Majithia's private papers are now in the Nehru Memorial Museum and Library, New Delhi.

Mohan Singh : *A History of Panjabi Literature, 1100-1932.* 2/e., Amritsar, 1956, 139, 28 p.

Survey of modern Panjabi writers, with publication lists.

Munsha Singh Dukhi : *Jivan Bhai Sahib Bhai Mohan Singh Ji Vaid.* (P) Amritsar, n/d., 807 p.

Biography of a colourful Sikh social and religious leader from Tarn Taran (1881-1936).

Nahar Singh, Gyani : *Azadi Dian Lahiran.* (P) Ludhiana, Punjab Gyani Press, 1960, 398 p.

History of political activities in India, 1900-1960, with particular reference to the Punjab and Sikhs.

_____: *Jivani Shahid Kartar Singh Sarahaba.* (P) Patiala, Punjabi University, 1967, 116 p.

Life of Sikh revolutionary, Kartar Singh.

Nahar Singh, Sardar : "Developments in Sikh Politics, 1900-1911," *Gurduara Gazette.* (P), April 1969. English section, pp. 7-60

Annotated C.I.D. note on Sikh politics prepared by the Assistant Director, Criminal Intelligence, Mr. D. Petrie.

_____: *Gooroo Ram Singh and the Kuka Sikhs.* 3 Vols. New Delhi, 1965-67.

Kuka documents, primarily drawn from British foreign department proceedings in the National Archives of India, New Delhi.

Narain Singh : *Kujh Had Biti, Kujh Jag Biti.* (P) Delhi, International Sikh Brotherhood, 1966.

Autobiography of a Sikh barrister, with background on the period 1900-1919.

Narinder Singh Duggal : *Panjabi Sahit.* (P) Jullundur, New Book Company, 1965, 215 p.

Survey of Panjabi literature.

Panjabi Sahit. (P) Amritsar, Kirpal Singh, 1941, 174 p.
Life and work of Bhai Mohan Singh Vaid (1881-1936).

Peace, M.L : *Sardar Kartar Singh Jhabbar.* Jullundur, n/d., 148 p.
Biography of a prominent Akali leader, with background on the growth of the gurdwara movement and communist activities in the Punjab.

Piara Singh Bhogal : *Panjabi Kavita Da Sau Sal.* (P) Jullundur, New Book Company, 1955, 154 p.
Survey of Panjabi poetry, 1850-1954.

Piara Singh Padam : *Kalam De Dhani.* (P) 2 Pts. Patiala, Sardar Sahit Bhavan, 1965-66, 308, 372 p.
Life and works of various Punjab writers.

Politico-Criminal Who's Who. Compiled in the Office of the Director, Criminal Intelligence, January 1914. Calcutta, 1914.
Information on over a hundred Punjab politicians, many of whom were Sikhs. Available in the India Office Library.

Prem Kahani. (P) Lahore, Punjab Press, 1932, 376 p.
Short biographies of Punjab poets, with the life of Budh Singh by Hira Singh Dard.

Principal Teja Singh Abhinandan Granth. (P) Patiala, Mahikma Panjabi, 1956, 300 p.
Series of articles and notes on the life of Principal Teja Singh, theologian and historian.

Professor Puran Singh Ji Jivan Te Likhat. (P) Amritsar, Likhari Book Depot, 1938, 185 p.
Life and writings of Professor Puran Singh, poet and historian.

Sachindar Nath Sanial : *Jujhar Shahidian Di Amar Gatha.* (P) Ludhiana, Desh Bhagat Parkashan, 1963. 260 p.
History of Ghadr activities, 1914-15.

Serebryakov, I : *Punjabi Literature.* Moscow, 1968.
Highly readable survey of Punjabi literature, with emphasis on the social and political writers of the twentieth century.

Shamsher Singh Ashok : *Bhai Kahan Singh Nabha.* (P) Gurar (Sangrur), Ashok Pustak Mala, 1966, 128 p.
Life of Bhai Kahan Singh of Nabha (1852-1938), encyclopedist, historian, and theologian.

____: *Panjabi Dian Lahiran.* (P) Niamatpur, Kaviraj Narain Singh Vallabha, 1954, 295 p.

Discussion of modern Sikh political and intellectual developments.

Sikh Itihas Te Kuke. (P) New Delhi, New Hindustan Publishers, 1964, 288 p.

Sikh history and the Kuka sect.

Suri, Vidya Sagar: *A Brief Biographical Sketch of Sohan Lal Pathak.* Patiala, Punjabi University, 1968, 62 p.

Life of a Sikh revolutionist.

Surindar Singh Narula : *Bhai Vir Singh.* (P) Ludhiana, Lahore Book Shop, 1950, 123 p.

Short life of Bhai Vir Singh.

Talwar, K.S : "The Anand Marriage Act," *Punjab Past and Present,* II, Pt. 2 (October 1968), pp. 400-410.

Survey of events leading to the passage of a controversial bill which legitimized the Sikh marriage ritual supported by the Tat Khalsa section of the Sikh community.

Teja Singh, Principal : *Arsi.* (P) Amritsar, Lok Sahit Prakashan, 1958, 159 p.

Autobiography of a prominent Sikh social and religious leader.

Teja Singh, Sant : *Jiwan Katha Gurmukh Piare Sant Atar Singh.* (P) 2 Pts. 3/e., Chima (Sangrur), Sant Teja Singh, 1958, 232, 315 p.

Life of a Sikh reformer and religious leader, Attar Singh.

Trilok Singh : *Varatman Sikhha Itihas.* (P) Amritsar, Bhai Jawahar Singh, 1962,

Survey of Sikh history, 1850-1962.

INDEXES

INDEX A

SUBJECT-TITLE INDEX

This index consists of titles from the first two sections, arranged alphabetically by select subject headings. Titles have been placed under two or more headings where appropriate. Because of the complexities of arranging items by subject, readers are requested to look under related headings. For example, although controversial works have been divided into Sikh and Sikh-non-Sikh lists, both should be checked carefully for specific titles. Fiction generally has been distributed under the subjects to which titles pertain.

Subject-Title Index

BIOGRAPHY

The Sikhs Gurus

Sikh Martyrs and Saints

Biographies of other Sikhs

CONTROVERSIES AMONG SIKHS

CONTROVERSIES BETWEEN SIKHS AND NON-SIKHS

CUSTOMS AND RITUALS

General Works

Baptism

Marriage

Maintenance of Hair

Purification and Penance

Worship of Holy Spots, Idols, and Saints

Miscellaneous

EDUCATION

Address :

FESTIVALS

Tegh Khalsa, 353.

Upkar Khalsa, 450.

Wadha Ghalu Ghara, 983.

HISTORY

The Annexation of the Punjaub, and the Maharajah Duleep Singh, 71.
Azmat-i-Khalsa, 746.

Bait Shah Muhammad, 608.
Baran Mislan, 186.
A Brief History of the Golden Temple, Amritsar, 225.

The Dawn of Nanak Saheb's Religion, 717.

The First and Second Sikh Wars, 110.

The Growth of Responsibility in Sikhism, 682.
Gur Gira Ragmala Mandan Parbodh Granth, 232.
Guru Singh Itihas, 80.
Guru Singh Sabha Itihas Nawin, 81.

Hind Da Puratan Itihas, 802.
History and Philosophy of the Sikh Religion, 359.
The History of the Golden Temple, Amritsar, and the Shrines Around, 644.
A History of the Sikhs from the Origin of the Nation to the Battles of the Sutlej, 125.
History of the Sikhs : or, Translation of the Sikhan De Raj Di Vikhia—Together with a Short Gurmukhi Grammar, 124.
How the Sikhs Became a Militant People, 391.

Kattak Ki Visakh ? 341.
Khalsa Panth, 559.
Khurshid-i-Khalsa, 487.

The Law of Inheritance to Chiefships As Observed by the Sikhs Previous to the Annexation of the Panjab, 202.

Maharaja Khalsa, 858.

Parsang Siri Nanakana Sahib Ji Da, 888.
Phul Namah Tawarikh, 93.
Prachin Panth Parkash, 553.

Ramgarhia, 133.
Risalai Chechak Wah Jangi Singhan, 198.

Short History of the Hari Mandar, 640.
A Short History of the Sikhs, 503.
Sikhan Di Raj Di Vithiya, 584.
Sikhon Ka Utsthan Aur Patan, 457.

The Sikhs, 200.
The Sikhs and the Sikh Wars, 201.
Singhan Namdharian Da Shahid Bilas, 339.
Sri Amritsar Darshan, 105.
Sri Darbar Sahib Ji De Sankhep Hal, 948.
Sri Gurmat Digvijai, 291.
Sri Gurmat Mandan, 281.
Sri Tarn Taran Mahatam, 250.
Sur Bir Khalsa Ya Baran Mislan, 90.

Tarikh-i-Patiala, 446.
Transformation of Sikhism, Or How the Sikhs Became a Political Power, 196.
Tawarikh-i-Guru Khalsa, 243.

LANGUAGE

Benati, 425.

History of the Sikhs : or, Translation of the Sikhan De Raj Di Vikhia...Together with a Short Gurmukhi Grammar, 124.

Jhok Jamia Panjab Da, 823.

Khalse De Bole, 307.
Ki Panjabi Nal Sada Piar Hai ? 377.

Panjabi Ate Hindi, 85.
Panjabi Ate Urdu Da Takara, 86.
Panjabi Boli De Prachar Te Sawar Lai Panjabi Vidyan Istriyan Te Purkhan Age Apil, 102.
Panjabi Da Bhandar Bharo, 87.
Panjabi Di Unnati Di Lor Te Sadhan Parthai Lekh, 433.

Saukhi Vidya Parthaye Lekh, 324.
Sawaiye Sri Mukh Wak, 930.
Sri Guru Granth Ji Ke Madh Se Paryai Farsi Padon Ke, 113.

ORGANIZATIONS AND INSTITUTIONS

(Also see "Controversies", "Social Reform")

Amritsar Versus Lahore, Or the Controversy about the Location of the Khalsa College, 506.

Chehra Dekhan De Shishe Da Zamima (CKD), 38.
Chief Khalsa Diwan De Central Khalsa Yatimkhana Da Majuda Halat De Asli Photo, 372.

Dasahira Bhav Panth Jagawa Arthat Panth Dasawa (Panch Khalsa Diwan), 669.
Deputation (Golden Temple), 632.
Desh Kuchal (Singh Sabhas), 376.
Dharamsalan Da Prabandh, 563.
Dharmik Khabran (Khalsa Pracharak Vidyala), 781.
Dhokha Nivar Pattra (Amritsar Singh

POLITICS

RELIGION

Theology and General Works

Ethics and Conduct

Scriptures and Prayer

SECTS AND SUB-DIVISIONS IN SIKH SOCIETY

SOCIAL REFORM

General Works

Caste

INDEX B

GENERAL INDEX

This general index contains references to individuals, institutions, and topics discussed in the four bibliographic sections. To avoid unnecessary duplication, names of authors or lists of newspapers and organizations already presented in alphabetized form in the third and fourth sections have not been included. The introduction contains additional background information.

General Index